The
U.S.
Shipbuilding
Industry

THE
U.S.
SHIPBUILDING
INDUSTRY:

Past,

Present,

and Future

By Clinton H. Whitehurst, Jr.

NAVAL INSTITUTE PRESS
Annapolis, Maryland

Library of Congress Cataloging-in-Publication Data

Whitehurst, Clinton H., 1927–
    The U.S. shipbuilding industry.

    Bibliography: p.
    Includes index.
    1. Shipbuilding industry—United States. I. Title.
II. Title: US shipbuilding industry.
VM299.6.W48   1986   338.4'76238'0973   86-18082
ISBN 0-87021-723-2

To those who built,
and to those who will build again,
great ships to carry the American flag
to the far corners of the earth

Contents

Preface

In his classic study *The Influence of Seapower Upon History: 1660–1783*, Alfred Mahan set down a philosophy of naval strategy and international politics "that in its way and its place, was to have as profound an effect on the world as had Darwin's *Origin of Species*." Thus noted Louis M. Hacker, dean of general studies at Columbia University in the 1957 edition Introduction to Mahan's internationally acclaimed treatise.

While Mahan's contribution to naval strategy requires no defense, it is still fair to point out that a major element of seapower—the shipbuilder—was not discussed. This omission is probably best explained by the fact that maritime nations in general, and those cited by Mahan in particular, were shipbuilding nations as well as naval and maritime powers, and that this would be implicitly understood by the reader.

While undoubtedly true 200 years ago, such is not the case today. The registration of large merchant fleets in "flags of convenience" nations having no shipbuilding/ship repair capability is a fact of life in the maritime world of the 1980s. Liberia, Honduras, and Panama are typically cited in this regard. Moreover, the practice of traditional maritime nations purchasing their vessels in foreign shipyards is growing.

In peacetime the dichotomy is not especially important. In fact, economics suggests that in a free market, that is, one without government intervention of any sort, the shipowner *must* purchase his vessel at the best world price to stay competitive. However, the problem comes not in peacetime but in time of national emergency. And while in Mahan's day a maritime nation could be assumed to possess a sufficient shipbuilding capability to support its fleet in time of war, that is not always a fair assumption now. In the case of the United States, it is far from clear whether the nation possesses a shipbuilding/repair capability sufficient to meet wartime demands.

This book proceeds from the assumption that the shipbuilder and ship repairer are essential elements of seapower, particularly in time of national emergency. If a key element in U.S. military planning is for the Navy to secure ocean lines of supply (sea control) and the merchant marine to keep the pipeline filled, including imports of essential raw materials, then it follows that a sufficient shipbuilding/repair mobilization base must be kept permanently in place—the more so because future conflicts will initially be fought with assets in being. The vexing question is, *how* can the United States ensure such a capability in the complex and competitive maritime environment of the 1980s? A chief purpose of the book is to provide insights into this question.

Early chapters place the shipbuilding industry in historical perspective and examine its rise to a dominant place in the colonial and early American economies. The long-term decline of the industry is analyzed, including government policies designed to aid shipbuilding but which in reality probably hastened its demise. Historical parallels are also duly noted and examined. A case in point is that following the American Revolution, innovative designs that significantly increased vessel speeds did much to secure America's place at sea. It is sometimes forgotten, however, that these innovative ships were built in innovative and efficient shipyards. Today, American design innovations such as the lighter aboard ship (LASH), the containership concept, and the liquid natural gas carrier (LNG) are copied worldwide. The question arises of whether it is unreasonable to expect a nation that can conceive and design highly complex vessels to be able to design and operate economically efficient shipyards as well.

Middle chapters describe and place the industry in its present-day setting. Industry structure and shipyard operations are treated extensively. Noted in particular is the competitive and complementary relationship that exists between the country's public (naval) and private shipyards. Later chapters examine the industry as an integral part of American seapower. Finally, the essential elements of a national shipyard policy are reviewed and fitted into the whole.

As in my earlier work, the *U.S. Merchant Marine: In Search of An Enduring Maritime Policy*, several knowledgeable authorities have contributed their thoughts and ideas. The result is a book containing differing views on some issues, but also, and more important, a book where much common ground is identified.

In the best of all worlds, a study on the U.S. shipbuilding/ship repair industry would be widely adopted as a classroom text and found on the desk of every member of Congress and every bureaucrat, as well as in the world's major libraries. That is a heroic goal at best. Rather than aiming for large numbers in one or more categories, this book is written for those smaller numbers of concerned individuals in every category who believe that American shipyards are an essential element of American seapower and that ways must be found to ensure their long-term viability. This book is for them, and may their numbers multiply!

Many people and organizations made this book possible. First, the financial and logistical support of the Strom Thurmond Institute of Goverment and Public Affairs was assistance beyond price. In this respect, the encouragement of its director, Horace Fleming, and his willingness for me to balance the demands the book made on my time with my responsibilities as a senior fellow of the Institute, are gratefully acknowledged.

Special thanks go to Christine Simonetti, my graduate research assistant, for her untiring work in the Clemson University libraries, and to Betty Woodall for her typing and editing skills. Bob Bryan, Chief, Reserve Fleet, at the Maritime Administration has been unfailing in his support, as has Al May, Executive Vice President of the Council of American Flag Ship Operators. Elizabeth Jones, editor of *News Briefs*, published by the American Maritime Officers Service, has been most helpful in keeping me current with regard to the Washington maritime scene. And to the extent that this book is intelligible, Constance MacDonald deserves much credit for a superb job of manuscript editing. Closer to home I thank my wife Marion for her continuing interest and unfailing optimism that the book would, in fact, be completed on time. To those many others too numerous to cite individually, I can only say that your assistance is appreciated and not forgotten.

The opinions, conclusions, and recommendations made in the book are solely those of the authors and not those of the Naval Institute Press. By the same token, a contributor's inclusion in the book does not imply that he agrees generally or specifically with the opinions, conclusions, and recommendations made in the book by the author or other contributors.

About the Contributors

Captain Ralph V. Buck, USN, is Deputy Director For Systems Analysis in the Office of the Assistant Secretary of the Navy (Shipbuilding and Logistics). He is a graduate of the Naval Academy and received a Master of Science degree in Operations Research from the Naval Postgraduate School. Other assignments include duty as a naval aviator (anti-submarine warfare) and as a member of the management faculty of the Naval War College at Newport, Rhode Island.

John T. Gilbride is Chief Executive Officer of Todd Shipyards Corporation. In addition to his responsibilities as CEO of one of the country's large shipyard complexes, he has lectured and written extensively on the U.S. shipyard industry. Upon graduating from the University of Pennsylvania in 1938, Mr. Gilbride joined Todd Shipyards as a draftsman. From that position he moved progressively up the corporate ladder, being named president of the company in 1958 and chief executive officer in 1975.

David H. Klinges is Vice President, Marine Construction, Bethlehem Steel Corporation. His academic credentials include an undergraduate degree from Franklin and Marshall College, a law degree from Yale, and attendance at Harvard University's Advanced Management Program. He is a former board chairman and executive committee chairman of the Shipbuilders Council of America and presently serves on the board of trustees of Franklin and Marshall College and the Webb Institute of Naval Architecture.

Captain Wilbur J. Mahony, USN (Ret.), is an instructor in the Department of Management at Clemson University while concurrently working toward a Ph.D. degree in Engineering Management at that institution. Prior to his retirement he served as Submarine Logistics Manager at the Naval Sea Systems Command, and was Commander, Naval Shipyard, Charleston, South Carolina, 1978–82. He is a graduate of the Naval Academy and also received a Master of Science degree from the Webb Institute of Naval Architecture.

Abbreviations Used in the Text

ASIB	Active shipbuilding industrial base (sometimes shortened to ASB)
CAD	Computer aided design
CAM	Computer aided manufacturing
CAR	Construction, alteration, and repair
CBO	Congressional Budget Office
CCF	Capital Construction Fund
CDS	Construction differential subsidy
CNA	Center for Naval Analyses
ConUS	Continental United States
DoD	Department of Defense
DoT	Department of Transportation
dwt	Deadweight tons
EDO	Engineering Duty Officer (sometimes shortened to ED)
EUSC	Effective U.S. control (shipping)
GAO	General Accounting Office
GT	Gross tons
LASH	Lighter aboard ship
LNG	Liquid natural gas carrier
MarAd	Maritime Administration
MSC	Military Sealift Command
MTMC	Military Traffic Management Command
NACOA	National Advisory Committee on Oceans and Atmosphere
NADES	National Defense Shipyard Study
NATO	North Atlantic Treaty Organization
NavSea	Naval Sea Systems Command
NDF	National defense feature
NDRF	National Defense Reserve Fleet
NRC	National Research Council of the National Academy of Science

OBO	Ore–bulk–oil carrier
ODS	Operating differential subsidy
OECD	Organization for Economic Cooperation and Development
OPEC	Oil Producing Exporting Countries
OTA	Office of Technology Assessment
RO/RO	Roll-on/roll-off
RRF	Ready Reserve Force
SLEP	Service Life Extension Program
SIC	Standard Industrial Classification Code
SYMBA	Shipyard Mobilization Base Study
UNCTAD	United Nations Conference on Trade and Development
USITC	United States International Trade Commission

The U.S. Shipbuilding Industry

1

Introduction

IN THE MID-1980s, increasing concern is being voiced about the general economic viability of U.S. shipyards and their adequacy to meet mobilization requirements—in particular, to meet requirements should a full-blown war break out in Europe. Probably at no time since World War II has concern for the nation's shipbuilding/repair industry been so visible.* Not only have industry spokesmen become more vocal, but responsible government agencies have taken a greater interest in what is happening and what might happen. Seven major government reports in the past four years and several nongovernment studies, in addition to numerous congressional hearings, have focused attention on shipbuilding and ship repair problems as well as those of the merchant marine.[1] Appendix A summarizes the findings of recent government studies. All note that shipyards are undergoing a marked contraction in terms of numbers and size, and directly, or indirectly, raise the question of whether they could play their expected roles in an emergency. Total employment in private shipyards decreased by approximately 21,000 from 1980 to 1984. (See below, Table 8.1.)

Three questions can be reasonably posed by the American citizen who is concerned about national security but uninformed about maritime matters in general, and shipyards in particular. First, why are shipyards so important to our national security? Second, if there are present or impending problems with respect to the shipbuilding/ship repair industry, what brought them about? And third, assuming serious problems are identified, what can be done to rectify them?

Shipyards and National Security

A joint Navy–Maritime Administration Shipyard Mobilization Base (SYMBA) study published in 1984 identified 119 shipyards in the United

*As a general proposition, a shipyard may have a shipbuilding capability, a ship repair capability, or both. Throughout the book the terms shipyard industry and shipbuilding/ship repair industry are used interchangeably.

States that have a *potential* national security value, that is, have the capability to perform mobilization tasks such as building, drydocking, and topside repairs. Of the 119, nine were government-owned, while the remaining 110 were in the private sector.[2]

Whether this number is adequate, however, depends upon a number of assumptions. One question is whether the United States would be engaged simultaneously in a NATO (European) war and one or more other major or minor conflicts, a situation that has been referred to as the ability to fight a ½, 1, 1½, 2, or 2½ war. Typical examples cited are simultaneous wars with the Soviet Union and the People's Republic of China, wars in Europe and Korea, Europe and Southeast Asia (Thailand, Vietnam), Europe and the Persian Gulf, or a combination of conflicts, some not yet visualized. Another consideration is the assumed length of the conflict. If a short war is forecast, then requirements become essentially reactivation and repair work, in addition to completing construction already under way. The longer the conflict, the greater the demand on shipyards, including the laying down of new tonnage to replace losses. In the SYMBA study, peak demand is forecast to occur one and one-half years into the conflict.

The final assumption concerns whether a NATO war would include a nuclear exchange between the United States and the Soviet Union. In such an exchange, most of the major shipyards in the United States would be destroyed, and the emphasis would shift from conventional conflict concerns to general nuclear recovery.

In summary, the SYMBA study concludes that a shipyard mobilization base should:

1. Ensure that ships of the naval fleet can be maintained in a high degree of material readiness and are modernized with appropriate new equipment.
2. In peacetime, retain sufficient capability to maintain or increase the size of the naval ship fleet and to build and maintain merchant ships consistent with the objectives of the Merchant Marine Act of 1936, as amended.
3. In time of conflict, be capable of handling activation, overhaul, repair, and battle damage of naval and merchant ships.
4. Ensure that the shipbuilding base provides the capability to build combatants and cargo ships to wartime requirements and to support the goal of a merchant marine that is suitable in time of war or national emergency.[3]

Shipyards in 1986

With the exception of World Wars I and II, the U.S. shipbuilding/ship repair industry has been in a long-term decline since 1848–57, a decade when American builders were averaging an output of approximately 390,000 tons a year.[4] (See Chapter 3.) However, a floor or safety net for the industry has been maintained by the federal government almost since the founding of the republic. Laws in the late eighteenth and early nineteenth centuries granted a monopoly to U.S. shipyards with respect to building merchant ships for the American domestic trades, that is, trade between U.S. ports. This policy has been periodically reaffirmed in various U.S. statutes down to the present day. Acts passed in 1936 and 1970 authorized direct subsidy payments to shipyards building vessels for the U.S. foreign trade. Historically, U.S. naval construction, repair, and overhaul work was reserved to domestic yards. This triad of direct and indirect government support is mainly responsible for keeping an American shipyard industry in place.

What then happened to disturb a support arrangement of almost half a century? To answer this question it is necessary to summarize events over the past decade.

In 1975–76, defense spending in real terms fell to its lowest point since the Korean War. Naval building programs were not spared. In this period, merchant ship construction for the domestic and foreign trades contributed substantially to shipyard industry well-being. In 1975, for example, federal government construction subsidies were being paid on 39 new ships and 5 reconstructed ships for the U.S. foreign trade. Overall, American yards had orders for 83 new vessels, aggregating 8 million deadweight tons, with an order book value of $4.4 billion.[5]

In 1981, when President Reagan took office, the active naval fleet stood at 491 ships. Almost immediately the new administration inaugurated two policies of profound importance to the shipyard industry. First, in keeping with Reagan campaign pledges, the goal of a 600-ship Navy was set firmly in place. This meant a substantial increase in government work for shipyards. The second policy had an opposite effect. No funds were requested to subsidize the difference between U.S. and foreign building costs for ships engaged in foreign trade.[6] (See Chapters 4 and 11 for a discussion of construction differential subsidies.) This is a classic illustration of how federal policy both giveth (in inaugurating the largest naval building program since World War II) and taketh away (in ending direct subsidy payments to shipyards for foreign trade merchant ship construction).

The Reagan administration has defended its non–construction differential subsidy (CDS) policy by pointing to increased naval work for shipyards, work it argues more than makes up for the loss of merchant ship contracts to foreign yards. While the argument is supportable considering total government shipyard expenditures, the policy's effects have been uneven over the industry. Naval construction, of necessity, had to be placed in larger yards with the capability of building technically complex vessels.[7] And even with increasing dollars going to overhaul and repair ($4–6 billion annually since FY 1982), the small and medium-size yards have had to share this work with the government-owned, naval shipyards, provided they had the technological capability to bid on the work in the first place. Moreover, private-sector repair work remained in the doldrums as the worldwide shipping recession for many sectors of the industry, notably tankers, continued into the mid-1980s.

But what of building for the domestic U.S. trades, business long reserved for American shipyards? Except for some new tanker construction to transport oil from Alaska to the lower 48 states and a scattering of other orders, shipyards faced declining protected trade business. In 1975 there were 205 ocean-going ships in the domestic trade. In March of 1986 the number was 179 although total deadweight tonnage was higher (i.e., there were fewer but larger vessels).

The Reagan administration has repeatedly stated its support for requiring domestic tonnage to be built in the United States. However, a growing number of maritime observers are calling for a relaxation of some of the restrictions; for example, allowing this shipping (or some part of it) to be built in the vastly cheaper foreign shipyards. (See Chapter 5.) In this respect, the president of one of the most active U.S. maritime unions, the Marine Engineers Beneficial Association, and a member of the National Maritime Council of the Department of Transportation, added his support for such a policy change.[8]

Coupled with a general uncertainty about whether Congress (and the administration) will continue to support the present shipyard monopoly with respect to domestic trade ship construction, and the acknowledged fact that land transportation systems are becoming increasingly competitive with the traditionally low ocean shipping rates, ship operators are hesitant to commit the necessary capital to replace an aging domestic trade fleet. In his 1984 year-end message, M. Lee Rice, president of the Shipbuilders Council, noted that the potential market for domestic tonnage replacement is "essentially dormant" and went on to point out that as of 1 January 1981 there were 34 domestic trade vessels on shipyard order books, in 1983 there were 15, and in 1984 only 10.[9]

Alternatives

Few persons in or out of government question the need for a shipbuilding ship/repair industry sufficient to meet mobilization requirements. Differences arise over the size of the shipyard mobilization base (i.e., numbers and capability), and how to ensure the survival of an industry that is overpriced in world commercial shipbuilding markets by between 100 and 150 percent.

In 1985, while there was some disagreement, most authorities concurred that the United States had a shipyard mobilization base sufficient to meet the most likely conflict demands. Disagreement, however, became sharper over whether the present shipyard base can be maintained down the road under present policies—and even sharper over the question of whether the industry can be substantially smaller and still meet mobilization requirements.

The alternatives are:

1. Maintain the shipyard industry as presently sized. Under this alternative *additional* government support would be needed. Forms it might take include renewing the construction subsidy program for foreign trade cargo vessels, reserving a specified amount of foreign trade cargo to American-built vessels, and building merchant ships for government account, such ships to be either leased to private operators or placed in a reserve status, that is, become a part of the National Defense Reserve Fleet.[10] Government-owned shipyard capability would remain the same.
2. Allow the present shipyard base to shrink to some agreed-upon minimum. This minimum would be maintained with government support, if necessary, as described in (1). This alternative assumes an excess shipyard capacity with respect to mobilization requirements. Naval shipyard capability would remain the same.
3. Allow the present shipyard base to shrink to a size that would rely entirely upon U.S. shipyards building for the domestic trade and naval work. Any shortfalls would be made up by maintaining one or more "mothballed" shipyards in a high state of readiness and/or expanding the capability of the government-owned, naval shipyards. Maintaining mothballed yards and an expanded naval shipyard capability would be a Department of Defense responsibility.

These alternatives will be discussed and analyzed in later chapters.

Conclusion

Analysts tend to focus on the large rather than the small, in shipyard studies as in other activities. It is the large yards such as Newport News, Electric Boat, Bath Iron Works, and the various Todd shipyards that get public attention. Together with the 80 or so medium-sized yards, they unquestionably constitute the most important part of U.S. shipyard mobilization capabilities in terms of national security.[11] But what of the several hundred smaller craft building and repair facilities located in the United States? Do they have a role to play in mobilization, and should their contributions be factored into the overall planning? Their possible roles and contributions are analyzed and commented upon in Chapter 8.

Another point that is self-evident, but one that can be overlooked, is that there is *no substitutability* in an emergency between shipyards located in NATO or other allied countries and shipyards located in the United States. At a particular time and place, a shipyard is a unique asset.

There would be relatively few problems in substituting a British-flag containership for an American one with respect to transporting military supplies to our forces in Europe, or substituting a West German roll-on/roll-off vessel under the same conditions, or a Japanese tanker for essentially the same type U.S. vessel in an emergency. Depending upon allied-flag merchant ships to meet part of our sealift requirements is not a new concept, nor is it without merit. Be that as it may, the same concept has limited applicability with respect to shipyards. In a NATO war, for example, a British shipyard in Liverpool would be of little help to a battle-damaged naval or merchant ship limping into Charleston, Boston, or Norfolk—or to a carrier entering San Francisco Bay in need of extensive repairs. A rule of thumb would be that shipyards in close geographic proximity *do have* a degree of substitutability. For example, facilities at Charleston can be substituted for those at Savannah or Jacksonville in many instances. However, the greater the geographic distance between shipyards, the less substitution is possible. And if a war in Europe is nonnuclear, U.S. shipyards may wind up as the only game in town.[12] Thus, should the U.S. shipyard mobilization base be at risk, the time to remedy the situation is while the assets are still within reach.

A final consideration worth noting in this introduction is that naval work by itself is insufficient to support the number of shipyards that would be needed in an emergency. The point was made by Secretary of the Navy John Lehman in an April 1983 interview when he said:

> No, there is not enough Navy business to hold the shipbuilding base. . . . We need more of a base than we are going to be able to hold on to with purely Navy building.[13]

The SYMBA study went into more detail:

> Navy work alone as projected in the study would not sustain an adequately diversified base, nor can the public yards sustain further decreases in workload and still maintain the capability for meeting mobilization demands. Although the Navy shipbuilding program has provided a substantial "shoring-up" of the base, Navy work tends to be concentrated in a few yards, while the vast majority of the 110 private yards modelled in the SYMBA study are engaged primarily in commercial work. A diverse shipyard base is essential for maximum flexibility and efficiency. Depart-

ment of Navy studies have shown that the Navy yards cannot sustain substantial decreases in workload without decreasing their capability for meeting mobilization requirements.[14]

Thus, while naval work is the cement that is presently holding together a shipbuilding base, it is simply not enough.

2 Shipbuilding: The Early Years

> And all I ask is a tall ship,
> And a star to steer her by.
> —John Masefield, "Sea Fever"

A SUCCESSFUL VOYAGE is the combination of a good vessel design, a good builder (shipyard), and good seamen. This chapter focuses on the shipbuilder, and to a lesser extent on the role of the designer—the conceiver of ships—in what has been called "America's Golden Age of Sail."

A study of American shipbuilding traditionally begins with the English North American settlements of the first part of the seventeenth century. While there is considerable logic to support this period as a departure point, shipbuilding is an art and a science that has evolved through hundreds of centuries, the last three and one-half being but a very small part of that evolution. And, more important, it is an evolution that is ongoing—a fact that gives the best, really the only, hope that the United States will one day achieve an economically viable shipbuilding/ship repair industry. We simply do not know what form the demand for ocean transportation will take 50 or 100 years from now—only that it will change. It is axiomatic that a maritime nation that acknowledges the inevitability of change, and ensures that its shipbuilders stay on the leading edge of shipbuilding technology, will, in the long run, be a nation that builds a fair part of the world's ships.

A Drifting Log to *Golden Hind*

Probably the first practical use that humans had for something that floated involved a drifting log. Perhaps someone used its buoyancy in crossing a stream or river, or to save himself after falling in the water. Logically, the first improvement on the log was a raft, that is, several logs bound together. From the log raft the Egyptians, the first shipbuilders of record, progressed to the lighter but larger papyrus reed raft, not greatly unlike the "Kon-Tiki" of relatively recent fame.[1] Some early drawings of Egyptian rafts date from 4000 to 3000 B.C., although no one is sure when these rafts were first used to transport people and goods along the Nile.

Or, perhaps, fishermen were the earliest users of rafts or boats—or if not the first, certainly among the first. Excavated dugouts from prehistoric times suggest this possibility. The early use of catamarans for fishing along the Indian Ocean coasts is another documented example.

In Egypt the concept of the pointed bow probably followed from use of a corklike tree, the *ambaj*, that tapered from a width of 5 or 6 feet at the ground to a pointed end at the top. At some later time, the *curve of the bow* could have evolved when the ends of the papyrus reeds were bound together to make a point, the binding tending to make the reeds curve upward.[2] Other improvements in ship and boat building would include substituting logs for planks, and pegging the planks together instead of tying them. Later, skins would be stretched over a wood frame to form a hull. The bark canoe, familiar to North American school children, was a natural result of this technological progression.

In the beginning, "ship" propulsion was accomplished with crude paddles. By 1600 B.C., the Egyptians had progressed from paddles to oars and to the use of sail. In this period, ships on the Nile reached lengths of 200 feet. They were broad of beam and of shallow draft.

The Phoenicians, and later the Minoan civilization centered on the island of Crete, probably put ships to their most practical commercial and military use. By 1000 B.C. their cargo and military sailing vessels were common in the Mediterranean. Technological improvements of this era included steering paddles (which defined a vessel's stern), stays to give strength to masts, and a crow's nest to aid in navigation.[3]

One of the earliest lessons on diminishing returns to scale in shipbuilding occurred shortly before the birth of Christ. In this period, roughly 500 B.C. to A.D. 100, the "power" of a ship was measured not only by the number of oars on a single tier, but by the number of tiers (or banks) of oars as well. Thus, a three-tier ship presumably was superior to a two-tier ship, a four-tier better than a three-tier, and so on. However, the more tiers, the higher the ship's freeboard, and the longer the oars required on the higher tiers. This made it difficult to coordinate rowing, a problem that, in turn, affected vessel maneuverability. According to the English historian and naval architect G. S. Baker, the point of diminishing returns was reached at the naval battle of Actium in 30 B.C., between Anthony and Caesar. Baker notes:

> Anthony's ships were mainly of four to ten banks, top heavy, and incapable of the rapid movement to breach or board an enemy and [in the ensuing action] each of them was forced to sustain the attack of three or more of

Caesar's two and three bank ships and many were sunk. . . . After the battle the three bank ship became the [standard] rowing vessel for a very long period.[4]

Across the Mediterranean in this same period, Greek galleys were being propelled by oars and sails. These, and the typical Phoenician ship, were three-bank oar/sail vessels, generally on the order of 100 to 200 feet in length with a 20 to 25 foot beam.

As the successor civilization, Rome improved upon the Greek galley. By A.D. 200 Roman ships generally had a main mast with two sails and a bowsprit, and were considerably larger and of deeper draft than earlier Greek and Phoenician vessels. It is worth noting that Rome was the first civilization to invest in a standing navy.

In Scandinavia, the Viking ships of the period A.D. 600 to 1000 brought the oar/sail-powered ship to its pinnacle. These vessels ranged from 75 to 100 feet in length with a beam of about 15 feet. That they were well constructed is attested to by the early Norse voyages of discovery to Iceland, Greenland, and Newfoundland.

Oar and sail warship *circa* A.D. 1050. This type ship was used by William the Conqueror in crossing the English Channel in 1066.

In the twelfth century, for the first time, a rudder was mounted on hinges attached to a vessel's sternpost. Thus did the steering oar pass into history. And in the same century, Arab mariners perfected the triangular sail, known then and now as a lateen. The advantage of a lateen was that is enabled ships to sail closer to the wind.[5]

In the fourteenth and fifteenth centuries, ship technology was exemplified by Columbus's *Santa Maria* (110 feet long, with three masts and a bowsprit), the ships of Prince Henry the Navigator, which were similar, and Francis Drake's *Golden Hind*, in which he circumnavigated the globe in 1577. Table 2.1 shows the dimensions of some typical sixteenth-century English-built ships.

The North American Colonial Period: 1607–1785

A short 30 years after Drake's *Golden Hind* sailed around the world, the first ship built in America, the 30-ton bark *Virginia*, was launched on the Kennebec River in what is now the state of Maine. Twenty-four years later, on 4 July 1631, the first seagoing vessel, *Blessing of the Bay*, slid into the waters of Massachusetts Bay.[6]

Early ships built in the American colonies undoubtedly followed European designs of that time. The standard in the fifteenth and sixteenth centuries was the Portuguese "carvel," essentially the design of the *Golden Hind* and most sixteenth-century European merchantmen. In the seventeenth century, ship designs were modified as the importance of vessel stability was increasingly recognized. The result was lower sterns and greater hold depth.

Table 2.1. Sixteenth-century English ship dimensions.[a]

Ship	Year	Keel length	Beam	Hold depth	Burden tons[b]
Elizabeth	1558	100	38	18	684
Victory	1560	95	35	17	555
Triumph	1561	100	40	19	760
Dreadnough	1573	80	30	15	360
Merhonor	1589	110	37	17	691

[a]SOURCE: G. S. Baker, *The Merchant Ship: Design Past and Present*, p. 31.

[b]Historically, the tonnage of a ship has been the measure of what a ship should pay for public services such as harbor dues, lighthouse costs, pilot and canal transit fees, etc. In medieval times, the wine cask was the measure of vessel carrying capacity. Two casks were considered one ton (tun) and were reckoned to occupy approximately 60 cubic feet of space. A ship of 500 burden tons (or 1,000 wine casks) was estimated to carry 500 tons of wine.

In the fifteenth century, English law required that ships be measured in terms of tonnage. In today's terms, a 200-ton, fifteenth-century English vessel would be considered a ship of approximately 200 net tons, net tonnage being the volume of a ship's enclosed space less space for non-cargo requirements such as crew quarters.

English warship *circa* A.D 1500 . Sir Francis Drake's *Golden Hind* was similar in design and construction.

As a general proposition, few industries, or major economic endeavors, blossom into overnight successes. Capital, the necessary technology, skilled labor, and a marketing strategy to gain buyer acceptance must all come together, a development that usually takes time. However, shipbuilding in North America was an exception to this rule.

A number of reasons are generally cited as to why shipbuilding took such a quick hold in the English colonies. One was that the material for building ships—wood and wood products, such as tar and turpentine—was plentiful. Another was that the colonists had come from a seafaring nation, where the ocean, and the opportunities it afforded for a livelihood, were known and appreciated. It was also important that the prevailing economic doctrine of the time—mercantilism—lent itself to colonial shipbuilding. Mercantilist theory supported the concept of colonies being the suppliers of raw materials for the commerce and industry of the mother country. England, long a shipbuilding nation, was already importing timber from Scandinavia at the time of the first North American settlements. With an abundance of timber, literally right down to the shoreline, it was logical that colonial shipbuilders early on would supply a large part of England's tonnage. And so they did.[7]

Fishing and Whaling

The fishing industry on the Newfoundland Banks predated the *Mayflower* by a century. And as demand for fish increased in Europe, so too did demand for New England–built ships, a demand later augmented by an increasingly important whaling industry. As the fishing and whaling fleets

Table 2.2. Colonial shipbuilding, 1769–71.

Colony where built	Number[a]	Tonnage
1769		
New Hampshire	54	2,452
Massachusetts	137	8,013
Rhode Island	39	1,482
Connecticut	50	1,542
New York	19	955
New Jersey	4	83
Pennsylvania	22	1,469
Maryland	20	1,344
Virginia	27	1,269
North Carolina	12	607
South Carolina	12	789
Georgia	2	50
West Florida	1	80
1770		
New Hampshire	47	3,581
Massachusetts	149	7,274
Rhode Island	164	2,035
Connecticut	46	1,522
New York	18	960
New Jersey	—	—
Pennsylvania	26	2,354
Maryland	17	1,545
Virginia	21	1,105
North Carolina	5	125
South Carolina	3	52
Georgia	3	57
West Florida	1	10
1771		
New Hampshire	55	4,991
Massachusetts	125	7,714
Rhode Island	75	2,148
Connecticut	46	1,483
New York	37	1,693
New Jersey	2	70
Pennsylvania	21	1,307
Maryland	18	1,645
Virginia	19	241
North Carolina	8	560
South Carolina	7	543
Georgia	6	450
West Florida	2	24

SOURCE: "U.S. Merchant Shipbuilding: 1607–1976." *Marine Engineering/Log*, August 1976, p. 65.

[a]Includes sloops, schooners, and top sails.

moved farther away from shore, more and larger ships were required.[8] Not surprisingly, this demand, added to tonnage required to service a growing trade between Europe, North America, the West Indies, and South America, ensured the continued prosperity of the shipbuilder.

By 1750 over 125 shipyards were located in the colonies. But more important, these yards were world-price-competitive. Vessel construction costs were from 30 to 50 percent less than in England. North American yards could build their best ships for 3 to 4 pounds sterling a ton compared to 5 to 7 pounds sterling a ton in Great Britain.[9] One estimate is that colonial shipbuilders were turning out 300 to 400 ships a year, and it was calculated that fully one-third of registered British tonnage was American-built.[10] Table 2.2 summarizes colonial shipbuilding statistics for 1769–71.

American Shipbuilding Supremacy: 1785–1855

The edge that the colonial shipbuilder had over the competition with respect to building costs was great enough to more than compensate for the higher wages paid American seamen. However, European builders (Scandinavia and Baltic Sea countries) with easy access to timber were also competitive in terms of cost; so cost alone was not enough to ensure continued supremacy of American-built ships in the marketplace. It was *design* that made American-built vessels unique, particularly designs that increased speed.

It has been suggested that the earliest demand for fast ships was the result of a growing propensity on the part of the colonists to engage in smuggling—for example, rum, sugar, and molasses from the non-British West Indies in exchange for colonial manufactures and tobacco. Both directions of this trade were prohibited by English law. For instance, in 1699 legislation forbade the "shipment of wool, woolen yarn, or cloth produced in the colonies to any other plantation or colony."[11] As a rule, colonial goods that competed with British-made goods were subject to similar restrictions. Or, as in the case of tobacco, the product could only be sold in England. In such a political–economic environment, as one writer suggests: "One did not go a smuggling or venture into piratical waters in 'slow coaches.'"[12]

When war with England came in 1775, and before the arrival of French assistance, it was the colonial merchant vessel in the role of privateer that achieved the early American successes. In 1776, for example, 229 English ships were captured, a figure that increased to 331 in 1777.[13] While the speed of an American privateer was, at best, not over 12 knots, she was still considerably faster than her prey, whether merchantman or warship.[14]

Twenty-seven years later in the nation's second war with England

(1812–15), the fast American-built privateers again played havoc with British shipping. Their effect can best be seen in a resolution adopted on 14 September 1814 at a public meeting in Glasgow. It stated:

> The number of privateers with which our channels have been infested, the audacity with which they have approached our coasts, and the success with which their enterprise has been attended, have proved injurious to our commerce, humbling to our pride and discreditable to the directors of the naval power of the British nation. . . . there is reason to believe that in the short space of less than 24 months above eight hundred vessels have been captured by the power whose maritime strength we have hitherto, impolitically held in contempt.[15]

One maritime authority concludes that "the close of the War of 1812 found the Yankee mariner with a respect for speed that amounted to reverence," and went on to say that "For as many years as they could remember, several thousand men regarded swift ships as synonymous with life, liberty, and the pursuit of happiness."[16] However, swift ships paid a price:

> The fast sailing ships were not only small but their cabins were mere closets, dingy, ill ventilated and uncomfortable beyond description. Many of them were so sharp that they were able to stow little cargo, and their between decks so low (less than five feet in height, usually) as to be unsuitable for steerage quarters.[17]

While historians agree that it would be stretching the facts to give American ingenuity the entire credit for designing and building the fast ships of the late eighteenth century,[18] it is still fair to say:

> It is to America's distinction, not that she alone possessed the secret [of a fast ship], but that at an early date she took, and on the whole successfully maintained, a position of world leadership in the development of vessels of this type.[19]

With the Treaty of Paris in 1815, a major reason for having fast ships ceased to exist. The needs of commerce took center stage, and the requirement was for a greater carrying (earning) capacity. The typical American fast schooner, brig, or frigate, was on the order of 200 to 400 tons. On the other hand, British yards had long been building vessels of 1,000 or more tons, the slow (3–5 knot) but profitable East Indiaman being a good example. The only remaining commercial enterprise of any consequence where vessel speed was of primary consideration was the African slave trade, which was outlawed in 1808 but continued to flourish nevertheless.

Needed now were new markets (trades) where vessel speed was important and sufficiently profitable to encourage the building of not only fast ships but *larger* ships. In essence, it was a case of fast ships in search of a mission.[20]

One of the first trades to match a fast ship with demand was the growing North Atlantic packet (passenger) business, spurred by an increasing number of European immigrants. In 1820 Europeans arriving in the United States totaled 7,691. By 1835 the number was almost 42,000, and in 1850 it reached 250,000.[21] Supplementing passenger earnings were mail and general cargo revenues. A fast passage brought prestige, and prestige brought full bookings and profits. Thus did the fast ship find an early commercial niche.

The best-known of the American packet companies was the Black Ball Line, which inaugurated service to England in 1818 with four ships. Early transit times averaged 18 to 25 days eastward bound, with best times at 14 to 16 days. The first Black Ball packet was the *James Monroe* of 400 tons with a maximum capacity of 25 passengers. Within ten years, however, average vessel size had increased to 500 to 600 tons, and in the 1840s it reached 800 tons. By 1850 the well-known builder and designer Donald McKay had built 16 packet ships of over 1,000 tons. His sister ships *Star of Empire* and *Chariot of Fame* exceeded 2,000 tons.[22]

Almost simultaneously, another developing trade, half a world away, also put a premium on fast ships. This was the Orient, or so-called China, trade. Here a fast vessel had at least two things in her favor. First, she could make a trip over the great distances involved in two-thirds the time of a slower ship. Second, the generally high value of the cargo carried could pay the premium freight rates charged by a fast ship but one with less carrying capacity. Moreover, a fast ship was good insurance in waters where pirates abounded.

A third employment for swift ships was the California trade that flourished after annexation in 1846. With the discovery of gold in 1848, the demand for fast ships increased tenfold. One estimate is that between 200,000 and 300,000 tons of shipping was employed in the California trade between 1850 and 1853.[23] Over 100,000 persons came to California by ship. For obvious reasons, the ships employed were fast. Passage times were on the order of 100 days from New York and 110 days from Boston.[24]

An additional market was added when, in 1849, the last of the British Navigation Acts were repealed. This allowed American participation in the English tea trade (India–Ceylon to England), where speed was at a premium. Another route was opened when gold was discovered in Australia in 1851. Many voyages combined these trades; for example, the American east coast to California, thence to China, either returning home with traditional spice cargoes or loading tea for England.[25]

Authorities disagree over when the clipper ship era (as it is known to school children today) actually began. In other words, which was the first clipper ship? Some argue that it began with the relatively small Baltimore clippers of the 1820s such as the *Ann McKim* (437 tons). Others insist the era truly began with much larger and faster ships, and cite the 750-ton *Rainbow*, built in 1845, as the first. One thing is certain, however: the American clipper evolved in an economic environment where speed was a paramount consideration. Moreover, it was sustained by equal ingenuity in putting speed to a profitable purpose. Appendix B lists a number of typical American clippers, together with their design specifications, for the period 1845–60. Also included is a representation of British-built clipper ships of the same period.

In the decade prior to the Civil War, the output of American shipyards reached the highest levels of the nineteenth century, with a peak output of 580,000 gross tons attained in 1855. This period proved to be the high-water mark not only for American shipbuilding, but for shipping as well. Table 2.3 lists gross tonnages built and documented in the United States between 1798 and 1855. Some notable shipbuilding successes would occur later, particularly in time of war or emergency, but they would simply be exceptions to a continuing long-term downward trend.

Conclusion

The period of American preeminence in world shipbuilding, which reached its zenith with the large California clippers, was all too brief,

Table 2.3. Merchant vessels built and documented in the United States for selected years, 1798–1855.

Year	Number of vessels[a]	Gross tons
1798	635	49,435
1800	995	106,261
1805	—[b]	128,507
1810	—	127,575
1815	1,329	155,579
1820	557	51,394
1825	1,000	116,464
1830	648	58,560
1835	725[c]	75,107
1840	871	118,309
1845	1,038	146,018
1850	1,360	272,218
1855	2,024	588,450

SOURCE: U.S. Bureau of Census, *Historical Statistics of U.S., Colonial Times to 1957*, Washington, D.C., 1960, p. 448.

[a]Includes canal boats and barges.

[b]Not available.

[c]Nine-month period.

perhaps 40 years at best. However, history is still the best teacher, and lessons can be learned from this period. One is that Americans, for whatever reasons, are at their innovative best in time of adversity. It is fair to say that while the ocean was their greatest benefactor in the colonial period and first part of the nineteenth century, the gift was not given freely. English navigation laws severely limited opportunities for them to profitably employ their shipbuilding talents. Pirates and the continued harassment by ships of England's enemies, and later England itself, threatened their very survival. Out of this came a penchant for fast ships but also the understanding that a fast ship must be viable, not only in conflict but in commerce. The first lesson gives rise to the second: if you have a better product, force the world to meet your standard. The British did not adopt the clipper ship out of admiration for American genius but out of necessity. The same point could be equally well made a century later. World shipping embraced the American-innovated containership because of the need to remain competitive, and for no other reason.

Assuming the American virtues of innovativeness and competitiveness are still factors, the lesson to be learned is that dollars spent on innovation in vessel design are dollars well spent. The second is that limiting a shipowner's opportunities with respect to employing an innovative creation is foolish in the extreme.[26] And should innovative investment in the private sector temporarily subside, it is a proper role of government to lead the way. The federally funded nuclear-powered *Savannah* (1962) and the innovative *Mariner*-class vessels of the 1950s were good, potentially profitable, long-term investments. The chief problem with respect to nuclear-powered merchant ships was lack of follow-through. A second-generation *Savannah* should have been launched in 1970, and a third in 1980. Had the concept of nuclear-powered merchant ships been aggressively pursued, even in the face of controversy and hostility, one could reasonably ask, where might vessel technology (and the American merchant marine) be today? Unlike the case of the clipper ships where we forced the world to our standard, in the case of nuclear power for merchant ships, we lowered ours to that of the critics, forgetting the predictions of numerous authorities of a century past who argued that a tall ship, narrow of beam, with a full spread of canvas, was inherently unstable and might capsize.

In the case of the *Mariners*, the object lesson was learned. A fast, large ship was shown to be profitable when much conventional wisdom at the time held that a 20-knot ship was uneconomical. The *Mariner* program proved the critics wrong, and the world adjusted accordingly.[27]

3

Shipbuilding:
The Long-Term
Decline

By strong brains laboring on the thought unwon,
They mark our passage as a race of men,
Earth will not see such ships as those again.
—John Masefield, "Ships"

AT THE HIGH POINT of American shipbuilding (and shipping) fortunes, about 1847–57, almost 3.4 million gross tons of shipping was built in the United States, the greater part of it the wooden sailing vessels described in Chapter 2. In this period, Great Britain produced about 1.8 million gross tons, and British possessions, chiefly Canada, another 1.7 million gross tons.[1] Clearly, the United States was the world's leading shipbuilding nation. However, figures can be deceiving. Looking only at market share, ignoring the underlying and always changing economic forces at work in the marketplace, is done only at one's peril.

Historically, the American wage, whether for seaman or shipwright, has tracked considerably higher than that of his foreign counterpart. Wages for foreign seamen in the first half of the nineteenth century were 25 to 50 percent lower than for Americans. However, this disadvantage was generally offset by smaller American crews. For example, a 1,000-ton British vessel was typically crewed by 40 men and 10 boys, while a comparable American ship would have a crew of between 20 and 30.[2] A small, American, fast-sailing vessel in the 400-ton class could be handled by 18 officers and men. And while she could carry only half the cargo of larger British vessels, the latter were burdened with a crew of 125.[3]

However, such an advantage could hardly be maintained forever. As the British began to build their own clipper ships in the late 1840s, for example, the *Sea Witch* in 1848 and the *Sea Queen* in 1849, crew sizes became more comparable.

On the shipbuilding side, the European builder again had the advantage of lower wages, about 50 percent less than in the United States.[4]

Offsetting this advantage was the lower price of American timber and generally superior American shipyard technology, which translated into a higher output per employee. However, the timber advantage progressively lessened as European builders began to import lumber from such diverse sources as Germany, Russia, Scandinavia, and Canada. In 1830 the cost of a wooden sailing ship per gross ton favored the American builder by almost one-half; by 1844 the differential had decreased to approximately 20 percent, and by 1860 it was almost gone.[5] But by this time a large part of British new construction was iron-hulled.

Iron and Steam Ships: British Ascendancy in Shipbuilding

It is generally conceded that Great Britain and the European nations never equaled the American builder in constructing fast-sailing vessels, an art and science that reached its height with the design and building of the extreme clippers in the 1850s.[6] However, pieces were falling into place that ultimately would lead to British shipbuilding supremacy.

A number of major, and several minor, factors explain this success. One age-old obstacle to an efficiently designed British ship was the means by which a vessel's tonnage was measured, and hence the basis for government taxes. Until 1836, a ship was measured in terms of length and breadth only, not depth.[7] Since the owner wanted a ship with the least measurement tonnage, efficient designs took second place to tax considerations. Eighteen years later, the measurement laws were codified in the Merchant Shipping Act of 1854. Basically, tonnage measurement (for tax purposes) was predicated on the capacity of a ship to earn revenue, her gross tonnage, essentially leaving the design and building of a ship to those who knew it best. This is the approach used in most maritime countries today.

One of the most important factors contributing to British shipbuilding success was willingness to invest in steam propulsion at a time when the American clipper ships and the American shipbuilding industry were the envy of the world.

The first English commercial employment of a steam vessel was the 56-foot *Charlotte Dundas* on the River Forth in Scotland.[8] In the United States, Robert Fulton demonstrated the practicality of steam propulsion when, in 1807, his *Clermont* made the 150-mile trip up the Hudson River from New York. This was followed in 1819 by the Atlantic crossing of the American steamship *Savannah*, although steam was used for less than 10 percent of the passage time. However, this American flirtation with steam in ocean service was short-lived and not seriously taken up again until 1845 when Congress offered mail subsidies to establish a steam packet service on the North Atlantic. By and large, American owners and builders were more than satisfied with the profits from wooden sailing ships.

Nevertheless, steam propulsion in the North Atlantic was an idea whose time had come. In 1838 scheduled steamer service was begun by the British flag *Sirius* and *Great Western*. Crossing times were 17 and 15 days respectively, considerably shorter and more predictable than that of the typical sailing packet.[9] Seven years later (1845) the 360-passanger *Great Britain* entered service. By 1860, England and steam power stood almost alone in the North Atlantic.

Another major factor that contributed to British shipbuilding and shipping success was the repeal in 1849 of the last of the Navigation Acts. English shipowners had long complained about the cost advantage held by American-built ships, a large part of the advantage being the low cost of lumber in North America. Yet British duties on foreign imported lumber in the first half of the nineteenth century were still in place, their avowed purpose being to foster a British colonial lumber industry. However, the Engligh-built ship was protected from foreign competition in that foreign ships were excluded not only from England's colonial trade but from home trade as well. The result of this protectionism was, at best, a mixed blessing. While these statutes ensured English shipping profits, they acted as a tranquilizer with respect to improvements in building wooden sailing ships. As one British authority points out:

> Protection from foreign competition resulted in British ship design of 1845 differing little from the style to be found in 1815. [And] . . . statistics confirm the overall stagnant nature of the British shipbuilding industry in the 35 years before 1850.[10]

With repeal of the Navigation Acts, the shipowner was free to buy his vessels anywhere he chose. But a policy of "free ships" also meant the shipbuilder must be competitive. No longer could he take a year or more to construct a vessel for a trading opportunity that could be gone before the ship was delivered to her owner. The competitive British clipper ship was fair evidence of the success of the new policy.

Concurrent with the introduction of steam as a means of propulsion was the increasing use of iron in vessel construction. This was an undeniable British advantage. England had large deposits of coal, which in turn attracted and fostered an iron, and later a steel, industry. Moreover, Great Britain had led the world into the Industrial Revolution with all that such leadership implied—an acceleration of engineering and technical skills, management of large-scale industries, and continuing innovations in things mechanical. By 1831 iron steamship building was well established, and such was its rapid advancement that 30 years later it could be considered a mature industry.[11] Innovation, however, was not limited to iron hulls and single-cylinder steam plants. In 1836 the screw propeller was perfected, and nine years later it was accepted by the British Admiralty. Lighter and smaller steam engines, but with more power, were built. These innovations moved the steam vessel from primarily a river and coastal trade vessel to an ocean carrier.

In 1862, thirty percent of the British merchant marine was of iron construction. England's technological superiority was recognized in a Select Report submitted to the Hanseatic League shipowners in 1847:

> Supposing the abolition of all protection. England must always possess a superiority in shipbuilding, owing to the greater cheapness with which she can build iron vessels. At present, the cheaper rates of materials and labour enable foreign nations to build wooden vessels perhaps cheaper than the English, but if the iron system should be found on a fair trial to succeed (and to steamers the point has not been denied), Great Britain must ever possess the power to underselling the foreigner.[12]

The effect of British technological superiority in iron and steam vessels, and the consequent results with respect to American shipping and shipbuilding, were described by historians Samuel E. Morison and Henry S. Commager:

> By 1857 the British Empire had an oceangoing steam tonnage of almost half a million tons, as compared with ninety thousand under the American flag. England had won back her maritime supremacy in fair competition, by the skill of her engineers and sturdy courage of her shipbuilders.[13]

British-built ships would dominate the world's trade routes for another century.

1865–1918

The Civil War is sometimes considered a major reason for the decline of American shipping and shipbuilding. This is a simplistic notion at best; as historian Harold Faulkner has observed:

> As chances for profit declined in shipping, capital found new and more profitable fields for investment. Manufacturing, which grew rapidly after the War of 1812, absorbed some of it; and considerable amounts were drawn into such internal improvements as canals and railways. The minds of the venturous and ambitious turned from the sea to the unexploited West, and capital turned from shipbuilding and the carrying trade to the development of natural resources. The elements contributing to the decline of the merchant marine were already apparent before the Civil War, and the result would undoubtedly have been the same if that conflict had not occurred.[14]

If one single intra–maritime-industry cause of the decline must be cited, it is probably that the American shipowners and shipbuilders were content with the profits being made on their fast, wooden sailing ships, profits that reached their height with the large California clippers. Historian John G. B. Hutchins notes that "the huge freight revenues of some clippers, which ranged from $75,000 to $125,000 were nearly sufficient to pay off the capital cost of the ship in one voyage." He goes on to conclude that never had the American shipowner seen such a profitable era.[15]

Table 3.1 indicates the extent to which wood and sail dominated American ship construction for most of the nineteenth century.

Table 3.1. U.S. merchant vessels built and documented, by type, for selected years, 1797–1900 (5 gross tons and over).

Year	Number of vessels[a]	Total gross tons	Steam/motor GT	Sailing[b]
1797	—[c]	56,679		56,679
1800	995	106,261		106,261
1805	—	128,507		128,507
1810	—	127,575		127,575
1815	1,329	155,579		155,579
1820	557	51,394	5,572	45,822
1825	1,000	116,464	9,171	107,293
1830	648	58,560	8,269	50,291
1835	725	75,107	12,347	62,760
1840	871	118,309	19,811	98,498
1845	1,038	146,018	40,926	105,092
1850	1,360	272,218	56,911	215,307
1855	2,024	588,450	78,127	505,323
1860	1,071	214,798	69,370	145,428
1865	1,789	394,523	146,433	248,090
1870	1,618	276,953	70,261	146,340
1875	1,301	297,639	62,460	206,884
1880	902	157,410	78,854	59,057
1885	920	159,056	84,333	65,362
1890	1,051	294,123	159,046	102,873
1895	694	111,602	69,754	34,900
1900	1,447	393,790	202,528	116,460

SOURCE: U.S Bureau of Census, *Historical Statistics of U.S., Colonial Times to 1957*, Washington, D.C., 1960, pp. 448–49.

[a]Including small vessels built at small boatyards is justified on the ground that *total* figures best reflect the total activity at the nation's shipyards during the period under consideration, a period when vessels were much smaller in size than they are today.

[b]Includes canalboats and barges prior to 1868.

[c]Not available.

In England the price of iron steamships continued to fall, and by 1845 they had gained a 10 to 15 percent cost differential advantage over wooden vessels. By 1860 the much more efficient compound steam plant was in wide use. While it was undoubtedly an exaggeration, the editor of the New York *Times* nonetheless wrote in 1866 "that shipbuilding in this country [United States] is all but completely destroyed."[16]

The principle of steelmaking had been understood since 1850. The problem was its expense and the generally uneven quality of output. With the introduction of the open hearth and the Bessemer process in the 1870s, and improved rolling processes, steel as a vessel construction material came into its own. Its chief advantage over iron was its lighter weight and the relative ease of shaping it to design specifications.

It should also be said that the British shipbuilder could switch to steel ships a lot more cheaply than could his American counterpart. In 1882 shipbuilding labor costs were 44 percent less in England than America, while the price of steel plate was about 25 percent less.[17]

In 1888 the British-built, twin-screw triple-expansion-engine *City of New York* and *City of Paris* entered transatlantic service under the U.S. flag. These 10,000 + gross ton vessels had a speed of 20 knots. Table 3.2 indicates the growth in size and speed of the North Atlantic iron (and steel) steamships between 1862 and 1914.

Following the Civil War the American navy was woefully neglected. Long after the conflict ended, Civil War–design monitors were still in use

Table 3.2. Growth in size and speed of North Atlantic ocean liners, 1860–1914.

Date	Vessel/Where built	Gross tonnage	Passenger lift	Speed, knots
1862	*China* (Br)	2,638	1,039	12
1888	*City of New York* (Br)	10,499	1,740	20
1888	*City of Paris* (Br)	10,499	1,740	20
1893	*Campania* (Br)	12,950	2,000	21
1893	*Lucania* (Br)	12,950	2,000	21
1899	*Auguste Victoria* (Gr)	8,479	980	18
1903	*Carpathia* (Br)	13,555	1,704	14
1905	*Amerida* (Gr)	22,225	2,508	18
1905	*Lusitania* (Br)	31,500	2,165	25
1905	*Mauretania* (Br)	31,500	2,165	25
1912	*Imperator* (Gr)	52,000	3,643	22
1912	*Titanic* (Br)	46,328	3,902	23
1914	*Acquitania* (Br)	45,647	3,263	23
1914	*Vaterland* (Gr)	54,282	4,050	23

SOURCE: N. R. P. Bonsor, *North Atlantic Seaway*.

at a time when other world navies were building faster, heavier, and more powerfully gunned warships. Aware of the fleet's deteriorating condition, the Navy Department in 1881 appointed its first Naval Advisory Board.[18] With congressional support, the move to the modern, steel warship began, and in 1883 the first four contracts for a new class of fighting ship were authorized. An additional 30 warships would be built in the next 10 years.[19] By the time of the Spanish–American War in 1898, the Navy had become a major shipyard customer, even though much of the new construction was being done in naval shipyards. But if the shipbuilders had a new, potentially large, customer, orders from U.S.-flag operators in foreign trade were almost nil. The reason was not hard to find. In 1830 ninety percent of American foreign commerce was moved in U.S.-flag vessels; by 1915 it was less than 10 percent.

The first effect of World War I was felt by the shipper as the European belligerents moved their ships from normal peacetime trades to wartime service. The result was ten- and twentyfold freight increases. For example, rates on cotton from a U.S. port to the United Kingdom that were 25 cents/hundred pounds in July 1914, reached $5 in December 1916. Coal tonnage shipped from the United States to Argentina increased by a factor of 25.[20] There were no American ships to fill the void, and the law of supply and demand exacted its inexorable price.

With American commercial interests threatened and the probability of the United States entering the war increasing, the country embarked upon a program to acquire, construct, and operate, for government account, shipping sufficient to ensure that its vital interests were protected. The Emergency Fleet Corporation, a government agency authorized by the Shipping Act of 1916, was assigned this responsibility. After America's entry into the war of 1917, ship production eventually rose to unprecedented levels. Some 150 yards, manned by 300,000 workers, were able to deliver 391,000 tons of shipping in a single month (October 1918), considerably more than in most entire prewar years. All told, over 17,400,000 tons were under contract.[21] It was a remarkable achievement, even granting the slow start, given an almost nonexistent shipbuilding industry on which to build.[22]

1919–1945

While only a fraction of the tonnage commissioned by the government was delivered before the Armistice (approximately 600,000 tons), launchings of new ships under the program continued through 1920. In that year the U.S. Shipping Board, the agency that operated the government-built fleet, held title to 1,502 ships of 9,358,421 deadweight tons.[23] Table 3.3 shows vessels built and documented in the United States during 1918–45.

Table 3.3. Merchant vessels built and documented in the United States, 1918–45 (2,000 gross tons and over).[a]

Year	Number of vessels	Gross tonnage
1918	386	1,671,962
1920	450	2,312,658
1925	11	81,012
1930	16	151,208
1935	2	19,022
1940	53	444,727
1945	1,067	7,663,362

SOURCE: Shipbuilders Council of America, *Annual Report* (New York, 2 April 1956). Cited in Wytze Gorter, *U.S. Shipbuilding Policy* (New York: Harper Brothers, 1956), pp. 211–12.

The end of World War I, like most previous wars, found shipping routes overtonnaged. The U.S. building program, which continued after the end of hostilities, in no small measure contributed to the problem.[24] The year 1920 saw the beginning of a shipping depression that reached its peak in 1922 when 75 percent of the government-owned fleet was idle. To complicate matters, the 1916 legislation that authorized the building program was also quite specific with respect to having the government get out of the role of shipowner as soon as possible. This, however, was easier said than done, and it was not until almost the beginning of World War II that the last government-owned ship was sold.

As might be expected, overtonnaging in world trades brought on hard times for shipbuilders. With war-built ships selling at bargain prices, there were few new orders. The year 1935 was the low point for new merchant ship construction in the interwar period. Many old and established shipyards either went out of business or suspended operations. Others existed almost entirely on repair work. Moreover, the higher cost of building ships in the United States had to be reckoned with. During congressional hearings in 1920 on how best to dispose of the government's war-built fleet, it was noted that the cost of building a comparable steel ship in the United States exceeded that of Great Britain by $60/ton ($70/ton vs. $130/ton).[25]

Things improved somewhat with legislation passed in 1928 that reestablished mail subsidies on a number of foreign trade routes. This brought about some new construction and the refurbishing of some existing tonnage. Also, orders for vessels operating in the domestic ocean trades, trades reserved exclusively for American-flag, American-built ships, provided a safety net for many yards, particularly on the Atlantic coast. (See Chapter 5.) Eight years later legislation provided for direct subsidy payments to shipyards building for U.S.-flag, foreign-trade operators. The start of President Roosevelt's two-ocean naval policy in his second term also was important in maintaining a shipbuilding base during the Great Depression.

During the interwar period, building and design innovations were primarily confined to the great transatlantic and Mediterranean-route passenger vessels such as the *Normandie, Queen Mary, Bremen, Ile de France, Rex, Conte di Savoa,* and *Queen Elizabeth.* Speed and luxury were the driving considerations. In the North Atlantic, crossing records changed hands often. At different times the Blue Riband was held by France, Germany, and Great Britain.[26] The largest U.S. new build in the decade preceding World War II was the 33,500-ton *America,* small compared to the 80,000-ton *Normandie* and *Queen Mary.*

On the whole, general cargo vessels, although small by today's standards (around 7,000 gross tons), had great utility in that they could carry many types of freight. While some improvement occurred in the building and design of tankers, economy of operation dominated engine-room considerations. Most freighters and tankers were in the 10 to 12 knot range.

When the United States entered World War II, its most noteworthy maritime contribution was not in vessel design but in the ability to mass-produce ships. The best-known merchant ship of World War II was the Liberty ship, and the first of this class was the *Patrick Henry,* built by Bethlehem Steel's yard in Baltimore, and launched on 27 September 1941, some three months before Pearl Harbor. All told, 2,742 were built.[27] The Liberty was followed by the Victory ship, of which 531 were constructed. Some 6,400 merchant-type ships, including 1,200 small craft, were built between 1937 and 1945. At the war's end the government-controlled merchant fleet stood at over 5,000 vessels.[28]

Equally impressive was the naval building program, the more so because a warship is a much more technologically complex vessel than a merchant ship. Naval chroniclers Phillip Andrews and Leonard Engel fairly summed the achievement of shipyards in this respect:

On 1 July 1940 the Navy had 383 battleships, carriers, cruisers, destroyers, and submarines, aggregating 1,313,000 tons. Including auxiliaries, the fleet numbered 1,076 vessels of 1,875,000 tons. In the next three years 333 combatant vessels aggregating 1,117,054 tons were built. Other completions in this period were: 1,274 mine and patrol craft of 199,765 tons, 161 auxiliaries, 654 yard and district craft and 610,781 tons of landing craft (12,964 vessels). Consequently, despite war losses and transfer of a great many vessels to allied navies, on 1 July 1943 the Navy had upwards of 13,000 vessels of over 4,500,000 tons, including more than 600 combatant ships of some 2,000,000 tons. Deliveries during June, 1943 alone totalled 1,200 vessels, in comparison with five in June, 1940.[29]

1946–1986

America's maritime supremacy, if it could be called that, lasted for but a short time after the end of World War II. High U.S. operating and building costs increasingly had to be offset by direct payments (construction and operating subsidies) and indirect support such as cargo reservation and cargo preference legislation. The United States remained a maritime nation only with massive government support.

Between 1936 and 1983 construction differential subsidy payments to shipyards amounted to $3.8 billion. No new constructin subsidy funds have been authorized since 1981.

The nonsubsidized shipowner, particularly the large oil companies, were the first to flee the flag because of high operating and building costs. In 1984, U.S.-owned but foreign-built and foreign-manned ships totaled 525 ships of 50.9 million deadweight tons.

In the postwar period two distinct trends began to develop after 1960. First, all ships, but particularly tankers, were getting larger. For tankers, this was primarily due to the economics of operating larger ships on the Persian Gulf–North America, Europe oil routes via the Cape of Good Hope. These routes became critically important with the frequent closings of the Suez Canal following Arab–Israeli conflicts.

The second trend was a movement to increased ship specialization. The general cargo ship that had served commerce for centuries was being replaced by the containership, roll-on/roll-off (RO-RO) vessels, and lighter aboard ship (LASH) vessels. The liquid natural gas carrier (LNG) was a design milestone in itself. Producing these technologically complex vessels in American yards posed no problem. In fact, all were U.S.-inspired and U.S.-developed. The disadvantage was construction cost (twice as much as an average foreign yard) and delivery time (3 to 18 months longer). Exacerbating the cost differential problem was the entry of Far Eastern shipyards into the competition. Japan, an early competitor, was followed by South Korea in the early 1980s, while cheap repair yards were to be found all the way from Japan and South Korea in the north, to the Malacca Straits in the south.

As noted above, construction differential subsidies, which allowed a significant portion of the American foreign trade merchant marine to be built in the United States, were dropped in 1981. The American shipyard was now almost entirely dependent on naval work and building and repairing ships for the U.S. domestic trades. However, a considerable part of naval work had to be shared with eight naval (government-owned) shipyards. While all new construction was assigned to private shipyards after 1967, naval repair and alteration work has consistently favored the navy yards by about 65 to 35 percent.

U.S. Shipbuilding and Design Achievements during the Period of Decline

Although the long-term trend in shipbuilding has been downward since the Civil War, there have been a number of bright spots. Some are recited below.

It has been noted that the United States lagged in the development and employment of the iron steamship, and to the extent that such ships were built in the United States, they were not cost-competitive. While this is generally true, the U.S. shipbuilder was still quite capable of turning out a competitive iron steamship when cost was not a consideration. With government mail subsidies as an inducement, the Collins Line in 1851 built the *Atlantic*, *Pacific*, *Baltic*, and *Arctic*, and later the *Adriatic*. They were fast, and regularly bested the passage times of their British competitors. The American penchant for speed had not subsided. Delaware Senator Bayard stated the case when he said: "Speed against which these British can never hope to compete. Speed of such magnitude as the Government of Britain, and its chosen instrument, this man Cunard, never visualized or could ever hope to achieve."[30] In 1852 the Collins ship *Pacific* made the first transatlantic crossing in less than 10 days.

Passenger accommodations in the Collins ships were exceptional for the era, and it could be said that American flag service introduced elegance into ocean travel. However, misfortune plagued the line from the outset. Two ships were lost in as many years, and when mail subsidies were withdrawn in 1858, the line went out of business.

On the inventor side, in 1836 the naturalized American John Ericsson patented an improved screw propeller and later designed the USS *Monitor*, an ironclad that went a long way to revolutionizing naval warfare. Aside from testing the value of iron plating, the classic battle between the *Monitor* and the CSS *Merrimac* at Hampton Roads in 1862 established the value of the turret, a swivel-type arrangement that allowed a gun to be trained through a wide arc. No longer did the number of guns a ship carried measure her strength, but rather the number of turrets and the size of the gun(s) she housed. (The USS *Monitor* had only two 11-inch guns mounted on a single revolving turret.)

The most successful Confederate warship was the commerce raider *Alabama*; and although she was built by Lairds Shipyard in Great Britain, the concept was American. The sea warfare lessons learned from the cruise of the *Alabama* carried down to World War II.[31]

In the period between 1880 and 1910, American shipbuilders enjoyed a brief renaissance with the design and building of large wooden sailing schooners. These were not clipper ships; they were not designed for speed, but to make a profit in the growing U.S. domestic bulk trade. By

1910 the size of these great wooden ships exceeded 3,000 gross tons, rivaling that of the moderate-size steel steamship of the period. The schooner's great advantage was its low construction cost and small crew size. Taken together, it was said that the American great schooner was "the most weatherly and economical sailing vessel in the world."[32] Between 1870 and 1914 over 950,000 tons of this type ship were built.[33]

The output of American shipyards in World Wars I and II (noted above) represented production achievements that hardly can be overstated—that of World War II an achievement the world will probably never see repeated.

Neither should the creativity that introduced the containership, LASH, and RO-RO to the world be forgotten; nor the launching of the world's first nuclear-powered merchant ship, the NS *Savannah*, and the Mariner program of the 1950s.

The United States in the mid-1980s is a second-order maritime power in terms of its merchant shipping and shipbuilding. This is hardly a new observation. However, high points of achievement and even brilliance are plainly discernible. Remembering this, an assessment of the American shipyard industry in 1986 might be that "It is not dead but only sleepeth."

Conclusion: Lessons Learned

What lessons can be learned from this period of our history—particularly, lessons that might help in developing a new public policy with respect to shipyards? The most important are here held to be the following:

1. Success in shipbuilding, as in all other economic endeavors, is not conferred by divine intervention or by the will of Congress; it must be sought. Great Britain won back its maritime supremacy because it wanted to do so. The United States can achieve a respectable ranking as a shipbuilding nation if it wants to, but only if all parties, not government alone, are willing to make the commitment. Certainly, the United States will not win back its shipbuilding place by enshrining the status quo. New ideas, new laws, or no laws at all must be given a fair hearing; and any ideas that pass muster should be given a fair trial.

2. The United States has repeatedly demonstrated that it can mobilize its shipyard assets quickly, and can rapidly expand shipyard output. This fact alone makes keeping an adequate shipyard capability in place a good defense investment.

Albeit slowly, the NATO alliance is moving toward having each nation contribute what it does best. In peacetime, probably all of the NATO partners individually can build merchant ships at less cost than the United States. What they cannot do is collectively match U.S. shipyard productivity in an emergency, a state of affairs where cost becomes less important. It is a point worth remembering should the United States ever be inclined to "negotiate away" its shipbuilding capability.

3. The genius of America is in its innovative spirit, its ability to recognize challenges as opportunities and capitalize upon them. American innovation with respect to ship design is recognized and copied worldwide. The next challenge is to push innovation in *shipbuilding and ship repair* to its limits, while recognizing that limits, in fact, do exist.

4 Legislation and Legislative Initiatives in Support of Shipyards

FROM THE TIME OF American independence, most major legislation and legislative initiatives in support of shipyards have been tied to support for the merchant marine, that is, the ship operator. From a political standpoint this was eminently logical. As a rule, the same statute would address both shipyard and vessel operator concerns in its different titles or sections. For example, Title V of the Merchant Marine Act of 1936 provides construction subsidies (aid to shipyards) while Title VI makes available operating subsidies for the shipping firm. The two titles were, in fact, tightly bound together, in that a vessel under an operating differential subsidy (ODS) contract was required to be American-built.

Chapters 2 and 3 chronologically traced the rise and decline of American shipbuilding from an economic perspective. This chapter will emphasize *legislation* and proposed legislation whose primary purpose was (or is) shipyard economic well-being. Somewhat less emphasis is placed on indirect support of the shipyard industry such as mortgage guarantees, cargo reservation, and the tax treatment of a ship operator's construction reserve fund (CRF).

Tables 4.1, 4.2, and 4.3 summarize (a) legislation directly impacting on shipyards, (b) legislation indirectly affecting shipyards, and (c) proposed legislative initiatives in direct support of shipyards. Following each table is a sketch of the political–economic setting in which the legislation's enactment took place, including opinions and concerns of lawmakers during the hearings stage of a particular statute, as well as concerns that occurred after a program's implementation.

Major Shipyard Legislation

Table 4.1 lists major enactments in support of the shipbuilding/ship repair industry since 1789.

Maritime legislation during the nation's first years was primarily concerned with where a ship was built and secondarily with vessel registry.

Table 4.1. Major legislation in support of U.S. shipyards, 1789–1985.

Legislation	Provision(s)
Acts of 4 July 1789, 20 July 1789, 1 September 1789, 30 July 1790	a. Discriminatory tonnage duties levied on non–U.S.-built vessels. b. Reserved U.S. coastwise trade to U.S.-built vessels.
An Act Concerning Navigation of the United States, 1 March 1817	a. Limited U.S. coastwise trade to U.S.-flag, U.S.-owned, and U.S.-built vessels.
Tariff Acts of 1890, 1894	a. Import duties on steel plate and iron removed for shipbuilders.
Panama Canal Act of 1912	a. Removed duties on all shipbuilding materials used to construct vessels for U.S. registry. The Simmons–Underwood bill of 1913 put all iron and steel on the free list.
Shipping Act of 1916	a. Legislative basis provided for establishing the Emergency Fleet Corporation. This government corporation would eventually build over 2,300 ships of all types, of approximately 14 million deadweight tons, at a cost of $3 billion.[a]
Tariff Act of 1930	a. Imposed a 50 percent *ad valorem* tax on nonemergency foreign repairs to U.S.-flag vessels.
Merchant Marine Act of 1920	a. Restated legislation that prohibits foreign-owned, -built, or -flag vessels in U.S. domestic trades. (Earlier prohibition was suspended on U.S. entry into World War I.) b. Section 30 of Act established policy of federal (preferred) mortgage guarantees for construction of vessels in U.S. shipyards. "A preferred mortgage shall constitute a lien upon the mortgaged vessel in the amount of the outstanding mortgage indebtedness secured by such vessel."
Acts of 27 July 1868, 1898, 1899	a. Alaska, Hawaii, Puerto Rico, and Guam trades reserved to American-built vessels.

Table 4.1. (cont.)

Legislation	Provision(s)
Merchant Marine Act of 1936	a. Title V provided for government payments to shipyards to make up difference between U.S. and foreign costs in building ships for U.S. foreign trade.
Merchant Marine Act of 1936	a. Act mandated that U.S.-flag ships in foreign trade receiving an operating differential subsidy be built in U.S. shipyards. b. Allowed ship operator to deposit earnings and revenues from ship sales into a tax-deferred construction reserve account until expended for ship construction.[b] c. Allowed a shipowner credit on obsolete vessel toward replacement construction in U.S. shipyards.
Act of 23 June 1938	a. Title XI "Federal Ship Mortgage Insurance" added to Merchant Marine Act of 1936. Replaced Ship Mortgage Act of 1920. In 1986 this title authorizes federal government to insure private loans used to finance construction/reconstruction of vessel in U.S. shipyards, including vessels in domestic trade and offshore drilling rigs, barges, and tugs.[c]
Public Law 911, 6 January 1951	a. Provided funds to build for government thirty-five 13,400 dwt 20-knot vessels. This became known as the "Mariner" program because each ship's name was followed by the word "Mariner" (e.g., *Keystone Mariner*).
Long Range Shipping Act of 1952	a. Construction differential subsidy option extended to all ships operating in U.S. foreign trade that are "suitable for national defense purposes in time of war or national emergency."

Table 4.1. (cont.)

Legislation	Provision(s)
	b. Section 507 amended to allow domestic trade ship operator to trade in old ships for credit on new construction; established a construction reserve fund for this shipping.
Merchant Marine Act of 1970	a. Set goal of building 300 ships for U.S.-flag registry over next 10 years. Construction subsidies were to be primary financing mechanism. Goal was to reduce CDS to 35 percent.
	b. Extended construction assistance to bulk carriers, *not* necessarily suitable for national defense in time of war or national emergency.
Public Law 97-252, 8 September 1982	a. Established that no naval vessel or major component may be constructed in a foreign shipyard unless authorized by the president in the interest of national security.

[a]There are as many estimates of the size and cost of the World War I shipbuilding program as there are writers in the maritime field. During the 19 months the United States was in the war, 875 vessels of 2.9 million gross tons were reportedly built. At the peak of the U.S. shipbuilding effort, 17.4 deadweight tons were held to be under contract. If government ownership of war-built vessels is accepted as a proxy for the number of vessels built under the program, then the maximum-size government-owned fleet was 1,792 ships of 11 million deadweight tons. Estimates of the cost of the building program range between $3 billion and 4 billion.

[b]In 1986 this fund is designated as a capital construction fund (CCF).

[c]In 1985 the Title XI program was badly shaken by the default of the Phoenix Corporation of Houston, Texas on two oil-bulk-ore (OBO) carriers. The revolving fund of the Title XI program was reduced by over $125 million. Total loan defaults through 1985 totaled $675 million. In February 1986 the Maritime Administration faced the possibility of an additional $220 million default from the Houston-based Global Marine, Inc. The firm filed for protection under the bankruptcy laws in January 1986.

Thus, until 1817 it was still possible for a foreign-flag vessel to participate in the U.S. coastal trades, although that was a relatively expensive option.[1]

As noted in Chapter 2, after the War of 1812–15 and up to the American Civil War, American shipyards, concentrating on wooden sailing vessels, were more than competitive in world markets. There was little need for government actions to support the industry. In the first part of the nineteenth century it was the British shipowner, restricted by his country's Navigation Acts to purchasing the relatively inefficient, high-cost, wooden British vessel, who was the advocate of a "free ship" policy.

After the Civil War, when the world's merchant fleets were moving to iron steamships, the relative cost advantage changed. British shipbuilders achieved a cost advantage that widened as the nineteenth century progressed. It was now the American foreign-trade shipowner, restricted to purchasing his vessels in higher-priced American yards, who suffered a competitive disadvantage. Throughout the latter part of the nineteenth century the issue of "free ships" (i.e., allowing foreign-built ships to be registered under the U.S. flag) periodically surfaced in American politics.

The period from 1865 to World War I was an era of generally high American tariffs on foreign imports, and on steel in particular. At different times, both Democrats and Republicans supported lower duties, but, as a rule, tariffs remained high. However, some relief with respect to importing shipbuilding materials was forthcoming. An act in 1872 allowed materials used in the construction of wooden vessels to enter duty-free. After 1912 all materials used in the construction of ships for U.S. registry were on the free list.

The Shipping Act of 1916, as noted in Chapter 3, established the Emergency Fleet Corporation (EFC), whose primary purpose was to acquire, through building and other means, sufficient tonnage to meet America's vital shipping needs. However, launching a massive building program was easier said than done. Internal bureaucratic bickering with respect to contract awards and material priorities delayed the program for almost six months, a circumstance that evoked both administration and congressional criticism. In fact, vessel output did not reach its peak until late in 1918. Moreover, the largest shipyard built from the ground up, the Hog Island shipyard near Philadelphia, was not completed until after the Armistice.[2] One lesson for the future was abundantly clear—it is extremely difficult to build ships in a hurry without prior planning, particularly when a shipbuilding base is lacking.

If getting a wartime shipbuilding program into high gear proved difficult, it was equally difficult for the government to dispose of its mammoth war-built, taxpayer-owned merchant fleet after the war. Debate primarily centered on how (equitably) to dispose of war-built tonnage. Many in Congress objected to selling at bargain prices ships that cost $200/ton to build. A major problem was that while many of these ships were not suitable for American trades, they were quite suitable for a number of others (e.g., Mediterranean and Baltic Sea uses). Ultimately, the U.S. Shipping Board, the agency charged with disposing of government-owned ships, was given discretion to sell the ships "consistent with good business practices." The enabling law was the Merchant Marine Act of 1920. Section 11 of the legislation created a construction loan fund that was to be funded by revenues from the sale and operations of government-owned ships.

The Merchant Marine Act of 1936 and Later Legislation

The Merchant Marine Act of 1936, sometimes called the "Magna Charta" of the American maritime industry, was the most comprehensive piece of shipping and shipbuilding legislation in American history. Title V had the most direct impact on shipbuilding in that it provided a mechanism for the government to pay a shipyard, contracting with an American foreign-trade ship operator, the difference between the higher American cost and the lower foreign one. Perhaps the most debated part of Title V during congressional hearings concerned the actual differential between American and foreign costs. In 1935 it was widely held that the cost differential was in the neighborhood of 40 percent. When the act was finally passed, the base differential was fixed at 33⅓ percent, excluding the cost of national defense features, but with the stipulation that the Maritime Commission could by an affirmative vote approve a 50 percent differential.[3]

In 1938 a blue ribbon commission appointed by the U.S. Maritime Commission pursuant to the Merchant Marine Act of 1936 noted that it was quite possible the cost difference might exceed 50 percent. In this respect the commission concluded:

> A less expensive remedy would be to permit construction abroad in all cases in which the foreign costs are less than half the costs here, registry here being required as soon as practicable, and the vessel so built and registered being eligible for an operating-differential subsidy as if built here. Domestic shipping, however, should be protected from the competition of a vessel so registered to the full extent that it is protected from the competition of vessels receiving a construction differential subsidy.
>
> This suggestion the Commission recommends. It would, where applicable, relieve the Government from the necessity of providing cash either as a loan or as a contribution (except as to national defense features). It would prevent the development and maintenance of our merchant marine being checked by the rise of shipbuilding costs here to levels more than twice as high as those abroad.[4]

All things considered, the Merchant Marine Act of 1936 made shipyard investment a reasonably attractive option for private capital. This was so primarily because the privately owned, foreign-trade fleet in the late 1930s was approaching statutory obsolescence. (The Merchant

Marine Act of 1936 required subsidized operators to replace vessels over 20 years of age.) In 1937 it was determined that 87 percent of this fleet would reach obsolescence in 1942.

In 1938 written assurances were received by the Maritime Commission for 60 ship replacement orders. The recommendation of the commission was that a 50-ship-a-year program be undertaken. After war broke out in Europe in 1939, and it became more and more apparent that the United States would be directly involved, President Roosevelt, in 1941, announced an emergency 200-ship-per-year building program. Prior to Pearl Harbor, the figure was increased by 300 additional ships. This construction was in addition to a greatly expanded naval construction program. Thus, *prior* to America's entry into the war, a shipbuilding base was being put into place.

In the pre–World War II period, specialized dry cargo ships were not the rule. While tankers and coal colliers had long been on the scene, much bulk cargo was still carried in the lower holds of general cargo vesels. This situation changed rapidly after World War II. Contracts for bulk carriers, large tankers, and specialized vessels of all types made up an increasing share of the work on shipbuilder order books. Legislation in 1952 and 1970 recognized this change and extended the construction differential subsidy option to operators of these vessels.

In 1951 Congress appropriated funds for the construction of 35 large, high-speed cargo vessels to be built for government account. Seven shipyards were awarded contracts of five ships each. In this instance it was the Maritime Commission (government) that was on the leading edge of technological innovation, as a number of shipping firm executives at the time believed that a 20-knot ship would prove uneconomical to operate. Events, however, proved the pessimists wrong. This $350 million commitment on the part of the federal government was one of its better investments, even though the ships built under the program were sold to ship operators at bargain prices.[5]

The last major piece of legislation that made the construction differential subsidy the centerpiece of shipyard support was the Merchant Marine Act of 1970. The stated purpose of this enactment was to build 300 ships under CDS over a 10-year period. The goal was never achieved. Since 1981 no funds have been requested for construction differential subsidy payments, a situation that has left all American-flag operators free to purchase their vessels in foreign yards. Thus did the "free ships" policy advocated by many nineteenth-century legislators come to pass 100 years later.

Indirect Government Assistance to Shipyards

Indirect aid to shipyards over the years has taken many forms. Major legislative enactments in this respect are summarized in Table 4.2.

Table 4.2. Legislation indirectly aiding U.S. shipyards.

Legislation	Legislative Provisions
Acts of 1792, 1813, 1818	a. Federal government provided a bounty for construction of fishing vessels. b. Subsidies granted to cod fishing fleet.
Act of 3 March 1845	a. Mail subsidies provided to selected shipping firms to encourage an American flag presence on certain routes. Ships were to be American-built. The subsidy was canceled in 1858.
Act of 23 December 1852	a. Foreign vessels wrecked on U.S. coasts could be admitted to U.S. registry if repairs (made in United States) were equal to three times the salvage value of the vessel. Act amended in 1894 to allow registry of foreign vessels wrecked anywhere on same conditions.
Act of 28 May 1865	a. Mail subsidies reinstated.
Act of 18 July 1866	a. Shipowners who transferred their vessels to foreign flag during Civil War could not re-register them under U.S. flag.
Ocean Mail Act of 1891	a. Comprehensive system of subsidized mail services authorized. Ships on these routes were to be U.S.-built.
Act of 28 April 1904 (Military Transportation Act)	a. Military cargo reserved to U.S.-flag ships and, by definition, to U.S.-built vessels.
Merchant Marine Act of 1920	a. Section 11 established a construction loan fund of $25 million. It was to be used to "aid in the construction of vessels of the best and most suitable types for U.S. foreign commerce." Funds were available to ship operator on favorable terms.

Table 4.2. (cont.)

Legislation	Legislative Provisions
Merchant Marine Act of 1928	a. Construction loan fund increased to $125 million. b. Mail subsidies made dependent on replacement (in U.S. shipyards) of obsolete vessels.
Merchant Marine Act of 1936	a. Vessel operator receiving an operating differential subsidy required to build ships in the United States.
Ship Sales Act of 1946	a. Surplus war-built ships sold to U.S. firms on a preferred basis and on favorable terms. Modification to peacetime configurations, repairs, and overhaul of these vessels done in U.S. yards. (See Tariff Act of 1930 and Merchant Marine Act of 1920, Table 4.1)
Cargo Preference Act of 1954	a. Fifty percent of government-sponsored cargoes must move in U.S.-flag ships, if available. The act induced a demand for U.S.-built ships. Shipments under the Agricultural Trade and Development Act of 1954 were also included in above-described cargo-sharing arrangement.
Act of 7 July 1960	a. Government share of construction cost raised to 55 percent for a two-year period. Purpose was to encourage replacement of U.S.-flag tonnage in U.S. shipyards.
Act of 13 September 1961	a. Act of 7 July amended to include *reconstruction* of ships at 55 percent subsidy level.
Trans-Alaska Pipeline Act of 1973	a. Prohibited export of domestically produced crude oil unless the president certified that such would

Table 4.2. (cont.)

Legislation	Legislative Provisions
	not imperil domestic supplies and was in national interest. Note that Section 27 of Merchant Marine Act of 1920 (Jones Act) restricts cargo movement between U.S. ports to U.S.-flag/built ships.
FY 1975 Defense Appropriations Authorization Act (Title VIII)	a. As a matter of national policy legislation required that "major combatant vessels for strike forces of the U.S. Navy be nuclear powered." Given the secrecy constraint on U.S. nuclear ship technology, the amendment effectively limited this work to U.S. yards.
Export Administration Act of 1979	a. Restricted the export of Alaska North Slope oil until 30 September 1983. Note: Congress granted two-year extension in 1983, i.e., until 1985.
Shipping Act of 1984	a. This legislation "deregulated" to a certain extent American-flag liner companies. To the extent these companies were better able to compete in international ocean shipping, U.S. shipyards indirectly benefited.
House—Joint Resolution 648 of Continuing Resolution Appropriations for FY 1985	a. Extended prohibition against Department of Defense purchasing any military vessel, not just naval vessels, from a foreign shipyard. (See Table 4.1, Public Law 97-252.)
An Act to Reauthorize the Export Administration Act of 1979 (Public Law 99-64, 12 July 1985)	a. Restricted the export of Alaska North Slope crude oil. Legislation required a review of the export restriction provisions of the act along with a review of other federal and state taxing and leasing policies.

The indirect (support) approach that has received the greatest visibility consists of various cargo reservation programs, mainly the 1904 Military Transportation Act, the 1954 Cargo Preference Act, the Agricultural Trade Development and Assistance Act of 1954 (Title II), and, to a lesser extent, Public Resolution Number 17 (March 1934), which provides that where government loans are made to foster exports, such exports must be carried in U.S.-flag ships. That there is an additional cost in using American-flag, American-built ships is well understood, although what the actual cost is, is debatable. In a 1978 Report to Congress, the U.S. General Accounting Office cited a study that estimated the cost to exceed $5 billion over a 20-year period.[6]

The most successful of the indirect approaches to aid shipyards is probably the Federal Ship Financing Guarantee Program (Title XI) of the Merchant Marine Act of 1936. The program insures the full payment to a private lender should the mortgagee (vessel owner) be in default. In FY 1983, 254 deep-draft vessels were covered to the extent of $4.7 billion dollars. When other, smaller eligible builds are included (e.g., drilling rigs, tugs, shipboard lighters), the vessel total is 6,491 with a commitment of $7.8 billion. Title XI historically has been self-supporting. In FY 1984 the Federal Ship Financing Fund, under Title XI, had a net income of $27.4 million. However, during this period the Maritime Administration paid out $101 million on nine defaults, leaving a year-end balance of $149 million.

Historically, American naval vessels have been built in U.S. yards; and since 1967 all new naval construction has been placed in *private* shipyards. As might be expected with multi-billion-dollar contracts, disagreements between the contracting parties (the Navy and the shipyards) have arisen over the years. In 1974, however, disputes became bitter, acrimonious, and public with respect to cost overruns and the question of who was at fault. The 1974 House of Representatives hearings (three volumes) were the most contentious in recent memory. Subsequently, on different occasions, the option of returning some new construction work to naval shipyards was raised, or threatened, depending upon one's viewpoint. In 1980 a naval "build foreign" alternative was openly discussed.[8] However, in 1982 Congress closed the door on this option with passage of Public Law 97-252.

Legislative Initiatives in Support of Shipyards, 1983–86

As noted in Chapter 3 and above, an already declining shipyard industry had to contend with further bad news when the Reagan administration in 1981 refused to ask for construction differential subsidy funds in its maritime budget request.

However, the decline of the U.S. shipyard industry has not gone without congressional notice. Table 4.3 lists recent legislative initiatives in this regard.

The most contentious of the initiatives proposed are those that focus primarily on *commercial* cargo sharing. While any additional cost of using American ships under this approach would be passed on to the consumer and would not require a government outlay, it is unalterably opposed by the Reagan administration. Admiral H. E. Shear (USN, Ret.), the maritime administrator (1981–85), stated administration policy in this way:

> While this administration supports existing laws that require U.S. flag participation in the carriage of U.S. government sponsored cargoes, it is opposed to any attempts to impose preference allocations on the movement of *commercial* cargoes. This is consistent with the administration's opposition to the cargo allocation scheme embodied in the U.N. Code of Conduct For Liner Conferences.[9]

In a major policy statement in early 1985, Representative Mario Biaggi, chairman of the House Merchant Marine Subcommittee, seemed to accept the administration position. In part, he said:

> The year 1984 has passed into history and still many of the ills of the maritime industry remain. If 1985 and 1986 are to bring any hope of revitalization to this declining and beleaguered industry, it must be with the help of all interested parties. . . . I believe we simply have to work within the budgetary and trade policies that have been enunciated by this Administration, which are similar to those of prior administrations.[10]

Others in the Congress are not so conciliatory. They point out the cargo reservation laws already in place with respect to government-impelled cargo, and that these costs are indirectly passed on to the taxpayer.[11]

Conclusion

Given the centuries-old history of legislation and legislative initiatives, it might seem surprising that few firm conclusions can be drawn about how best, through legislation, to support an admittedly high-cost U.S. shipyard industry. Yet some things can be said.

First, it is the responsibility of government to ensure that there is a sufficient shipbuilding base *on which to build* in a war or a national emergency. While a correct and legitimate goal of government policy is to foster efficiency in all private-sector undertakings, first things still must come first. In this context, having a shipbuilding industry comes before having a nonexistent, cost-competitive shipbuilding industry. This is a

Table 4.3. Legislative and individual proposals in support of U.S. shipyards, 1983–86.

Direct Support of Shipyards	
Maritime Redevelopment Bank Act	Establish a Maritime Redevelopment Bank to finance, cofinance, refinance maritime projects through loan guarantees. Loans to be secured by ship mortgage or other firm assets. Legislation would restructure Title XI of the Merchant Marine Act of 1936 and encourage series production of commercial vessels.
****	Various proposals made to increase the share of naval repair and alteration work awarded to private shipyards. Proposals range from mandating 40 to 50 percent of this work to private yards.
****	Investigate the possibility of having U.S. shipyards export diesel-electric submarines to allied naval forces. Report on feasibility of this option requested by Senate Armed Services Committee.[a]
****	Allow American flag operators who build two ships in U.S. yards to build three ships in foreign yards. These foreign-built ships would be considered "U.S.-built" with respect to Title XI, operating differential subsidies, and cargo preference laws.
****	Fund a grant program to upgrade propulsion machinery of U.S.-flag vessels in U.S. yards. Requirement is that fuel savings be on the order of 25 percent and that engine rooms be automated.
****	Department of Defense to finance construction in U.S. shipyards of militarily useful vessels. Vessels built in series would be sold or

Table 4.3. (cont.)

Direct Support of Shipyards	
	chartered to U.S. citizens. A variant of this proposal would make funding a Department of Transportation responsibility.[b]
****	Authorize $250 million in construction subsidy monies. Allow construction differential subsidies to exceed 50 percent.
****	Authorize $300 million in construction subsidies for FY 1986, raise permissible CDS payment to 60 percent, and increase Federal Ship Mortgage Guaranty from $12 billion to $15 billion.

Indirect Support of Shipyards	
Competitive Shipping and Shipbuilding Act	Would require that exporters and importers of dry cargo and liquid bulk commodities increase use of U.S.-built, U.S.-flag ships. Percent of this trade going to U.S. ships would begin at 5 percent and increase to 20 percent.
****	Extend capital construction fund (CCF) to include domestic trade vessels. CCF now only allows U.S. foreign-trade operators to deposit monies into tax-deferred accounts for purpose of ultimately constructing/reconstructing tonnage in U.S. shipyards.
****	Allow a tax credit, similar to present 10 percent investment tax credit, for work performed in U.S. shipyards when both labor and management reduce construction costs; e.g., if management reduces profits by 15 percent and labor reduces labor costs by 15 percent,

Table 4.3. (cont.)

Indirect Support of Shipyards

	then a full tax credit of 15 percent would be given. Estimated total savings in U.S. building costs is 30 percent.
Conference Report, House Joint Resolution 465, Continuing Resolution for FY 1986	Established "a revolving Mariner [type] Fund for the construction and lease of cargo vessels configured for the military sealift mission."
	Start-up money for the fund would come from $852 million of unused naval appropriations. While the Conference Report set aside the $852 million, it cannot be spent until further enabling legislation is passed by Congress.

[a]On 23 May 1985 the Department of Defense recommended against the option on the grounds of "unacceptable loss of . . . irreplaceable submarine technology." Congress must now act on that recommendation.

[b]Numerous suggestions have been made both in and outside of government that U.S. shipbuilding costs can be significantly reduced if a series of at least 10 ships is built in a single shipyard. (See Chapter 9.)

continuing responsibility and must be recognized as such until such time as the nation beats its swords into plowshares and its spears into pruning-hooks.

Earlier chapters noted that the ability of a nation to expand its shipbuilding base in an emergency is directly dependent upon (a) the size of the existing base and (b) the existence of a prearranged and well understood plan to expand the base. The problems encountered in World War I, and the relatively few in World War II, fairly bear out this contention.

A second conclusion might be: "If it ain't broke, don't fix it." In 1981 construction differential subsidies were abandoned—not because they were proved to be an ineffective vehicle for supporting a shipyard industry when contrasted with other options, or very large when compared with other defense expenditures, but rather as a way to reduce the federal budget deficit. While the point can be correctly made that undisciplined subsidies can breed inefficiencies, it is still questionable policy to "throw out the baby with the bathwater." In other words, it is not a contradiction in terms to have *efficient* taxpayer-funded defense programs.

If one reviews the rationalizations for all the legislation, and proposed legislation, put forward in support of U.S. shipyards since the founding of the republic, national security is the only one that can be consistently defended. Other rationalizations for government financial support ebb and rise, dependent only on the circumstances of the moment. But, consistently, hundreds of long-dead observers of the maritime scene believed that shipyards were essential to the nation's security. Were they wrong?

5

The Jones Act: Retain, Amend, or Repeal

AS THE 1980s BEGAN, Section 27 of the Merchant Marine Act of 1920, commonly referred to as the "Jones Act,"* was but one leg in the historic tripod of government shipyard support, the other two being construction subsidies for U.S. foreign trade shipping, and naval building and repair work. Section 27 essentially reaffirmed a century-old American policy that reserved the U.S. domestic ocean trade to American-flag, American-owned, and American-built ships. It states:

> That no merchandise shall be transported by water, or by land and water, on penalty of forfeiture thereof, between points in the United States, including Districts, Territories, and possessions thereof embraced within the coastwise laws, either directly or via a foreign port, or for any part of the transportation, in any other vessel than a vessel *built in and documented under the laws of the United States and owned by persons who are citizens of the United States* [italics supplied].[1]

In the half century of American shipbuilding supremacy, roughly from 1815 to 1857, America's merchant shipping was world-competitive. Total registered tonnage rivaled that of England, and in foreign trade, American vessels carried the lion's share of the country's foreign commerce. Some writers estimated this portion to exceed 90 percent. However, as U.S. shipbuilding gradually lost its competitive advantage in a world fast turning to iron steamships, and one where higher operating costs could no longer be countered by greater productivity, the protected domestic trade fleet became the backbone of the U.S. merchant marine. In this respect, at a time when the U.S. share of its foreign trade had fallen to less than 10 percent, the tonnage on U.S. rivers and the Great Lakes and along the coasts increased, from 2,960,633 gross tons in 1863 to 6,818,363 gross tons in 1914.[2]

*The Merchant Marine Act of 1920, commonly known as the "Jones Act," was named for Senator Wesley L. Jones of Wisconsin, a long-time supporter of U.S. maritime interests.

With the opening of the Panama Canal in 1914, a significantly increased intercoastal trade added further tonnage to the domestic fleet. Moreover, the Panama Canal Act of 1912 constrained railroads from interfering with the highly competitive intercoastal shipping industry; that is, the railroads were prohibited from acquiring any water carrier with which they competed or might compete.[3] Thus, while railroads could compete with intercoastal shipping for transcontinental freight, they essentially had to compete on ocean carrier terms.

However, domestic ocean shipping prosperity exacted its price. As one historian notes:

> The high cost of the coastwise shipping service was definitely paid by the shippers, who in turn forced the burden either forward onto consumers or backward onto producers. In general, as for example in the coal, lumber and building-materials trades, the burden was shifted forward. In those cases in which the demand was highly elastic, the high costs of service either prevented cargo from moving or caused it to move overland.[4]

Figure 5.1 shows principal Jones Act trading routes.

The surge in shipbuilding brought on by America's entry into World War I was noted in Chapter 3. The long-term result, with respect to the foreign trade merchant marine, was a moderate increase in the U.S.-flag share of its foreign commerce. The percent share of this trade for the interwar years was:

Year	U.S.-flag share (imports)	U.S.-flag share (exports)
1921	70.7%	38.2%
1925	49.2	31.6
1930	52.2	30.0
1935	41.6	22.9
1940	38.8	21.2

However, one thing did not change: the United States remained a high-cost shipbuilding nation.

Jones Act Beneficiaries

Section 27 of the Merchant Marine Act of 1920 lent direct support to the U.S. shipyard industry and the workers it employed in mandating that domestic-trade ships be built in the United States. And since these ships traded between American ports, repairs and overhauls were also, by and large, done in U.S. yards.

However, shipyards and shipyard labor were not the only beneficiaries of Section 27. The national security interest benefited to the extent that Jones Act shipping was militarily useful in time of emergency. While a

national defense value cannot be attributed to all domestic-trade shipping, a significant part fairly falls into this category.* In 1986, of the 179
active merchant vessels in the Jones Act fleet, the inventory of militarily
useful vessels was estimated to be:

Passenger vessels	2
Intermodal	24
Tankers[a]	55
	81

[a]Estimate based on age, speed, and tonnage.

A third benefiting group was the domestic-trade shipping firm. The
benefit here was straightforward. It did not have to compete with lower-
cost foreign-flag shipping. Twenty-three companies were engaged in this
trade in 1985. Not included are firms operating barges and integrated tug
barges (ITB). They were:

American Hawaii Cruises	Mobil Oil
American President Lines	Ogden Marine
Apex Marine	Pacific Gulf Marine
Atlantic Richfield	Puerto Rico Marine
Chevron Shipping Company	Sabine Towing and
Cove Shipping	Transportation
Exxon	Sea-Land Services
Gulf Oil	Sun Transport
Keystone Shipping	Texaco
Marine Transport	Trinidad Corporation
Maritime Overseas Corporation	Union Oil (California)
Matson Navigation Company	United States Lines

The fourth interest group that gained from the Jones Act was seagoing
labor. In 1984 it was estimated that 6,000 jobholders, with an annual
payroll of $670 million, were indebted to this statute.[5]

---

*A continuing problem in analyzing U.S. maritime industry data is differences between
reporting sources (e.g., between the Maritime Administration, the Military Sealift Command, and private sector operators and associations). For example, the Maritime Administration reported the Jones Act ocean-going tanker fleet as of 1 October 1985 to number 135
active and 70 inactive vessels, while data supplied by the Exxon Shipping Company listed by
name a grand total of 160 vessels. Historically, the Military Sealift Command and the
Maritime Administration report different figures for essentially similar vessel classifications
on the same dates, and/or categorize their data to make comparisons difficult, if not
meaningless. When maritime industry data are reported by the Naval Sea Systems Command, they generally differ from both of the above sources. Unless otherwise noted,
Maritime Administration data are used throughout this chapter.

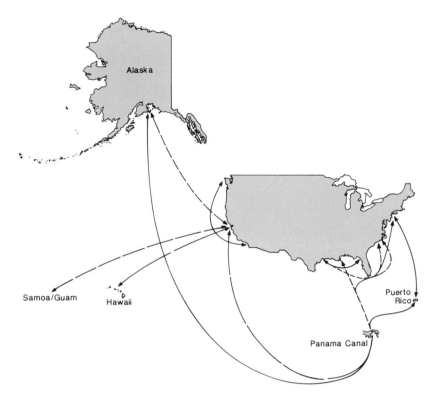

Figure 5.1. Domestic trade ocean commerce routes, 1986. Note: By definition, domestic Great Lakes trade routes are excluded from this figure, primarily because this tonnage, while protected by the Jones Act, has never been considered to have a national security role in an emergency (i.e., the tonnage is not suitable for logistically supporting deployed American forces overseas). As of 1 October 1985, the active Great Lakes fleet was composed of 54 bulk carriers, 3 tankers, and 1 car ferry, of approximately 1.7 million deadweight tons. In the period 1970–85, thirty Great Lakes ships were built in U.S. shipyards located on the Great Lakes.

U.S. Shipyards

At the beginning of this chapter, we observed that in 1980 the construction differential subsidy program, authorized under the Merchant Marine Act of 1936, was still a major government initiative in support of U.S. shipyards. But as noted in an earlier chapter, no funds for this program have been asked for or appropriated since 1981. Essentially, one leg of the government support tripod for shipyards has been cut off.

However, under the Omnibus Budget Reconciliation Act of 1981, American foreign-trade shipowners receiving an operating differential subsidy, who were once required to build in U.S. yards, were allowed to acquire their vessels overseas. Before this option expired on 30 September 1983, forty-nine vessels were constructed or reconstructed outside the United States. In 1984 and 1985 the Reagan administration asked for legislation to renew the "build foreign" authority.[6]

Thus, in the mid-1980s U.S. shipyards earned income from one major and two minor sources: (a) building and repairing/overhauling U.S. naval ships, (b) building and repairing ships for the protected U.S. domestic trades, and (c) repairing U.S. and foreign ships. Since many yards earn revenues from all these sources, estimating the value of the Jones Act to their economic well-being is not a simple exercise. However, estimates can be made.

Table 5.1 indicates Jones Act shipyard orders for 1983–85. Nine shipyards held contracts for this work. They ranged in size from the small to the very largest and, in terms of geography, were spread from the Atlantic to the Pacific coast and from the Great Lakes to the Gulf of Mexico.[7]

Assuming that Jones Act contracts average ten a year, the additional shipyard workers employed amount to about 10,000, generating a payroll of approximately $130 million annually.[8]

In January 1985, naval contracts to private shipyards, building or on order, totaled 100 ships of 886,000 light displacement tons. In the period 1981–84 inclusive, the initial shipyard contract value of naval orders was $18.5 billion. For the year 1984, the figure was $2.84 billion.[9]

However, construction contracts are but one part of the Navy's contribution to shipyard employment. Another is repair and overhaul work. In FY 1985, $6.37 billion was requested in this respect. Assuming the private shipyard share of this to be 30 percent, then an additional $1.9 billion must be added to the Navy's contribution to shipyard economic viability.

If Jones Act construction and repair work is estimated at $750 million annually, a total that is quite high, it still is small in comparison to the sum of all naval contracts. Nonetheless, Jones Act work historically has been quite important, particularly at the margin. In this context, even though the contribution is small, it can be the difference between profit and loss for a shipyard. And as the goal of a 600-ship navy nears completion in the mid-1990s, and naval contracts decline, theoretically Jones Act builds and repairs should take on increasing importance. The problem is that there is little economic incentive for new Jones Act construction.

Jones Act Exceptions

While Section 27 of the Merchant Marine Act of 1920 is specific in its intent, initially and over the years exceptions have been written into the law.

Table 5.1. Domestic-trade tonnage delivered or scheduled for delivery, 1983–85.[a]

Vessel type[b]	Number[c]	Deadweight tons	Contract price
Product tanker	3	127,500	$255.0 million
Tanker	5	150,000	288.0
Tanker	1	35,000	80.0
Barge/tug	2	94,000	143.5
Incinerator ship	2	24,800	150.0
Dredge	2	10,800	50.0
Research vessel	1	4,800	30.0
	16	446,900	$996.5

SOURCE: Maritime Administration, *Annual Report, 1982*, Maritime Administration, *Merchant Marine Data Sheet, June 1, 1984*, and Maritime Administration, *Shipbuilding Progress Report*, 30 June 1984.

[a]As of 30 June 1984. No new Jones Act orders were placed in 1985.

[b]Major construction only. Does not include barges, lighters, ferries, excursion boats, or small craft in general.

[c]In late 1984 three containerships and two large tankers were ordered for employment in the U.S. domestic trade. The total contract price for these ships was $430 million. Delivery was scheduled for 1986.

The original act exempted the Philippine and Virgin islands. In 1946, when the Philippines were granted independence, that particular exception became a moot issue. However, the Virgin Island exemption has remained in place, with that trade open to foreign-flag shipping.

Some minor exceptions were also included in the original legislation, with respect to the movement of foreign cargo vans, shipping tanks, and barges between U.S. ports.[10]

Since the enactment of the so-called coastwise laws in the late eighteenth century, ships operating between U.S. ports have done so without benefit of either direct or indirect government financial support (e.g., mail subsidies or construction and operating subsidies). As they were sheltered from foreign competition, Congress saw no need for such assistance. Thus, with respect to ship cost, the domestic trade operator, being required to purchase his vessel in the United States, in 1986 paid over twice the world price for his asset.

However, ships are "movable" assets; that is, are capable of being employed in *different* trades. Therefore, a vessel built with a construction subsidy wherein the vessel operator paid only one-half the cost and the government the rest, had a significant economic advantage in competing with a vessel wherein the owner paid the entire U.S. cost. As a general proposition, vessels built with a construction subsidy are not allowed to engage in domestic ocean commerce. However, Section 506 of the Merchant Marine Act of 1936 provides an escape clause. If the Maritime

Administration determines that there is no "Jones Act" ship available, then a CDS vessel may obtain a six-month (in a 12-month period) waiver to engage in a protected trade. In the most recent five-year period, FY 1978–84, waivers were granted to 28 tankers moving crude oil from Alaska to the lower 48 states. Historically, waivers have been granted to Canadian vessels operating between U.S. Great Lake ports and, on the west coast, between Alaskan ports. A recent exception (1984) is that foreign-owned, -built, and -crewed vessels may transport passengers between the U.S. mainland and Puerto Rico when no U.S.-flag vessel is available.

A catchall, general-exception provision is authorized in Public Law 891, in that a waiver may be granted "upon the request of the Secretary of Defense to the extent deemed necessary in the interest of national defense by the Secretary of Defense."[11]

Proposals for Jones Act Exceptions

Periodically, bills are introduced in Congress for a particular Jones Act exception, or an administrative decision is taken to waive a specific Jones Act provision. By and large, these exceptions have been of minor consequence and for limited periods of time.[12]

However, in 1983 and 1984 two proposals were made that had long-term, far-reaching consequences. The first, though not directly tied to a Jones Act exception, would have a major impact on both shipbuilders and domestic ship operators.

The Trans-Alaska Pipeline Act of 1973 prohibited the export of domestic crude oil. Only the president could waive the provision, and then only for reasons of vital national interests. The Export Administration Act of 1979 extended the export prohibition until 30 September 1983. Efforts in 1984 to extend the prohibition or reach a compromise failed. However, export restrictions remained in place under provisions of another statute, the International Emergency Economic Powers Act.

Those desiring repeal or modification of the export restrictions argue that it would be more cost-effective to ship Alaska crude oil to Japan and other Pacific buyers and replace it with crude from other foreign sources (e.g., the Persian Gulf or Venezuela) than to ship it domestically. Under this arrangement the relatively long and expensive movement of Alaska crude to the U.S. east and Gulf coasts via the Panama Canal would be avoided. Estimates of possible savings range from $2 to $3 a barrel.[13]

The impact of removing export restrictions on Jones Act shipping would be considerable. In FY 1984, fifty-four U.S.-flag tankers were engaged in the movement of Alaska oil to the lower 48 states, Hawaii, and Puerto Rico. A majority of this tonnage is new and was built in U.S. shipyards.[14]

A 188,500-dwt *San Diego*–class tanker being hauled from graving (construction) dock of National Steel and Shipbuilding Company of San Diego, California, in 1977. This tanker was the first of four designed and built by NASSCO for the Alaskan oil trade. (Courtesy of Shipbuilders Council of America and National Steel and Shipbuilding Company)

The second major Jones Act exception was proposed in 1983. It would allow registration under the American flag of two foreign-built passenger ships. The ships would be used in the growing cruise ship business between American ports. While foreign-flag cruise ships can and do operate between U.S. and foreign ports, they cannot carry passengers between U.S. ports. By the mid-1980s, however, a strictly U.S. cruise market had been identified and recognized as potentially profitable. Routes included the U.S. west coast to Hawaii and Alaska, east coast ports to Puerto Rico, and coastwise cruises between east and Gulf coast ports as well as cruises along the Atlantic coast. In 1985 two large cruise ships and two smaller ones were actively employed in this trade, while plans had been announced for additional ships.[15]

Thus, the request of Cruise America Line for a Jones Act waiver to operate the foreign-built *Cunard Princess* and *Cunard Countess* under the U.S. flag between U.S. ports met solid opposition from U.S. ship-yards. They argued that "reflagging" the two ships, whose purchase price was less than half the cost of building similar ships in an American yard, would set a precedent that would end any chance of American shipyards again building passenger ships, a market they had not participated in for over 20 years.

The 1984 debate over granting these waivers pitted maritime union against maritime union, shipyards against shipowners, and split the Congress. The chairman of the House Merchant Marine Subcommittee, Mario Biaggi, was a strong supporter of reflagging but was unable to prevail in a House–Senate conference that considered the needed waiver. The issue was again before Congress in 1985. A hardly startling conclusion is that as long as a potentially profitable cruise market between U.S. ports exists, the issue of reflagging lower-priced, foreign-built passenger vessels will not go away.

Costs and Benefits

The benefits of keeping the Jones Act intact basically turn on national security concerns—having in place a U.S.-flag, citizen-manned merchant fleet and support for a shipyard mobilization base. This benefit is difficult to measure in dollar amounts because in a national emergency ships and shipyards are assets beyond price.

The cost to the nation of granting a domestic ocean commerce monopoly to U.S. ships and shipyards, while difficult to estimate, can be approximated. A 1984 Congressional Budget Office study stated:

> It is estimated that the cost to the economy from cabotage in fiscal 1983 was about $1.3 billion. This is the cost to shippers for U.S. flag services above the cost of the same services from foreign flag ships. The major portion of this amount (about $1 billion) is attributable to the carriage of Alaskan North Slope crude oil to the continental United States.[16]

An earlier study that analyzed the Alaska–lower 48 state trade concluded that the total higher cost of using American ships would range from 10 to 40 percent, the higher percent being in the movement of crude petroleum.[17]

On the other hand, the Matson Navigation Company, a U.S.-flag liner firm operating in the U.S. west coast–Hawaii trade, maintains that if (its) "current Hawaii fleet had been built in foreign yards, the overall level of freight rates could be reduced by [only] 9.7 percent without impairing its rate of return on rate base."[18]

Retain, Amend, or Repeal?

Keeping the Jones Act essentially unchanged is a firm commitment on the part of the Reagan administration. This position was reaffirmed in 1985 by Admiral Harold E. Shear, USN (Ret.), then the maritime administrator, who stated:

First and foremost, it has been, and continues to be the fact that this Administration reaffirms the sanctity of the Jones Act. On May 20 and August 5, 1982, former Secretary of Transportation Drew Lewis announced the Administration's position: "The administration reaffirms the sanctity of the Jones Act." The present Secretary of Transportation, Elizabeth Hanford Dole, reemphasized this position at her confirmation hearing: "This administration has no plans to revise the Jones Act and on the contrary recently reaffirmed the sanctity of the Jones Act." As recently as April 14 of this year, I noted before the Senate Merchant Marine Subcommittee, the Administration's affirmation of the Jones Act, and in the same month, in remarks to the Society [of Naval Architects and Marine Engineers], I also noted the Administration's firm support of the Jones Act.[19]

While the administration's position on the Jones Act seems quite clear, it has made no such strong commitment with respect to keeping in place export restrictions on Alaskan oil. The diverse views that surfaced during 1984 represent attempts to extend the Export Administration Act of 1979; and President Reagan's response to a question at a 22 February 1984 news conference made this abundantly clear. The news conference exchange was as follows:

> Q. "Back home, Mr. President, this week the Senate will consider amendments to the Export Administration Act. One will be to lift the ban on the export of Alaskan oil . . . your administration has privately supported this. Will you campaign aggressively when it's being considered in the Congress?"
> A. "Well, we're still looking and studying at this. There are still some problems about it, and I share the view that it would be an asset to the United States to do this."
> Q. "May I ask you if one of your problems in making a final decision is the opposition that the maritime unions have expressed?"
> A. "Well, I have to say that consideration of our merchant marine, the maritime force, has to be one because they are essential to our national defense, and as an adjunct to the Navy. And we want to make sure that there is a merchant marine in existence in this country."[20]

During 1982–86, a number of proposals have been made to amend the Jones Act directly or indirectly. The major components of these initiatives are listed below:

1. Allow (new) U.S.-flag, U.S.-owned, foreign-built vessels to enter the domestic trades.
2. Allow existing foreign-built and -registered ships owned by U.S. citizens to engage in the U.S. domestic trades under the American flag.

3. Allow foreign-built, U.S.-flag passenger vessels into the domestic trades.
4. Allow U.S.-flag vessels built with construction subsidies to enter the domestic trade without repayment of the subsidy.

The above proposals contain provisions, where necessary, to ensure equity with respect to existing water and land carriers.[21]
Further initiatives include:

5. Allow U.S.-owned, foreign-flag, foreign-built, and foreign-crewed vessels into the coastal and intercoastal trades, but not in the U.S. noncontiguous trades, e.g., U.S.–Hawaii, U.S.–Puerto Rico, U.S.–Alaska. Under this proposal a U.S. owner desiring to operate a foreign-flag, foreign-built ship in the coastal and intercoastal trades would be required to build in the United States under a construction subsidy program, and to operate under the U.S. flag, a tanker or bulk carrier in an American foreign trade.
6. Restrict the U.S. Virgin Island trade to U.S.-flag vessels, but not necessarily U.S.-built vessels.
7. Allow U.S.-flag, foreign-built vessels into the noncontiguous U.S. domestic trades.[22]

Many of the above proposals are commented on in different chapters throughout this book, and specific recommendations with respect to several are made in Chapter 15.

Conclusion

This chapter has primarily focused on provisions of the Jones Act insofar as they affect the U.S. shipyard industry. However, many of the proposals to amend the Jones Act, such as the above, are linked with proposals for new or renewed government programs in support of a larger shipyard mobilization base and/or increasing the overall size of the active U.S.-flag fleet—as, for example, a proposal to build "X" number of merchant ships for government account and lease them to private industry and/or put them into the Ready Reserve Force of the National Defense Reserve Fleet in exchange for allowing foreign-flag/built vessels into the U.S. domestic ocean trades.

The option of outright repeal of the Jones Act has not been discussed for the simple reason that no such serious proposal has been made in recent times. Nonetheless, it is still a policy option. The current alternatives are to retain the act essentially in its present form; amend it to ease restrictions on foreign-flag, foreign-built vessel participation in the U.S. protected trades; or amend it in conjunction with the establishment of other programs in support of U.S.-flag shipping and shipbuilding.

6 Industry Organization

IT HAS BEEN SAID many times that on any particular day no one is certain of the number of trucking firms operating in the United States. The industry ranges from the very large Yellow Freights and Roadways to the so-called Mom and Pop operators of a single truck, the numbers of which change daily. Estimates sometimes have variances as great as plus or minus one thousand. Fixing numbers to the shipbuilding and ship repair industry is only somewhat easier.

The previously cited (Chapter 1) Shipyard Mobilization Base Study (SYMBA), released in 1984, identified 110 yards having a mobilization potential and an additional 567 smaller shipyards, all classified within the Bureau of Labor Statistics Standard Industrial Classification (SIC) Code 3731. The Congressional Budget Office (CBO) study, *U.S. Shipping and Shipbuilding: Trends and Policy Choices* (1984), used essentially the same figures. Shipbuilding and repairing (SIC 3731) is defined as:

> Establishments primarily engaged in building and repairing all types of ships, barges, and lighters, whether propelled by sail or motor power or towed by other craft. This industry also includes the conversion and alteration of ships. Establishments primarily engaged in fabricating structural assemblies or components for ships, or subcontractors engaged in ship painting, joinery, carpentry work, electrical wiring installation, etc., are classified in other industries.[1]

Other estimates of what constitutes U.S. shipbuilding and repair facilities tend to be somewhat lower. After subtracting duplicate corporate listings and the nine publicly owned shipyards from the 1983–84 *Marine Directory* (published by the authoritative *Marine Engineering/Log*), 485 yards are identified.[2] The Maritime Administration defines the private sector shipbuilding and repair industry as some 380 establishments having a minimum of 20 or more employees.[3] Standard and Poor's 1984 *Registry of Corporations* is the least generous of all with respect to shipyard numbers. It lists only 132 firms in its SIC 3731 classification.[4]

In 1984 the Shipbuilders Council of America, an industry trade association, petitioned the Small Business Administration to divide SIC Code 3731 into three subcodes. Sizes suggested were: (1) shipbuilding, 1,000 or more employees; (2) ship repair, 500 or more; and (3) small craft construction, 250 or more employees.[5]

While the numbers (and capabilities) of the nation's smaller shipyards at present are somewhat soft figures, major shipyards are relatively easy to identify. In this respect, 23 shipyards are considered to be the active shipbuilding industrial base (ASIB), the base being defined as yards *seeking*, as well as *having*, the capability of fulfilling contracts for constructing naval and/or large merchant ships.[6] These shipyards account for approximately one-half of the total shipyard employment in the United States. Table 6.1 lists ASIB shipyards in 1985.

The largest shipyards in the ASIB, with one exception, are not stand-alone investments. The two private-sector, nuclear-capable yards, which are also two of the largest yards, are parts of industrial conglomerates. Newport News is a division of Tenneco, while Electric Boat and the Quincy, Massachusetts shipyard are a part of General Dynamics. Of the

Table 6.1. Shipyards in the active shipbuilding industrial base, 1985.

Shipyard	Location
Alabama Drydock and Shipbuilding	Mobile, AL
Avondale Corporation	New Orleans, LA
Bath Iron Works	Bath, ME
Bay Shipbuilding	Sturgeon Bay, WI
Bethlehem Steel	Sparrows Point, MD
Equitable Shipyards	New Orleans, LA
General Dynamics/Electric Boat	Groton, CT
General Dynamics	Quincy, MA
Halter Marine	New Orleans, LA
Ingalls Shipbuilding	Pascagoula, MS
Lockheed Shipbuilding	Seattle, WA
Marinette Marine	Marinette, WI
National Steel and Shipbuilding	San Diego, CA
Newport News Shipbuilding	Newport News, VA
Norfolk Shipbuilding	Norfolk, VA
Pennsylvania Shipbuilding	Chester, PA
Peterson Builders	Sturgeon Bay, WI
Tacoma Boatbuilding	Tacoma, WA
Tampa Shipyards	Tampa, FL
Todd Shipyards	Galveston, TX
Todd Pacific Shipyards	Los Angeles, CA
Todd Pacific Shipyards	San Francisco, CA
Todd Pacific Shipyards	Seattle, WA

23 yards in the ASIB, 10 are subsidiaries of large corporations.[7] Only Todd Shipyards, Inc. and the employee-owned Avondale Corporation are nonconglomerate enterprises.

Historically, the ASIB tends to remain relatively constant although, over time, the list does change as yards close or give up construction work to concentrate on repair and overhaul, and hence, by definition, drop out of the base.[8] Figure 6.1 shows the geographic location of ASIB shipyards.

Naval Construction

While naval construction, by definition, takes place within the ASIB, yards within the base have differing capabilities and hence different earning opportunities from naval contracts. In descending order these capabilities are:

1. Building nuclear-powered vessels.
2. Building technologically complex naval combatants.
3. Building naval amphibious/auxiliary vessels plus merchant vessels.
4. Building merchant vessels.

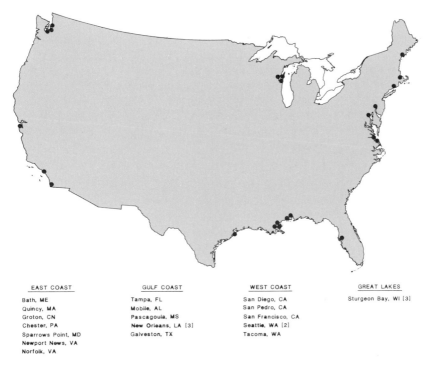

EAST COAST	GULF COAST	WEST COAST	GREAT LAKES
Bath, ME	Tampa, FL	San Diego, CA	Sturgeon Bay, WI [3]
Quincy, MA	Mobile, AL	San Pedro, CA	
Groton, CN	Pascagoula, MS	San Francisco, CA	
Chester, PA	New Orleans, LA [3]	Seattle, WA [2]	
Sparrows Point, MD	Galveston, TX	Tacoma, WA	
Newport News, VA			
Norfolk, VA			

Figure 6.1. Geographic location of shipyards in the active shipbuilding industrial base (ASIB), 1985.

Higher-order categories include the capabilities of lower-ranked ones. Table 6.2 lists types of construction in shipyards in the ASIB in 1984.

Table 6.3 lists naval construction awards to ASIB shipyards, 1980–84.

While the vast majority of construction contracts, in both numbers and value, went to ASIB yards, some contracts were awarded to smaller,

Table 6.2. Construction in ASIB shipyards, 1984.

Shipyard
Alabama Drydock and Shipbuilding, Mobile, AL
Avondale Shipyards, New Orleans, LA**
Bath Iron Works, Bath, ME*
Bay Shipbuilding, Sturgeon Bay, WI
Bethlehem Steel, Sparrows Point, MD
Equitable Shipyards, New Orleans, LA
General Dynamics/Electric Boat, Groton, CT [1]*
General Dynamics, Quincy, MA
Halter Marine, New Orleans, LA
Ingalls Shipbuilding, Pascagoula, MS*
Lockheed Shipbuilding, Seattle, WA**
Marinette Marine, Marinette, WI
National Steel and Shipbuilding, San Diego, CA**
Newport News Shipbuilding, Newport News, VA [1]*
Norfolk Shipbuilding, Norfolk, VA
Pennsylvania Shipbuilding, Chester, PA**
Peterson Builders, Sturgeon Bay, WI**
Tacoma Boatbuilding, Tacoma, WA**
Tampa Shipyards, Tampa, FL
Todd Shipyards, Galveston, TX
Todd Pacific Shipyards, San Pedro, CA*
Todd Pacific Shipyards, San Francisco, CA
Todd Pacific Shipyards, Seattle, WA*

[1] Nuclear-powered vessels.

*Ballistic missile submarines (SSBN), attack submarines (SSN), aircraft carriers (CVN), guided missile cruisers (CG), guided missile frigates (FFG), guided missile destroyers (DDG), destroyers (DD).

**Dock landing ship (LSD), mine countermeasure ship (MCM), ocean surveillance (AGOS), cable repair (ARC), oilers (AO), repair drydock (ARDM), salvage ship (ARS), patrol craft (YP), Coast Guard medium endurance cutter (WMEC), hospital ship (AH), vehicle cargo ship (AKR), amphibious assault ship (LHD).

SOURCE: "U.S. Navy Shipbuilding and Conversion Program, 1983," *U.S. Naval Institute Proceedings*, February 1984, pp. 122–23; "U.S. Navy Shipbuilding and Conversion Program," *U.S. Naval Institute Proceedings*, January 1985, pp. 140–41.

Table 6.3. Naval construction contracts, 1980–84.

Shipyard	Year/Contract Type				
	1980	1981	1982	1983	1984
Electric Boat	A,B	A,B	A,B	A,B	A,B
Newport News	B,C,D	B,C	B,C	B,C	B,C
Ingalls	E,F,G,H	E,F,G	E,F,G	E,F	E,H
Bath Iron Works	I	I	E,I	E,I	E,I
Todd (San Pedro)	I	I	I	I	I
Todd (Seattle)	I	I	I	I	I
National Steel	J	J,O	J,O	J,O	O
Avondale	L	L	L	L	L
Lockheed	K	K	O	O	O
Marinette Marine	M	M	—	O	O
Tacoma Boat	N,O	N,O	N,O	N,O	N,O
Peterson Builders	—	—	O	O	O

KEY

A Ballistic missile submarine (SSBN)
B Submarine (SSN)
C Aircraft carrier (CVN)
D Nuclear guided missile cruiser (CGN)
E Guided missile cruiser (CG)
F Destroyer (DD)
G Guided missile Destroyer (DDG)

H Amphibious assault ship (LHD)
I Guided missile frigate (FFG)
J Destroyer tender (AD)
K Submarine tender (AS)
L Oilers (AO)
M Fleet ocean tug (ATF)
N Ocean surveillance ship (AGOS)

O Cable repair ship (ARC), salvage ship (ARS), Coast Guard cutter (WMEC), dock landing ship (LSD), mine countermeasure ship (MCM), patrol craft (YP)

SOURCE: "U.S. Navy Shipbuilding Program," 1980, 1981, and 1982, *U.S. Naval Institute Proceedings*, January 1981, 1982, and 1983, pp. 119–20, 121–22, and 120–21 and "U.S. Navy Shipbuilding and Conversion Program," 1983 and 1984, *U.S. Naval Institute Proceedings*, February 1984 and January 1985, pp. 122–23 and 140–41.

non-ASIB shipyards. Included were contract for construction of patrol combat missile ships (PHM) to the Boeing Marine Company of Seattle, contracts for construction of medium endurance Coast Guard cutters (W-MEC) to the R. E. Derecktor Company of Middletown, Connecticut, and one contract for a cargo ship (AK) to Boland Marine of New Orleans.[9] The value of these awards was less than 2 percent of the total for the five-year period.

In summary, as indicated in Table 6.3, approximately half (12) of the ASIB yards participated in naval construction work in the period 1980–84.[10]

Ship Repair and Overhaul: General

Between the ASIB yards and the smaller facilities there are approximately 200 medium to large repair shipyards. Slightly over half of these have the capability of drydocking an oceangoing vessel. In this regard, the SYMBA study identified 71 yards with a capability of drydocking vessels 400 feet or longer and 34 yards capable of drydocking vessels between 150 and 400 feet in length.[11]

Table 6.4 is a representative sample of non-ASIB repair yards together with repair capabilities. It should be noted, however, that the yards shown are a sample and not necessarily the largest facilities.

As a general rule, repair work tends to be more profitable than building, and in this respect a number of build-capable yards list only repair work on their order books. According to the Shipbuilders Council of America, (1) repair work now accounts for approximately 25 percent of all waterfront industrial activity, (2) the value of repair work doubled during 1974–84, and (3) repair employment grew by 20 percent in the same time period.[12]

Aside from naval contracts, which are discussed in the next section, the private sector spends about $1.5 billion a year for repair work, equally divided between U.S. and foreign-flag ship operators. With respect to U.S. firms, the Jones Act (domestic trade) fleet is the best customer.[13] If present Maritime Administration initiatives to have Congress repeal the 50 percent ad valorem tax on foreign repairs made by U.S. ships is successful, then the importance of Jones Act vessel repairs will substantially increase.

Naval Repair and Overhaul

Considerable attention has been focused on the Navy's building program and its ultimate goal of a 600-ship fleet, while less attention has been paid to the Navy's repair market. The latter, however, is of growing importance to a growing number of shipyards. M. Lee Rice, president of the Shipbuilders Council of America, noted this trend in an October 1984 address at a symposium sponsored by the American Society of Naval Engineers and the Commander in Chief, Atlantic Fleet:

> Make no mistake about it, the Navy ship repair market has become vitally important to the private sector. Since 1977–78, the commercial sector of the industry has declined by nearly two-thirds from its peak of 48,000 workers.

He went on to state:

> As further proof of how important the Navy repair market has become, it should be pointed out that Navy work now represents more than 75 percent of the total ship repair market. In 1977, when commercial shipbuilding was at its peak, Navy work comprised only about 50 percent of the ship repair market.[14]

Table 6.4. Representative U.S. repair shipyards, 1984.

Firm	Location	Capability
Atlantic Drydock/Marine	Jacksonville, FL	R,MD, MVC
Bender Ship Repair	Mobile, AL	R,SD,SVC
Blount Marine	Warren, RI	R,SD
Boeing Marine System	Seattle, WA	SVC (hydrofoils)
Boland Marine	New Orleans, LA	R,SVC
Boston Shipyard	Boston, MA	R,MD
Braswell Shipyards	Charleston, SC	R,MD
California Shipbuilding	Long Beach, CA	R,SD
Coastal Drydock and Repair	Brooklyn, NY	R,MD
Delta Shipyard	Houma, LA	R,SD,SVC
Detyens Shipyard	Charleston, SC	R,MD
FMC Corporation	Portland, OR	R,SVC
Galveston Shipbuilding	Galveston, TX	R,SVC
General Ship Repair	Baltimore, MD	R,SD,SVC
Gulf-Tampa Drydock	Tampa, FL	R,SD
Hoboken Shipyard	Hoboken, NJ	R,LD
Jacksonville Shipyards	Jacksonville, FL	R,LD
Jeffboat, Inc.	Jefferson, IN	SD,SVC
Marine Power & Equipment	Seattle, WA	R,SD,SVC
McDermott Shipyard Group	New Orleans, LA	R,SD,SVC
Metro Marine	Norfolk, VA	R,MD
National Marine Service	New Orleans, LA	R,SD
North Florida Shipyard	Jacksonville, FL	R,SD
Pacific Drydock and Repair	Oakland, CA	R,SD
Pacific Marine and Supply	Honolulu, HI	R
Port of Portland	Portland, OR	R,LD
Southern Shipbuilding Corp.	Slidell, LA	R,SD,SVC
Southwest Marine	San Diego, CA	R
Southwest Marine	Pago Pago, Samoa	R
Texas-Gulfport	Port Arthur, TX	R,SVC*
Triple A Shipyard	San Francisco, CA	R,MD
Twin City Shipyard	St. Paul, MN	R,SD,SVC
West Winds, Inc.	San Francisco, CA	R

SOURCE: Marine Engineering/Log, *Marine Directory 1983–84* and *Marine Engineering/Log*, May 1984, p. 57.
*Offshore drilling rigs.
R: repair.
SD: small drydock, 300–7,500 tons.
MD: medium dyrdock, 7,500–20,000 tons.
LD: large drydock, 20,000 tons plus.
SVC: small vessel construction.
MDV: medium vessel construction.

Ship repair work is a major part of shipyard revenues. The SS *Pennsylvania Sun* undergoes repairs in the former Sun Shipbuilding and Drydock Company's two-section floating dry dock. This dry dock accommodates vessels with widths of up to 197 feet and is capable of handling vessels of up to 400,000 dwt. The former Sun Shipbuilding facility is now operated by the Pennsylvania Shipbuilding Corporation. (Courtesy Sun Shipbuilding and Drydock Company and Pennsylvania Shipbuilding Corporation)

However, naval repair and overhaul work is shared with eight naval shipyards, yards devoted exclusively to repair and conversion work since 1967. Thus, the extent to which the private sector benefits from naval work depends upon the share of naval work it is awarded. Over the last

The SS *Cpl. Louis J. Hauge, Jr.* became the first ship of the U.S. Navy's Maritime Prepositioning Ship Program upon delivery from Bethlehem Steel Corporation's Sparrows Point, Maryland, shipyard on 7 September 1984. (Courtesy Bethlehem Steel Corporation)

decade the proportion has ranged between 33 and 39 percent for private yards. A congressional mandate directs that private-sector share not fall below 30 percent.

The amounts involved are not small. In FY 1983, the bill for naval ship maintenance and modernization was $4.994 billion, whereas in FY 1984, it was $5.279 billion, and in FY 1985, the request was for $6.37 billion.[15] If $5.5 billion is taken as a likely average figure for the period FY 1986–90, and if the private sector share is held to average 35 percent, then the value to U.S. shipyards of naval repair work tends around $2 billion annually.[16]

In 1984 the House Armed Services Committee recommended a 60–40 split between naval and private yards, or a 50–50 split excluding work on nuclear-powered ships. The House Appropriations Committee also endorsed the concept. With a 60–40 split, an additional $275 million in repair contracts would go to the private sector, assuming a $5.5 billion repair appropriation. In 1984, Congress also mandated a limited amount of competition between naval and private yards. The Navy was to put two ship overhauls out for bid. All direct and indirect costs of both private and naval yards were to be included. One overhaul will go to the low bidder, the second to next lowest. During the overhaul period the performance of the winning yards (naval or private) will be evaluated. Table 6.5 lists 39 U.S. private shipyards that do the vast majority of shipyard repair work. The table shows the number of employees allotted to naval work and to private sector employment.

Table 6.5. Shipyards by number of employees doing repair work, 1985.

Shipyard	Total employment	Government work	Private work
East Coast			
Atlantic Drydock	21	21	0
Metal Trades, Inc.	177	177	0
Atlantic Marine	185	167	18
Hoboken Shipyard	236	236	0
Braswell Shipyard	245	245	0
Detyens Shipyard	250	239	11
Boston Shipyard	278	243	35
General Shipyard	309	309	0
Metro Machine	402	402	0
Penn Shipbuilding	612	539	73
Jonathan Corp.	725	725	0
Jacksonville Shipyard	810	237	573
Coastal Drydock and Repair	827	827	0
Norfolk Shipbuilding	1,692	656	1,036
Bath Iron Works	1,996	1,996	0
Newport News Shipyard	7,220	7,199	21
Gulf Coast			
Bethlehem Steel	294	267	27
Avondale Corporation	358	0	358
Tampa Shipyard	407	0	407
Todd Shipyards	525	61	464
Ingalls Shipyard	1,519	1,519	0

Naval Repair and Overhaul Work: Issues

In recent years several issues have surfaced with respect to the award of naval repair work in addition to how the overall appropriation is divided.

1. The issue of whether marginally qualified shipyards should be awarded repair contracts. The House Committee on Appropriations in its report on the FY 1985 defense appropriation bill took this position:

> The Navy is currently attempting to weed out marginally qualified shipyards which do not have piers or drydocks. The Committee notes that the Navy testified that some of these yards actually disrupt operational activities because they have to use Navy space to perform their work. Moreover, it is the Committee's belief that at a time when major shipyards are going out of business due to lack of work, it is questionable as to whether it makes good management sense in the event of mobilization to continue to award contracts to marginally qualified yards which are making no contribution to the industrial facility capability of this country.[17]

Table 6.5. (cont.)

Shipyard	Total employment	Government work	Private work
West Coast			
Pacific Drydock	74	20	54
Campbell Industries	87	71	16
Todd Shipyards (Seattle)	121	32	89
Southwest Marine (San Francisco)	123	52	71
Arcwel, Inc.	149	149	0
Continental Marine (San Francisco)	164	164	0
Triple A (San Francisco)	165	28	137
Southwest Marine (San Pedro)	193	100	93
Triple A (San Diego)	197	197	0
Duwamish Shipyard	200	200	0
Lake Union Drydock	200	200	0
Continental Marine (San Diego)	267	267	0
Rohr Marine Industries	286	286	0
Todd Shipyards (San Francisco)	395	37	358
Tacoma Boatbuilding	434	0	434
Service Engineering Company	620	588	32
National Steel	641	572	69
Todd Shipyards (San Pedro)	943	926	17
	24,347	19,954	4,393

SOURCE: "The Shipyard Mobilization Base and Interrelated Issues: Policy Dilemma—Security Risks," address by M. Lee Rice before Conference on American Merchant Marine, Center for Ocean Laws and Policy, Charlottesville, Va., 30 March 1985.

NOTE: In December 1985 it was announced that the Boston Shipyard would close in 1986.

The House Armed Services Committee was somewhat more flexible in that it cautioned the Navy not to decertify a yard holding a Master Ship Repair Contract solely because it lacks a drydock or pier space, if all other requirements are met.

2. The issue of the amount of repair and overhaul work that should be set aside for private shipyards in a vessel's homeport. The issue was succinctly stated by the House Committee on Appropriations:

Navy policy is to reserve 30 percent of ship maintenance, repair, and alterations for homeport private shipyards. However, currently, 58.7 percent of the private work is performed in homeport yards. As a result, once the Navy has set aside work for nuclear capable yards, and homeport shipyards, there is only 4.3 percent of the total Navy ship overhaul program left for 35 percent of the licensed shipyards in non-homeport areas to bid on. This imbalance is highlighted by the fact that San Diego and Norfolk together get half of the private repair work despite their having only one-fifth of the licensed private yards.[18]

3. Division of naval work between the higher-cost U.S. west coast shipyards and yards in the Gulf and on the Atlantic coast. Periodically, the Maritime Administration reports to Congress on the relative costs of shipbuilding in the coastal districts of the United States. A comparison of cost ratios in 1984 using the Atlantic Coast as a base (1.000) shows Pacific Coast costs as 1.039 and Gulf Coast costs as .954 of the base. The main difference between the districts is the direct and indirect cost of labor, a difference that would directly translate into higher repair costs on the west coast. In this respect, labor costs at naval shipyards are almost 17 percent higher on the west coast.[19] The case *for* west coast yards is analyzed in Appendix C.

4. The amount of government work, if any, that the Small Business Administration should set aside for small shipyards. Currently, shipyards with fewer than 1,000 employees are considered "small." This issue was summarized by L. M. Thorell, vice president and general manager, Todd Pacific Shipyards, in testimony before Congress in 1984. He concluded:

> . . . the ultimate effect of the SBA's "set aside" policy is to effectively eliminate any large capable contractor from even competing for Government set-aside work. As an example, the amount of set-aside work comprises about 67 percent of all Navy repair work issued in the port of San Francisco. Surely the intent of the regulations was not to eliminate large capable defense contracts.[20]

These issues and their implication with respect to defining a national shipyard policy will be addressed in more detail in later chapters.

Suppliers and Subcontractors

In the era of American shipbuilding supremacy, when vessels were made of wood and wind-driven, the number of shipyard suppliers was relatively few, and subcontractors were almost nonexistent. A shipyard's success and reputation was largely under its control. The maritime historian John G. B. Hutchins broke down the expense of building a medium-size vessel in 1857 as:

Labor (4,245 days work)	$ 6,395
Contract work (millwork, hauling, incl. labor)	2,196
Supervision and general expense	1,286
Oak timber	4,211
Hackmatack knees	403
Southern pine plank	3,389
Oak plank	812

Pine deck plank	747
Spars	654
Miscellaneous lumber	519
Iron fastenings, nails and castings	1,963
Oakum and paint, etc.	1,652
Equipment	643
Tools	131
Total cost (hull and spars only)	$25,001[21]

However, as ships became more complex, suppliers increased in number and the subcontractor became an important part of the industry in his own right. This change is best reflected in the statement of John P. Diesel, president of Newport News Shipbuilding and Dry Dock Company, in hearings before Congress in 1974. He said:

> Although we are the largest private employer in Virginia, the rest of the country certainly has a big hand in our shipbuilding programs. For example, more than 850 companies in nearly 40 States supply materials for a carrier.
>
> This involves 11,000 individual purchase orders which, needless to say, challenge our warehousing and storage facilities. We stock more than 35,000 different items.[22]

In a 1980 National Academy of Science report citing Maritime Administration data, the direct and indirect requirements of the U.S. shipbuilding industry from 20 leading supplying industries were identified. This information is shown in Table 6.6.

The Shipbuilders Council has compiled a list of shipyard suppliers by congressional district. Thirty-eight states and 281 congressional districts were represented. New York and California led the other states by wide margins. The total number of suppliers in this 1983 survey was 871. However, the Shipbuilders Council is the first to acknowledge that this list is incomplete, and, owing to the difficulty of defining and obtaining the data, compiling a definitive list of shipyard suppliers may never be possible.

Conclusion

Since 1982, the base date for the SYMBA study, 16 shipyards in the shipyard mobilization base have closed, either permanently or temporarily, while only one has been added. Four of these closures were in the ASIB.

As the shipyard base shrinks, the question of how many yards is enough in the context of national security becomes more pressing. The follow-on study to SYMBA, the National Defense Shipyard Study (NADES), begun in late 1983, suggests a base of 9 public yards and 57

Table 6.6. Direct and indirect requirements of U.S. shipbuilding industry from 20 leading supplier industries, 1970.

Supplier	Relative importance in terms of dollar purchases (%)
Primary iron and steel manufacturing	17
Primary nonferrous metal manufacturing	11
Heating, plumbing, and fabricated metals	9
Wholesale and retail	9
Engines and turbines	8
General industrial machinery	7
Other transportation	5
Business services	5
Other fabricated metal products	5
Real estate and rental	3
Electric/gas/water/sanitary services	3
Metalworking machinery and equipment	3
Lumber and wood products	2
Finance and insurance	2
Electrical transmission equipment	2
Motor vehicles and equipment	2
Business travel	2
Maintenance and repair construction	2
Machine shop products	2
Stone and clay products	1

Calculated from: Port Authority of New York and New Jersey, *Economic Impact of the U.S. Merchant Marine and Shipbuilding Industries: An Input–Output Analysis* (Washington, D.C.: Maritime Administration, 1977), p. 33.

private yards. Twenty-nine of the 57 have the capability of building and drydocking vessels over 475 feet in length.

The question of how many yards is enough was put to Larry French, president of the Society of Naval Architects and Marine Engineers, in 1984. Using the capability to build a ship 400 feet long as the basic criterion, French stated:

> This is a question really for the government to answer. But you can take a number from 17 to 21 and pick any one of those. I can't argue that 21 is a more valid number than 17. But I think that the number of yards that must be kept operating for national defense must be in that range.

He went on to comment upon the importance of shipyard suppliers:

> If you give me a shipyard in San Diego, and a trained crew of workers in San Diego, without any suppliers in the United States I couldn't build a ship

in time of war. You need the steel mills, you need the electrical manufacturers, you need the foundries, you need the forges, and you need them domestically.[23]

Perhaps as important as the question of how many is the question of which yards will survive as the base shrinks. One consideration that will play a large part in answering this question is whether a yard has a parent company with "deep pockets." In this respect, 4 yards in the ASIB base have parents that are among the top 15 firms in terms of defense contracts.[24] Other things being equal, the odds are good that these yards will survive. But that does not answer the question of how many, the necessary geographic dispersion, and the capabilities required. These are the important questions, and finding answers cannot be put off indefinitely.

7   Naval Shipyards

THE FIRST NAVY YARD was established at Portsmouth, New Hampshire in 1800. Along with Portsmouth, Congress also authorized, in 1799, the Washington, Boston, Philadelphia, and Norfolk navy yards.[1]

Portsmouth, which has been referred to as the "Cradle of American Shipbuilding," is the product of a shipbuilding tradition dating back almost 300 years; it was in 1690 that the British government selected Portsmouth as the site to build ships for the Royal Navy. Concurrently, a contract was authorized for the building of HMS *Falkland*, a 637-ton frigate of 54 guns, the first warship to be built in North America.[2] This is the historical foundation upon which an American shipbuilding and ship repair industry was built. In 1986, the currently active eight naval shipyards are a significant part of that industry. Historically, both private and public shipyards have provided shipbuilding and repair support to the Navy, complementing each other in essential, but different, missions.

Naval shipyards exist to provide immediately responsive ship repair support to the currently operating combatant fleet, and to be the nucleus from which necessary wartime shipbuilding and repair capability can be mobilized. Four are strategically located along the east coast and four on the west coast, including Hawaii, as shown in Figure 7.1.

Naval shipyards work closely with local naval base commanders and other area naval commands to provide the many crew support, administrative, and security functions required by ships assigned to a naval yard for overhaul or repair.

Responsibilities

Naval shipyards are a part of the operational navy, and are expected to be as immediately responsive to emergency requirements as commands afloat. Their skilled manpower can be, and often is, quickly organized to accomplish an urgent repair or operationally required ship alteration. Experienced workers in all shipyard crafts can be immediately dispatched

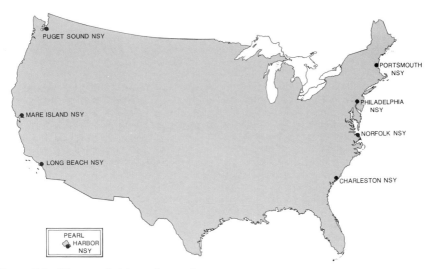

PUGET SOUND NSY

PORTSMOUTH NSY

PHILADELPHIA NSY

MARE ISLAND NSY

NORFOLK NSY

LONG BEACH NSY

CHARLESTON NSY

PEARL HARBOR NSY

Figure 7.1. The naval shipyard complex.

to the most remote locations on the globe, wherever U.S. naval ships are operating and emergency repairs required. Naval shipyard teams have been sent to such ports as Bahrain in the Persian Gulf; Diego Garcia in the Indian Ocean; Guam in the Western Pacific; Holy Loch, Scotland; and La Madellena, off Sardinia in the Mediterranean. Time after time, overseas repairs have been accomplished quickly and professionally, thereby demonstrating one of the great strengths of the present naval shipyard system in projecting its capabilities where and when they are needed.

The primary way in which naval shipyard work differs from private shipyards was stated by the Commander, Naval Sea Systems Command before Congress some ten years ago:

> While private shipyards have received all of our new construction work for the past few years, we have traditionally assigned most of the major combatant ship overhaul and repair work to naval shipyards where unique capabilities for fleet support exist.[3]

While all new construction for the Navy is accomplished in private shipyards, the majority of repair and conversion work, especially for major combatants, is performed by naval shipyards. The official mission statement, applicable to all naval shipyards, is:

> To provide logistic support for assigned ships and service craft; to perform authorized work in connection with construction, conversion, overhaul, repair, alteration, drydocking and outfitting of ships and craft, as assigned; to perform manufacturing, research, development, and test

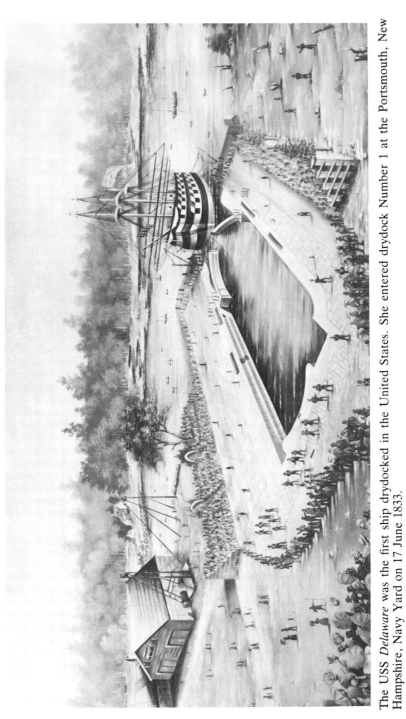

The USS *Delaware* was the first ship drydocked in the United States. She entered drydock Number 1 at the Portsmouth, New Hampshire, Navy Yard on 17 June 1833.

work, as assigned; and to provide services and material to other activities and units as directed by competent authority.[4]

Management Organization and Evolution

Naval shipyards are commanded by U.S. naval engineering duty (ED) officers, of the rank of captain or commodore, The reporting chain is directly to the Commander, Naval Sea Systems Command (NavSea) in Washington. A vice admiral (engineering duty officer) headed NavSea from 1974, when the command was established, until 1985, when a line officer was assigned as commander.[5]

The management team that operates the various shipyard departments, offices, and divisions is a fairly even mix of naval officers and senior civil servants. Civilians provide local continuity, while the naval officer role is to ensure that vital operational needs of the fleet customers are understood and managed within the shipyard organization. Thus, the shipyard line organizations are generally headed by naval officers, while, with some exceptions, staff responsibilities are filled by civilians. The system of management now in place is the result of years of evolution and will continue to change in the future to accommodate new technology and management practices. Naval officers from most of the branches within the Navy occupy positions of shipyard authority and leadership. Engineering duty officers head two of the major shipyard departments, production and planning. The Supply and Civil Engineer Corps furnish officers to head and staff the supply and public works departments. Unrestricted line officers work side by side with their staff corps and restricted line counterparts, an arrangement that guarantees heterogeneity to the officer management team.

Where continuity of management and specialized backgrounds are important, senior civilians of general schedule levels GS-14 and GS-15 head specific offices and departments, such as industrial relations, the nuclear engineering department, and the production shops.

Civilian managers of a naval shipyard can be classified into two groups. Members of one group have traditionally come from the ranks of the blue collar trades and occupy important management positions as heads of the shops, which are organized along the lines of production trades. The other group of supervisors consists of white collar professionals who are responsible for the shipyard's labor relations, finances, engineering, and material acquisition.

Both of these civilian management groups have displayed commitment and dedication to their work, in a spirit especially well personified by J. H. Whitthorne, known for years as "Mr. Mare Island." When Whitthorne finally retired in 1967, he had spent 59 years and 3 months in civil service, "the longest consecutive civilian employment record in U.S. Naval History."[6]

Since World War II, management of naval shipyards has been the responsibility of the engineering duty (ED) officers of the Navy. For the first 160 years, the responsibilities of today's EDs were split between two communities: engineers and constructors.[7]

In 1794, a naval constructor was appointed to supervise the building of the first six ships authorized by Congress, each of which was to be built in a different shipyard on the east coast. One of the six constructors was called the "Principal Constructor of the Navy." When international tensions eased in 1802, four of the six navy yards were closed, and most of the constructors were out of work.

The other community from which the current engineering duty officers trace their lineage was an outgrowth of the age of steam. The steam engineer first began to serve the technical needs of the Navy in 1836. A civilian engineer was appointed to the steamship *Fulton II*, then under construction. Later, the two technical communities were associated with different specific bureaus of the Navy. In 1842, the Navy Department was reorganized, and a Corps of Engineers and five bureaus were established:

- The Bureau of Yards and Docks
- The Bureau of Construction, Equipment and Repair
- The Bureau of Ordnance and Hydrography
- The Bureau of Provision and Clothing
- The Bureau of Medicine and Surgery

The bureau system was extended in 1862 when three new bureaus were added:

- The Bureau of Steam Engineering
- The Bureau of Equipment and Recruiting
- The Bureau of Navigation

By act of Congress in 1866 the Construction Corps was established. Under this legislation, naval constructors were authorized commissions as officers in a staff corps of the U.S. Navy.

From these two staff corps, Engineering and Construction, each affiliated with different bureaus (the Bureau of Steam Engineering and the Bureau of Construction), the engineering duty officers, through a series of steps over the years, eventually became part of the line of the Navy. In 1986, EDs are principally associated with the Naval Sea Systems Command, the successor to the Bureaus of Construction, Equipment and Repair, Ordnance and Hydrography, and Steam Engineering.[8]

In 1910, the Bureau of Steam Engineering became the Bureau of Engineering. Overlapping areas of responsibilities and some duplication of work between the Bureaus of Engineering and Construction created delays as the Navy's shipbuilding programs developed in the decade prior to World War II. On 5 October 1939, the Bureaus of Engineering and Construction were combined to form the Bureau of Ships. The authorizing action was passed by Congress in 1940.[9] While the merger of the two bureaus was taking place, there was disagreement with regard to the merger of the two technical groups, the EDOs and constructors. Admiral Robinson, head of the Bureau of Engineering and the senior EDO, favored their merger as restricted line officers. Admiral Van Keuren, head of the Bureau of Construction, favored their merger as a new staff corps. Admiral Van Kuren yielded to the logic that technically expert engineering officers needed to be as close to the line officers of the Navy as possible, when he stated:

> ... It is wiser to get closer to the line, to be better able to absorb their point of view and in turn to enable them [the unrestricted line officers] to appreciate better the technical point of view and career problems of the technical officers.[10]

On 25 June 1940, President Roosevelt signed the bill specifying that EDOs were to be combined with the former Construction Corps officers as an addition to the numbers of line officers allowed by Congress. EDOs (now EDs) are restricted line officers responsible for the management of naval ship and ordnance design, procurement, and maintenance.

In 1966, another command transition established the Naval Ships Systems Command, Naval Electronic Systems Command, and Naval Ordnance Systems Commands as subordinate to the Chief of Naval Material. The Naval Ships Systems Command and Naval Ordnance Systems Commands were merged in 1974 to form the Naval Sea System Command. Its commander is the reporting senior for all eight naval shipyards.[11]

Each of the eight naval shipyards has its own special character, expertise, and strength. The reasons for the variations are several. In some cases, traditions are traceable to pre–Revolutionary War days, as can be observed in the crusty saltiness of rugged New England shipyard employees and the proud southern traditions of Virginia or South Carolina. In other cases, hard work in response to current necessities has spawned other traditions. Workers at the Long Beach Naval Shipyard, which was established in relatively recent times (1943), are militantly proud of their capability and record. The recent activation of the battleship *New Jersey* gave ample evidence that Long Beach, along with the older naval shipyards, can be mobilized for large and difficult assignments, which will be done on time and within cost, and will meet quality standards.

Table 7.1 illustrates the various capabilities of the eight naval shipyards and the type of work that each may be assigned.

Appendix D, a brief history of each of the eight naval shipyards,

Table 7.1. U.S. naval shipyard strategic capabilities assignment.

	Atlantic Coast Shipyards				Strategic assignment	Type ships assigned	Pacific Coast Shipyards			
	PORTS	PHILA	NORVA	CHASN			LBEACH	MARE IS.	PUGET	PEARL
		X	X		Air warfare	Carriers	X		X	
		X	X	X	Anti-air warfare	Cruisers, destroyers	X		X	X
		X	X	X	Anti-sub. warfare	Destroyers, frigates	X		X	X
	X		X	X	Sub. warfare	Nuclear attack		X	X	X
	X			X	Sub. warfare (FBM)	Fleet ballistic missile		X	X	
				X	Sub. warfare	Diesel-powered		X		X
			X		Surface warfare, nuclear	Nuclear-powered cruisers/destroyers		X	X	
			X		Air warfare, nuclear	Nuclear carriers			X	

explains why naval shipyards have developed an individual character while maintaining similar organizations and general goals.

Role of the Naval Shipyards in a Changing Environment

The navy yard of the pre–World War II era encompassed a full range of ship support, including that required for the crew. Support included the provision of supplies, ammunition, medical services, housing, messing, berthing, recreational facilities, and financial services. In some cases the navy yard commandant served as the military commander in the area. Captain David Farragut at Mare Island actually acted as on-scene commander of naval forces for San Francisco Bay. The central function around which these essential services revolved, however, was the industrial capability to repair and, in most cases, construct naval ships and craft.

With the coming of a naval base organization in the post–World War II years, certain functions and facilities that were formerly the responsibility of the navy yard were reorganized and assigned to either a naval shipyard, a naval supply center, or a naval ammunition depot. These changes in organization and functions made the naval shipyard's role more questionable to those who saw the private sector as better able to fulfill the construction, conversion, and repair work that had been done in naval shipyards.[12]

In the debate over private and public sector capability, historical influences should be kept in mind. The shipyard complex of the mid-1980s is a product of many past decisions and realities that were at the same time political, economic, geographic, technical, and sometimes even patriotic and religious in character. The establishment and maintenance of the fleet support capability provided by naval shipyards is the product of not only the strategic need for these facilities in the locations at which they have developed, but also the realities of local politics and the economics of facility location. Strategic need and local support both had to exist, in just the right proportions, to explain the specific mix of our present eight naval shipyards. Almost mathematically predictable cyclic buildups of employment and skill levels during recent wars, followed by dramatic depletions of manpower resources after the peace, have occurred. These cycles molded the current capability base of the eight naval shipyards in an evolutionary way. However, the creation of these facilities, with their traditions, skills, and manpower base, could also have happened in the private sector.

The private U.S. shipbuilding industry includes a number of large building yards around the perimeter of the country, with some, but not all, having the capabilities of the naval shipyard complex. However, the level of ship support needed has not been provided by the private sector.

Launching of the USS *Mariano G. Vallejo* at the Mare Island Naval Shipyard. The *Vallejo* was a Polaris-type nuclear submarine and was one of a number of nuclear submarines built at Mare Island. The last ship constructed at the yard was the USS *Drum*, a nuclear attack submarine launched in 1970. (Official U.S. Navy photograph)

Naval shipyards are responsive to fleet needs, and their capability, in some cases, has taken decades to build. As vigorously as free market economists may advocate allowing the marketplace to function, it is highly questionable whether the United States can afford the luxury of abandoning this vital fleet support function to the vagaries of labor–management animosity, free market product selection, and regulation by the Securities and Exchange Commission. A modern, complex, nuclear and missile navy at sea requires the basic depot level support of the naval shipyards *in concert with private sector* capabilities.

Our current capability to overhaul, repair, modernize, and refuel nuclear-powered ships illustrates this point. It takes literally years to build the intricate network of facilities, procedures, skills, qualifications, discipline, and dedicated attitudes necessary to do nuclear work successfully. Only two private shipyards, Newport News Shipbuilding and Drydock Company and the Electric Boat Division of General Dynamics, are currently authorized to work on nuclear-powered ships. The Electric Boat Division has not done overhaul or refueling work since the mid-1970s, because it has been totally consumed with contracted new construction. Similarly, Ingalls built and overhauled nuclear submarines at one time, but is now totally committed to conventionally powered ships. Only Newport News has retained the capability to accomplish nuclear work in both new construction and repair.

On the other hand, six naval shipyards have the current capability and authorization to do nuclear work.[13] Acquisition of this capability has not been easy or accomplished without full dedication to the task.

In the case of Portsmouth, an interest in submarines dating to World War I was the basis for the present full dedication to overhaul, modernization, repair, and refueling of nuclear submarines. Likewise, the decision made after World War II that Charleston would be a submarine yard is not only the key to its current involvement in all phases of nuclear submarine repair work, but a major factor in explaining the very existence of the shipyard.

The requirements needed at Pearl Harbor cannot even be approached by any private sector capability. While one might wish for full and free competition with respect to shipbuilding and the ship repair industry (i.e., to have all shipyard support lodged in the private sector), the fact is that the nation cannot afford to abandon the security of the rock it stands on.

Naval shipyards are responsible for, and provide many facets of, crew support during overhauls. Crew berthing and messing near a ship are recognized as important to the efficient accomplishment of work that the crew must do—either because they can best perform the tasks, or because austere budgets do not provide funds for their shipyard accomplishment. In many cases, the tools, technical expertise, and materials provided by the naval shipyard are essential to the work of the ship's force. Fleet overhaul scheduling policies now in use provide continuity of experience in those technical areas needed to maintain required skill levels. The continuity of management expertise, technical skills, and engineering experience provided by the assignment of naval work to a particular

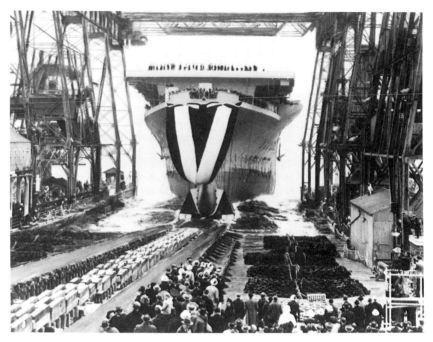

Launching of the attack carrier USS *Shangri-la* at the Norfolk Naval Shipyard in 1944. Over 100,000 persons attended the launching. (Official U.S. Navy photograph)

shipyard ensures its ongoing capability; whereas the selection of only work considered to be profitable—a necessary criterion of private industry—would not ensure that the required fleet support levels would be maintained as needed.

Mobilization Requirements

As important as the material support of the operating fleet in peacetime is, the most important characteristic of naval shipyards is their mobilization potential. World War II mobilization illustrates what mobilization requirements may be in the extreme: total shipyard employment increased tenfold between mid-1940 and the employment peak in 1943. However, a World War II mobilization experience is not envisioned in current plans. Present estimates are that a shortfall of 40,000 workers would exist at D day, with an additional 55,000 workers needed to reach a projected peak a year and a half after D day. This scenario assumes a global situation lasting about three years.[14] It includes a buildup in both naval and private shipyards.

An ongoing base of expertise and experience in nuclear and missile systems is essential for effective mobilization and support of ships now in the fleet. Naval shipyards have traditionally provided this kind of rallying potential. Each time a review of their role has been undertaken, the need for naval shipyards in mobilization has been reaffirmed.[15]

Current Issues

It is axiomatic that "Success leads to complacency, complacency to failure, and failure to success." One can never assume that the degree of success achieved is complete and that further improvement is unnecessary; the only two alternatives are to get better or to get worse. Maintenance of the status quo between an improving posture and deterioration is a tenuous and elusive goal. Thus, naval shipyards face an endless array of challenges that must be met resolutely to ensure the continued viability of these shipyards in a basically free market economy.

Three significant issues in the 1980s are: (1) coping with the mandate to contract out selected, nonessential-to-mission functions that are demonstrated by analysis to be less expensively accomplished by private industry; (2) responding to increasing pressures to improve productivity and reduce federal employment roles while still meeting the technical and workload demands of a complex and growing fleet; and (3) reacting to the demands of the private ship repair industry for an increased share of naval ship repair work.

Contracting Out

OMB Circular A-76 articulates a long-standing policy that the federal government should not start, or carry on, any commercial activity to provide a service or product for its own use if such product or service can be otherwise procured. Some examples of activities contracted out to private industry are:

Office equipment repair	Blueprinting
Gas manufacturing	Refuse collection
Tree and garden nurseries	Telephone services
Laundry services	Tugboat services
Cement mixing	Photographic services

The above list is neither exhaustive nor universally applicable to all shipyards; but it illustrates the types of activity, under the procedures used to meet the requirements of OMB Circular A-76, that are being studied as candidates for contracting out.

An elaborate and costly procedure has been mandated to: define the function, determine its cost when done by government resources, request bids from private industry, and, in comparing public estimated cost versus private bid, either award the work to private industry bidders or keep the function a government activity. However, if the award is made to private industry, the civilian positions in government devoted to that function are eliminated, and the facilities to accomplish the work using government resources are lost. If a tree or garden nursery, with a current contract to provide service to the government, went out of business or failed to perform after winning an award, no lasting damage would be done. However, functions as essential as gas manufacturing or refuse collection cannot be left undone for very long before the problems get out of hand.

One of the most disconcerting aspects of this program is the arbitrary manner in which the functions to be studied are selected. If sufficient nominations of functions are not forthcoming from the field activities, Washington bureaucrats dictate the functions to be studied. Each announcement of another commercial activity (CA) to be studied initiates an acrimonious meeting at the field activity level among the affected workers, their union representatives, management, and a "sympathetic" press. If a function is contracted out, the activity commander loses control of his own resources. This termite-like erosion of the field activity functions and structure causes those in policy-making positions to wonder whether it might be better to look at the activity as a whole and contract it out rather than to contract it out in small bites. The administrative procedures of this program are so onerous that participants are hard put not to give up out of sheer weariness.

The point is that we need naval shipyards. What then are the legitimate, mission-oriented functions that must be kept in-house and are not under any circumstances candidates for the OMB-A76 Chinese-torture brand of CA analysis? General shipyard functions that should be properly assigned to naval shipyards include:

- Provide a responsive, geographically dispersed, strike-free industrial capability in support of fleet readiness.
- Ensure a controlled ready, qualified workforce to support changing operational commitments and emergent work.
- Ensure sustained support of highly complex and classified workloads.
- Maintain an immediate capability to repair battle damage rapidly for all classes of naval ships.
- Provide an immediate mobilization base for rapid expansion to support extended combat operations.

The lists of functions for potential contracting out often include security, a function that could either be assessed as a candidate for contracting out or be classified as mission-essential. Since the truck bombing of U.S. marines in Lebanon in 1984, there has been increased interest in security,

in the continental United States. The feeling that "it could happen
generated specific actions to enhance the security stature of naval
ds. However, security is a function in which a field commander
/e precise control in order to safeguard classified matter, prevent
, and limit possible damage due to terrorist attack. The degree of
quired demands that security be one of the functions retained
The repair of office machines can be farmed out without
)ut the field commander should retain control over specific
, such as security, that are essential to mission effectiveness
without the need to repeatedly justify the action.

Budget Pressures

The debate over the DoD budget levels for the FY 1986 budget had
ramifications that affected the naval shipyards. The Naval Material Command established in the 1960s was, until 1985, in the chain of command
between the naval shipyards and the Chief of Naval Operations. The
reorganization of the Navy by which this entire management level was
eliminated in 1985 forcefully demonstrated the budget austerity of the
mid-1980s. Secretary of the Navy John Lehman discussed the decision in
this way:

> The reason for the command's elimination is twofold: First, the move
> will help trim the Navy's overgrown bureaucracy, . . . an incredible and
> unwieldy monster, and second the service's procurement procedures must
> be improved.[16]

In another change, naval shipyards employment levels were directed
to be reduced by 5,000. Table 7.2 shows, by yard, the number of employees, the projected (in early 1985) forced firings, the total reduction
ordered, and the employee totals expected for 31 December 1985.[17]

Table 7.2. Reductions in force, naval shipyards, mandated for 1985.[17]

Shipyard	Empls. 2/28	Proj. RIFs	Total red.	Empls. 12/31
Charleston	8,601	145	251	8,350
Long Beach	6,895	400	1,295	5,600
Mare Island	10,028	150	328	9,700
Norfolk	13,327	250	1,027	12,300
Pearl Harbor	6,778	550	628	6,150
Philadelphia	11,373	512	1,113	10,260
Portsmouth	8,528	225	228	8,300
Puget Sound	12,387	200	687	11,700
Total	77,917	2,432	5,557	72,360

In view of the cyclic variations in naval shipyard employment levels, the reductions mandated in 1985 should not be a surprise, given the high level of interest in budget deficit reductions in both the administration and Congress. The naval shipyards provide one of the best targets for cuts in the entire Defense Department. In one neat, eight-component package is a federal payroll of over 70,000 people with few defenders but plenty of free market critics from a private shipbuilding and repair industry beleaguered by a lack of commercial work.

To meet the challenge, naval shipyards, as a group, must establish a justifiable reputation for leadership in productivity and cost. In order of emphasis, the three major rallying points for naval shipyard management are: schedule adherence, cost, and quality. In recent years, schedule has been the most important of these parameters. Since "time is money," it has traditionally been assumed that if a shipyard were able to "make" schedule, and spend a little extra in the process, the cost savings from a shorter duration would offset any excess cost incurred. While this assumption is good in theory, the half-life of a reputation based on schedule alone is short.

A recent example of such a comparison was the initial assignment of the aircraft carrier *Saratoga* to the Philadelphia Naval Shipyard in the Service Life Extension Program (SLEP). Cost was the central issue. The political decision to assign this SLEP to Philadelphia would have generated less rhetoric had it been demonstrated that a cost comparison between Philadelphia and Newport News yielded a toss-up, or was clearly favorable to Philadelphia.[18]

In the past, cost differentials between naval and private shipyards have been attributed to several legitimate, legislated factors. Naval shipyard workers, because of high retention rates and the system of wage area surveys by which federal wage rates are established, are paid on average higher wages than private shipyard workers receive. Civil servants have generous benefits that must be paid for. The exemplary compliance with mandated environmental and social programs that is expected of large federal installations incurs a relatively high overhead. Private shipyards must turn a profit, pay for insurance, and bear the opportunity cost of investment. They can hire and fire to follow workload variations. Documented comparisons have been made between private and public shipyards, although conditions that prevailed at the time of the studies make any projection into the future questionable.[19] However, these studies are quoted frequently to demonstrate that everyone knows naval shipyards are more expensive than private yards.

More recently, a study comparing costs of private and public overhaul developed a different conclusion:

. . . in our sample, the total cost-production cost plus time cost of an "average" overhaul done in a naval shipyard was lower than the total cost of an "average" overhaul done in a private yard.[20]

There are many initiatives in process to achieve improvement in naval shipyard productivity and cost performance. Several, however, illustrate what can and should be pursued, as described below.

Management and Overhead Costs

Naval shipyards have rarely been able to operate at their optimum level. Workload, constrained by the Navy Operations and Maintenance (O&M) budget, has been below levels that would be considered optimum for assessing facility capacity and overhead requirements. Two yards are now experimenting with overhead function reorganization in attempts to reduce overhead costs. One shipyard has consolidated many of the overhead codes that previously reported directly to the shipyard commander. It is projected that increased effectiveness can be achieved by putting administration, occupational safety and health, equal employment opportunity, legal, and so on, under the direct supervision of a civilian deputy to the shipyard commander.

Another shipyard is in the process of eliminating the shop head level in the production and public works departments. The general foreman, instead of reporting directly to the shop head, with responsibility for only one shop (welding, electric, rigger, etc.), will report to the group superintendent, who has responsibility for several shops. In addition to eliminating a level of supervision, the proposal may afford opportunities for more efficient utilization of personnel in responding to varying workload by trade.

Technology Improvements in Ship Repair

Technology improvements have been identified that have resulted in savings in some shipyards, and in most cases could be used by others, both private and public. These include:

1. Removal of asbestos by use of impregnation and entrapment techniques.
2. Improved scrap metal management.
3. Use of brush electroplating.
4. Automatic gas metal arc welding application to main propulsion shaft repair.
5. Waterborne repairs to torpedo tube slide valves, rudder tiller arms, and so on.
6. Procedure for installing stripheaters.

7. Plasma cutting of nonferrous metals.
8. Use of air-supported structures to protect application of nonskid material.
9. Computer aided manufacture of ventilation fitting patterns.
10. Use of numerically controlled machines to eliminate hand chipping, grinding, and machining of propellers.

The above organizational and technological improvements can be of benefit to both public and private shipyards. The cost competition among public (naval) shipyards and between private and public shipyards can be beneficial if the overriding principle is that each shipyard exists to keep the fleet at sea.

Public versus Private Split of U.S. Ship Repair Work

The allocation of conversion, alteration, and repair (CAR) work between the public and private shipyards is a controversial issue that is frequently debated during annual budget hearings before relevant congressional committees. During the period 1974–83, the split was approximately 30 percent private and 70 percent public. Arguments to continue the 30–70 policy cite the need to perform as much overhaul and repair work as possible in a homeport, and the fact that naval shipyards are the only yards with the capacity and capabilities to do work on the number of complex combatants in the fleet. Private shipyard industry representatives maintain that cost advantages could ensue if a 50/50 split policy were to be adopted or legislated.

Although the subject has been reviewed with regularity during the past ten years, the basic split has not changed. Accommodation on this issue seems to depend on the lack of full capability in both skills and facilities to do the necessary work in the private yards. Another consideration is the necessity to maintain the required skills in the naval shipyards as a mobilization base.

While no significant change in this policy has occurred in ten years, the issue is not dead, and it will continue to be debated as long as the current dearth of commercial ship space construction and repair work prevails in the United States. The basis for a rational policy may lie in an analysis of the mobilization response expected from each of the sectors.

Conclusion

Naval shipyards have a long history of providing responsive fleet support where and when it has been needed. The massive mobilization required in World War II is not likely to be needed in the future, but a reading of history since World War II demonstrates the need for rapid expansion of *ship repair* capabilities.

The complexity of modern naval combatants requires that a ready base of technologically trained and experienced shipyard personnel be maintained for the existing, expanding fleet.

8   Shipyard Labor

DEPENDING UPON HOW one defines shipbuilding and repair, total employment in the industry in 1984 ranged between 235,000 and 250,000. (See Chapter 6 for definitions of the U.S. shipyard industry.) Table 8.1 estimates private and naval (public) shipyard employment over the five-year period 1980–84.

Under the Merchant Marine Act of 1936, as amended, the Maritime Administration is required to conduct an annual survey of private shipbuilder and ship repair yards in the United States, basically to determine the adequacy of the shipyard mobilization base. Fifty-one major shipbuilding/repair yards, employing 94,735 workers, were analyzed in the 1984 survey.[1] The total number of employees in the individual yards ranged from 35 to 28,112. The average number was 1,857 and the median 326.

Table 8.2 profiles employment at major U.S. yards in terms of production and nonproduction (staff, administrative, managerial) employees. It is evident from Table 8.2, as pointed out throughout this book, that while total private sector shipyard employment has increased in the past five years, the increase has been entirely due to increases in naval construction and repair/overhaul budgets.[2] On the other hand, employment on commercial work fell drastically, from 19,317 in 1980 to 7,926 in 1984.

Shipyard Labor Profile

The cost share attributable to labor in building a ship in the United States is high—between 35 and 60 percent with the average estimated at 45 percent.[3] Conversely, foreign labor-share costs range from 20 to 35 percent.

Wages

In the vast majority of U.S. shipyards, wages are time-rated, generally on an hourly basis. In the first six months of 1984, weekly shipyard hours worked ranged from 40.6 to 41.4.[4]

Table 8.1. Total private and naval shipyard employment, 1980–84.

Year[a]	Private shipyards	Naval shipyards	Total
1980	178,000	72,400	250,400
1981	186,700	76,500	263,200
1982	171,600	80,000	251,800
1983	147,300	82,000	229,300
1984	156,900	80,800	237,700

SOURCES: U.S. Maritime Administration, 1984 *Report on Survey of U.S. Shipbuilding and Repair Facilities*, p. 44 and Shipbuilders Council of America, *Statistical Summary* (January 1985), p. 11.

[a]Annual average.

Table 8.2. Employment by category at major private shipyards engaged in shipbuilding and ship repair, 1980–84.

Year[a]	Production-related employees		Other	Total
1980	86,787	(19,317)[b]	15,267	102,054
1981	89,729	(20,282)	15,937	105,666
1982	86,828	(21,233)	14,979	101,807
1983	86,558	(10,853)	15,924	102,482
1984	89,880	(7,926)	15,805	105,686

SOURCE: U.S., International Trade Commission, *Analysis of the International Competitiveness of the U.S. Commercial Shipbuilding and Ship Repair Industries*, p. 18.

U.S.I.T.C. figures for 1984 are approximately the same as those for the 23 shipyards that comprise the Maritime Administration's active shipbuilding industrial base (ASIB). In April 1984 total employment at ASIB yards was 105,501.

[a]Yearly average.

[b](____) Number of production workers engaged in commercial shipbuilding and repair.

Table 8.3 contrasts weekly earnings of U.S. shipyard workers, all U.S. durable goods workers, and Japanese shipyard workers in 1983.

Weekly earnings shown in Table 8.3 can be extrapolated for 1984 by using 1984 hourly wage data and assuming a common, across-the-board, 40-hour week. Under these assumptions, Table 8.4 contrasts weekly shipyard worker earnings in the United States, Japan, and South Korea.

Less recent, but still indicative of the labor disadvantage faced by U.S. shipyards, is a 15-nation comparison of hourly compensation for shipbuilding production workers, shown in Table 8.5.

Man-Hours to Build a Ship

Productivity, by any measure, has been the most discussed of any shipyard issue. (See Chapter 9.)

Table 8.3. Comparison of weekly earnings in U.S. shipbuilding and durable goods industries and Japanese shipbuilding industry, 1983.

Industry	Weekly Earnings
U.S. shipbuilding	$427.18
U.S. durable goods	378.95
Japanese shipbuilding	253.09

SOURCES: U.S. shipbuilding/repair data from Bureau of Labor Statistics: reprinted in Shipbuilders Council of America, *Statistical Summary* (January 1985), and U.S., International Trade Commission, *Analysis of the International Competitiveness of the U.S. Commercial Shipbuilding and Ship Repair Industries*, Table C-4, p. 79.

Table 8.4. Comparison of weekly earnings in U.S., Japanese, and South Korean shipbuilding industries, 1984.

Country	Total hourly compensation	Weekly hours	Weekly earnings
United States	$12.78	40[a]	$511.12
Japan	7.84	40	313.60
South Korea	2.06	40	82.40

SOURCE: U.S., Congress, Subcommittee on Merchant Marine, *Hearings, Maritime Redevelopment Bank Act*, p. 59.

[a]Actual number of weekly hours worked in United States in July 1984 was 40.3.

One well-publicized fact with respect to productivity is that it takes a considerably longer time to build a commercial ship in the United States than one overseas. One authoritative estimate puts the differential at between 38 and 65 percent additional man-hours.[5] Thus delivery times are often twice those of foreign yards, adding at least 10 percent to the cost of building a vessel, not including the opportunity cost of the shipowner's capital for the additional time or lost voyage profit possibilities.

Labor Organization

With the exception of Avondale Corporation in New Orleans, all shipyards in the active shipbuilding industrial base (ASIB) are unionized, and it is estimated that over 90 percent of all shipyard workers belong to a union. The major unions (in terms of numbers) representing shipyard workers are:

- Industrial Union of Marine and Shipbuilding Workers
- International Brotherhood of Boilermakers, Iron Shipbuilders, Blacksmiths, Forgers, and Helpers
- Metal Trades Council
- United Steel Workers

Table 8.5. Comparison of hourly earnings of U.S. and foreign shipbuilding
production workers, 1977–80.

Country	Compensation/hour (U.S. dollars)		Index (U.S. = 100)	
	1977	1980	1977	1980
West Germany	8.88	14.25	110	119
Sweden	9.76	13.22	121	111
Netherlands	8.63	12.69	107	106
Norway	9.20	11.97	114	100
United States	8.08	11.94	100	100
Denmark	8.01	11.33	99	95
Canada	8.48	10.76	—	—
France	6.44	10.73	80	90
Italy	5.55	9.10	69	76
United Kingdom	3.64	7.58	45	63
Spain	4.41	7.13	—	—
Japan	5.11	6.77	63	57
Greece	2.58	4.29	—	—
Taiwan	.91	1.86	11	16
South Korea	1.40	1.72	17	14

SOURCE: U.S., Office of Technology Assessment, *An Assessment of Maritime Trade and Technology*, Table 33, p. 104.
    When compared with Japanese and South Korean compensation in 1984, the U.S. position has slightly improved. In 1980, Japanese compensation was 57 percent of the U.S. figure; in 1984, it is 61.3. South Korea in 1980 was 14 percent; in 1984, it is 16 percent.

Numerous craft unions also represent smaller numbers of workers.[6] Appendix E summarizes the contract provisions of one of the major shipyard unions.

Increasing Efficiency In U.S. Shipyards: Labor and Management Viewpoints

Given that shipbuilding and ship repair is a labor-intensive industry, if the United States is going to improve its competitive worldwide position, savings must come from (a) lower wage rates, (b) fewer man-hours to build a ship, or (c) both.

    Before we consider the respective positions of labor and management on the general issue of increasing productivity, it must be pointed out that U.S. shipyard productivity has been increasing with respect to both domestic industries and foreign competitors. In the former case, it is estimated that shipyard productivity in terms of value added per production per hour increased 35 percent between 1970 and 1980.[7]

A welder works on a subsection of a vessel under construction at the former Sun Shipbuilding and Drydock Company in Chester, Pennsylvania. The successor company to Sun Shipbuilding is the Pennsylvania Shipbuilding Corporation. (Courtesy Sun Shipbuilding and Drydock Company and Pennsylvania Shipbuilding Corporation)

The Avondale Corporation has been extensively cited as a firm that is significantly cutting costs by adopting state-of-the art manufacturing and management techinques.[8] However, while American productivity is increasing, it is still far from being competitive in world shipbuilding markets.[9]

Most shipyard labor and shipyard management disagreements occur over the question of how to become competitive.

Shipyard management essentially makes two points. The first agrees with labor's general position that modern production and management techniques must be implemented to the greatest extent possible. In essence, the number of man-hours required to build a ship must be reduced. To accomplish this, management recognizes that, on its part, large capital investments must be made. However, it argues that historically cumbersome work rules that evolved along with different shipyard crafts and were sanctified by union agreements, must be changed. Otherwise, shipyard management argues that greater capital investments would be for naught, and certainly not enough to close the U.S.–foreign shipyard man-hour gap.

Second, management urges that shipyard worker wage rates must be reduced (givebacks), or, at a minimum, wage increases must be slowed significantly.[10]

Labor's general position is that while management initiatives, including greater capital investments, have enhanced productivity, there is still considerable room for improvement. Labor's position in this respect was clearly enunciated when the president of the Industrial Union of Marine and Shipbuilding Workers in 1985 called upon Todd Shipyards to concentrate on increasing productivity and cut profit margins rather than cut wages.[11]

Tacit support was given to labor's position in a wide-ranging review of the U.S. shipbuilding/repair industry by Raymond Ramsay, the director of the Office of Maritime Affairs and Shipbuilding Technology, Naval Sea Systems Command. In a 1983 paper, he noted:

> In Japan, when a company has to absorb a sudden economic hardship such as a 25 percent decline in sales, the sacrificial "pecking order" is firmly set. *First* the corporate dividends are cut. Then the salaries and bonuses of top management are reduced. Next, management salaries are trimmed from the top to the middle of the hierarchy. *Lastly*, the rank and file are asked to accept pay cuts or a reduction in the workforce through attrition or voluntary discharge. In the UNITED STATES, a typical American-owned firm would probably do the opposite under similar circumstances. . . .
>
> It is basic Japanese theory that about 80 percent of a company's productivity and product quality problems must be solved by top management action. American management has either not yet realized this or is reluctant to make a major adjustment.[12]

With respect to work rule changes, change has come, albeit slowly. In a contract negotiated with Pennsylvania Shipbuilding by the International Brotherhood of Boilermakers and Iron Shipbuilders in 1982, a number of long-time work rules were scrapped. In describing the work-rule changes, Page Groton, director of the union's Shipbuilding Division, said:

> We recognized the same as the company did that there was a lot of standby time in a lot of operations. Standby time doesn't do us any good and it doesn't do them [the company] any good. It was nobody's fault. It's just one of those things that grew up from World War II.[13]

The problem to be corrected was aptly described by a vice-president of Penn Shipbuilding:

> You had cases in which five tradesmen were required to do five minutes' worth of work each on a job. Four of them stood around and waited and watched one do his job and then they did theirs [one at a time].[14]

Whether the Penn Shipbuilding agreement will be a trend-setting one, and to what extent it will reduce the number of man-hours to build a ship, are not yet known. One indication that should bear watching is the yard's performance (productivity improvement) with respect to its recently awarded (May 1985) $222 million contract to build two naval fleet oilers.

National Security Issues

Table 8.2 broke down the shipyard workforce into production and non-production employees. In a national security context, it is the production worker who is the more critical. This criticality comes about for two reasons: first, the time needed to train/retrain a skilled shipyard production employee;[15] and second, the fact that a number of shipyard jobs are more or less unique to the industry.[16] Thus, if the earlier cited 1984 Shipyard Mobilization Study (SYMBA) is even fairly close to the mark in forecasting the possible shortage of 40,000 shipyard production workers in a 1988 mobilation, the importance of training time for critical shipyard skills becomes self-evident.[17]

Table 8.6 classifies shipyard production workers by skill/craft type. Ten skills that make up approximately 65 percent of the production workforce are held to be critical. These are welders, shipfitters, machinists, electricians, pipefitters, riggers, flame cutters, crane operators, marine draftsmen, and shipwrights.[18]

Table 8.7 shows training times for selected skills that are more or less unique to shipbuilding/repair.

The cost of replacing a skilled shipyard worker is estimated at between

Table 8.6. Shipyard production workers classified by type of skill.

Employee classification	Percent total workforce
Nonproduction workers[a]	15.0
Production worker: skill not particular to shipyards; e.g., machinist, painter, carpenter, electrician.	57.0
Production worker: skill unique to shipyard; e.g., pipefitter, rigger, shipfitter, loftsman.	28.0
	100.0

SOURCE: Maritime Administration and University of Michigan data developed in U.S., International Trade Commission, *Analysis of the International Competitiveness of the U.S. Commercial Shipbuilding and Repair Industries*, p. 19.

[a]The 1984 Maritime Administration–Navy Shipyard Mobilization Study (SYMBA) calculated that nonproduction employees ranged from 20 to 50 percent of total shipyard workforces.

Table 8.7. Training time for new shipyard employee to reach journeyman level in selected shipyard skills.

Skill	Training time (hours)
Crane operator	1,000
Shipfitter	8,000
Pipefitter	8,000
Rigger	8,000
Marine draftsman	10,000
Shipwright	8 to 10 years

SOURCE: Raymond Ramsay, "A Time for Shipbuilding Renaissance," *Naval Engineers Journal*, September 1983, p. 56.

$25,000 and $30,000.[19] However, there may be additional costs to the shipyard if an otherwise qualified craftsman is required to be additionally certified for shipyard work.[20]

Reducing the man-hours to build/repair a ship in the United States is both a peacetime and a national security goal. In peacetime the objective is to make the United States more competitive in world markets; in wartime or an emergency, the goal is to economize on skilled manpower.

Small Shipyards

In Chapter 6, it was noted that perhaps there are as many as 500 small shipyards and small boat repair facilities in the United States, most with 20 or fewer employees. The number of production-type workers in this less visible part of the industry can only be approximated. One approach is to accept total private shipyard employment as being around 156,000 (Table 8.1), deduct 24,000, or an average of 15 percent of this number, as nonproduction employees, and from this figure subtract the 90,000 production employees from the 51 shipyards included in the annual Maritime Administration survey of U.S. shipyards, that is, the larger yards. Thus (156,000 − 24,000 − 90,000 =) 42,000 production workers are estimated to be employed in small building and repair facilities.

In a national emergency when manpower allotments would be prioritized by the federal government, much of the skilled labor in smaller facilities would go to work in the major yards. These 42,000, however, would not make up for any numerical shortfall because they have already been included in the overall total. Rather, their value to a mobilization effort would lie in their diverse skills background, since small facilities are basically nonunion, and hence have few, if any, work-rule restrictions. These multi-skilled craftsmen would form a potential pool of instructors to teach new employees a variety of shipyard skills.

Many small facilities are located near major shipyards—the very yards where production worker shortages would likely occur. With relatively little effort, the Maritime Administration could identify a number of such viable facilities (i.e. those that might reasonably be expected to be in business down the line), and earmark them as potential "national emergency classrooms."[21]

Conclusion

As noted above, labor policies that enhance national security are also policies that will increase American shipyard competitiveness. If, as many analysts expect, there will be skilled labor shortages at shipyards at some problematic "M-Day" in the future, then policies in 1986 that make labor more efficient and/or reduce the number of workers (man-hours) needed for particular tasks, must be counted as pluses.

Actually, there are some firm foundations on which to build. A 1983 report by the Office of Technology Assessment noted that "labor productivity in terms of output-per-man hour for basic measurable jobs such as stick welding, is comparable and, in fact, often shows U.S. workers to be more productive."[22]

However encouraging, this information is but one of several building blocks that must be put in place. Others are less restrictive work rules (discussed above) and a recognition that incentive pay systems positively influence labor productivity.

If shipyard labor can make this contribution, then it fairly becomes management's responsibility to act upon the long-held knowledge:

> ... that in a labor intensive industry such as ours, with the high cost of labor in the United States as compared to the world market, it is absolutely essential that we pre-outfit and that we orientate our shipbuilding activities away from conventional "stick building" techniques and towards the use of group technology, flexible manufacturing, zone outfitting and all the other techniques which minimize the total number of production man hours required to build a ship.[23]

Approaches and problems in achieving a more competitive U.S. shipbuilding/repair industry are discussed in the next chapter.

9   Shipyard Productivity

> . . . the challenge to the industry is great . . . . because of past failures it has
> lost credibility . . . . it can succeed if it decides to do it rather than bewailing
> its present fate.*

IT IS WELL UNDERSTOOD that the cost of building and repairing ships is
significantly higher in the United States than in foreign countries. Building costs two to three times as much in the United States, while repairs are
from 25 to 100 percent higher. Some summary comments from recently
published (shipyard) studies suggest reasons for American noncompeti-
tiveness:

> Currently the U.S. shipbuilding and repair industry does not compete
> effectively with foreign shipyards because of generally higher labor and
> material costs and lower productivity in the United States.[1]

> At present, the technological status of U.S. shipyards is generally lower
> than that of comparable Japanese and Korean shipyards in terms of techno-
> logical investment, research and development (R&D) investment, use of
> labor, tooling, degree of automation and use of robotics, and application of
> modern automated management and control techniques, as well as in the
> methods of processing, joining, and assembly.[2]

> As the USA is an environmentally and sociologically rich nation, in-
> ternal labour costs are high—far higher than those faced by Far Eastern
> industries. Naturally, this factor increases substantially the cost of having a
> ship built in the U.S., and therefore favors the industries of the less
> developed countries such as Korea, Taiwan, Brazil, Spain and so on.[3]

> Many factors give other countries the competitive edge in shipping and
> shipbuilding: government subsidization, in particular, as well as advanced

*From remarks made by Andrew S. Prince, Assistant Director, Transportation and Traffic
Management, Department of the Navy on 30 March 1985 at a seminar on the American
Merchant Marine sponsored by the University of Virginia Center for Ocean Law and
Policy. Mr. Prince's remarks were made during his presentation of a paper by Everett Pyatt,
Assistant Secretary of the Navy (Shipbuilding and Logistics).

management systems and practices, different social structures, product diversification, and lower shipbuilding and material costs.[4]

The private sector of the industry is unable to compete on equal terms for commercial ship orders in world markets. Leading commercial shipbuilding countries foster commercial construction and repair with substantial direct and indirect subsidies. Thus, despite the best efforts of U.S. shipbuilders to improve their productivity, hopes for revival of commercial U.S. shipbuilding are not likely to be realized in the near future.[5]

Why are U.S. liner industry and the domestic shipbuilding industry both generally in precarious positions today? Primarily because they have been weakened by the very programs intended to help them—ODS and CDS. . . .

CDS, which is really a subsidy for the shipyards rather than shipowners (coupled with the domestic-source ship replacement obligation placed upon ODS recipients), relieved the shipyards of the need to find means to truly compete with foreign yards. Captive ship buyers and subsidy for the inefficiencies of the U.S. yards bred further inefficiencies and lack of competitiveness. Thus, not only are most U.S. yards physically below world standards—all lack the technology to build large slow-speed diesel engines, the most efficient and economical propulsion system available today.[6]

No knowledgeable individual would categorically deny the general validity of the above statements. Nor, for that matter, would any responsible shipyard official. The relevant question is, what, if anything, can be done to improve upon present circumstances? However, before we explore that question, one fact must be emphasized: U.S. shipyards have the capability to build any type of ship. And as pointed out in Chapter 2, *innovation in vessel design*, beginning with the fast-sailing ships of the post–Revolutionary War period and continuing to the present day, is an American hallmark. The heart of the problem is not shipyard capability but cost.

Market Segmentation: Technologically Complex and Less Complex Vessels

The shipbuilding and, to a certain extent, ship repair markets are highly segmented. On the very high end is the demand for technologically complex naval vessels such as nuclear-powered attack aircraft carriers of the *Nimitz* class and nuclear-powered ballistic missile and attack submarines. Most naval combatants would fall within the technologically complex category.

The degree of complexity in naval construction was well put by John Diesel, president of Newport News Shipbuilding, in 1974 when he noted that designing and planning an aircraft carrier involves "more than 2,400 miles of blueprints, 22,000 work packages, and 16,000 drawings."[7]

Ship subassemblies become assemblies and then modules as they move from right to left on Ingalls Shipbuilding Corporation assembly lines. The line in the foreground is producing destroyer bow modules; the second line is for the mid-body of the ships; and the third produces stern modules. (Courtesy Shipbuilders Council of America and Ingalls Shipbuilding Corporation)

Technologically complex commercial builds include liquid natural gas carriers (LNG), large barge vessels such as Lykes Lines' Seabee ships, and sophisticated offshore drilling rigs. Further down the scale would be naval fleet auxiliaries, commercial containerships, and roll-on/roll-off vessels, and at the low end would be single-commodity bulk carriers such as oil tankers and ore carriers. It might be noted that complexity is not necessarily a function of size. An oil tanker, for example, whether one of 80,000 dwt or 250,000 dwt, is still a relatively uncomplicated vessel.

As a general proposition, technologically complex naval vessels are built in series. Recent series builds include nuclear attack submarines (SSN), guided missile cruisers (CG), and guided missile frigates (FFG). The productivity gains in series building is that average vessel costs decrease as numbers (output) increase from the lead ship onward.[8]

On the other hand, technologically complex merchant vessels tend to be built in quite limited numbers. The explanation is quite simple. While the United States has just one Navy, generally working from a five-year building program, there are a number of U.S.-flag shipping firms, each with different design requirements, limited vessel numbers, and different delivery dates.

As a rule, the more technologically complex the vessel, the more competitive is the U.S. shipyard. In fact, there is probably only one shipyard in the entire world capable of building a nuclear-powered aircraft carrier—much less the three simultaneously under construction at the Newport News Shipbuilding and Drydock Company in the mid-1980s.[9]

Productivity and Lower Costs

Observers of the plight of the U.S. shipbuilding/ship repair industry consistently stress the fact that foreign shipyards can build vessels cheaper than U.S. yards and that this is due to (1) greater productivity and (2) lower wages. The conclusion that usually follows is that U.S. yards, to the greatest extent possible, should reduce labor costs by replacing higher-priced American workers with automated, capital-intense manufacturing techniques. A follow-on conclusion is that American shipyard management could profitably benefit from studying and emulating the management practices of its most successful competitors. It is often pointed out that productivity in building commercial vessels in the best foreign shipyards is 100 percent better than in major U.S. shipyards[10]—and that percent increases in U.S. shipbuilding productivity have lagged increases in some other American industries.

The above conclusions are correct in the general economic sense that a firm should invest more of its resources in inputs that generate higher marginal products and correspondingly less on other inputs. But the conclusion is naive when applied to shipbuilding without qualification. (Appendix F is a theoretical, but understandable, explanation of how a firm decides on the mix of inputs in its production function.)

First, it must be understood that shipyards are at one and the same time both capital-intense and labor-intense. In 1985 the total number of private sector shipyard production workers was 81,227. The production employees of yards doing naval work accounted for 69,919 of this total. The average number of workers at the 12 yards doing naval contract work was 5,826; the median workforce was 2,860. (See Table 6.3 for the yards doing naval contract work in 1984.) The largest of these yards in terms of production workers was the General Dynamics Electric Boat Division with 22,103 employees.[11] On the other hand, private U.S. shipyards have made considerable capital improvements. Table 9.1 indicates the extent of this investment over the past decade.

However, Table 9.1 can be misleading in two respects. First, capital expenditures are not evenly distributed over the industry. The great majority of this investment has been from yards extensively engaged in, or expecting to engage in, naval work. For example, two shipbuilders accounted for 44 percent of the $329 million invested in 1982.[12] The second caution is that capital improvements have not been spread evenly with respect to shipbuilding and ship repair. In 1983, $300 million of the $321 million invested went to improving repair and overhaul capabilities.

In 1986, the general direction in which the U.S. shipyard industry is heading is becoming much clearer. Capital investment is being geared toward improvements in repair and overhaul facilities, particularly the repair and overhaul of technologically complex naval vessels. As the 600-ship naval building program winds down in the early 1990s, the

Table 9.1. U.S. shipyard capital improvement expenditures, FY 1975–84.

Fiscal year (FY)	Capital expenditure ($million)
1975	$221.0
1976	252.9
1977	135.0
1978	176.0
1979	208.0
1980	263.0
1981	190.0
1982	329.0
1983	321.0
1984	217.8 (est.)
	$2,313.7

SOURCE: Maritime Administration, *Annual Reports*, for fiscal years 1975–83. Page numbers in FY order, beginning with FY 1975, are 8, 10, 19, 19, 21, 7, 6, 11, 9, 9.

Navy's appropriations for repair and overhaul will, of necessity, increase (to maintain a much larger fleet than that which existed in 1980). New construction will be done to replace obsolete vessels, not to increase overall numbers or tonnage, and hence will decrease. This division of naval funds will be reinforced over the long term by a continuation and expansion of the Service Life Extension Program (SLEP), a program whose primary purpose is to extend the normal life of large and expensive combatant vessels.

If major shipyards see naval repair work as their primary source of revenues down the road, it follows that the number of production workers at a yard primarily engaged in repair work will remain relatively constant.[13] This is so basically because repair and overhaul work on technologically complex vessels is labor-intensive.[14]

At the beginning of the chapter it was noted that authorities both inside and outside the shipbuilding/repair industry recognized the need to increase shipyard productivity. Recognition of the problem has led to a number of initiatives on the part of industry and government to address the issue. One of the more promising initiatives is the naval contract incentive program wherein a shipbuilder has the incentive to modernize his facilities with the goal of building ships at below the target cost. Two examples are illustrative:

> In the 2 years after the Navy changed its contracts to give more incentives to improved performance, a builder of surface combatants received $40 million of what it saved the Navy as a bonus on top of its contract target profit of $95 million. From 1978 to 1983, another naval shipbuilder modernized its facilities and made numerous improvements in its ship production processes which resulted in fewer manhours on the job and shorter construction times. With the new contract terms, the shipbuilder's improvement has been directly reflected in corporate earnings, which rose from 1.9 percent in 1978 to 8.4 percent in 1983.[15]

Other programs have also been inaugurated to improve productivity in a number of areas, including improved exchange of technical information and cooperation in the shipbuilding industry, applying new and improved production techniques, designing integrated manufacturing systems, utilizing computers in shipbuilding [e.g., computer aided design (CAD) and computer aided manufacturing (CAM)], and developing a set of usable shipbuilding standards.

Shipyard Suppliers

The role of the shipyard supplier was briefly noted in Chapter 6, on industry organization. Suppliers are an even more important consideration in matters of shipyard productivity.

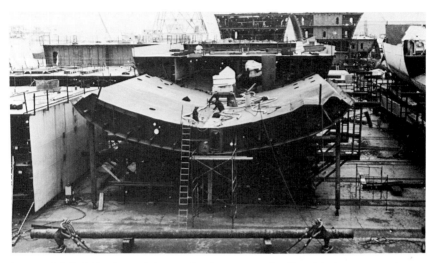

Ingalls Shipbuilding's modular production process begins with the construction of assemblies, which are later joined to form modules. This photo shows the early stages of work on a *DD-963*–class destroyer. (Courtesy Shipbuilders Council of America and Ingalls Shipbuilding Corporation)

As much as two-thirds of the cost of a major naval combatant ship acquisition is value added by suppliers, with the remainder the value added by the shipbuilder. When applied to the Navy current five year plan, $29.6 billion of the $88.8 billion program therefore is the value added by the shipbuilder. A productivity improvement of, for example, 10 percent by shipbuilders could save $2.96 billion in the five-year program. Consider as well achieving the same hypothetical 10 percent in the supplier's two thirds of the program. This could be $5.92 billion, twice the savings potential in shipbuilding for the same productivity gain.[16]

However, the importance of the shipyard to suppliers varies. "For some . . . the yard is a key customer whose needs take priority; for others the yard is almost a nuisance customer in terms of volume and dollar value of order and the technology required."[17]

Supplier items are considered critical in shipbuilding if:

- They are installed on most ships.
- The manufacturing lead time exceeds 18 months.
- Their production is characterized by low volume or unique production processes.
- The time is critical to the ship's construction schedule.

As noted in early chapters and throughout this book, naval work has become the mainstay of shipyard revenues; hence the number of suppliers for the naval shipbuilding/repair market is a fair estimate of the number of suppliers overall. This number is estimated to be 5,000.[18]

However, the supplier industry, defined as those firms furnishing material, equipment, or service, is characterized "by inadequate profit and growth potential, insufficient production volume, and undependable forecasts of future volume."[19]

Recommendations to improve the economic viability of the shipyard supplier industrial base include:

1. After the initial competitive buy, the Navy should consider the use of a sole source supplier for a specified production run (improve production volume).
2. Periodically, perhaps every 10 years, the Navy should obtain from suppliers (and shipbuilders) ideas for improving productivity.
3. The Navy should develop a system to simplify and speed the implementation of changes in specifications.
4. Government policies must be such that the suppliers' right to data is respected.[20]

Perhaps the most important suggested change insofar as improving productivity is concerned is developing a contracting system that encourages product improvement. It is argued that:

> In fixed price situations characteristic of procurements from shipbuilding suppliers, there is no incentive for the supplier to improve his product by means of the value analysis machinery, which is cumbersome, because he is required to share the benefit of the improvement with the Navy. Since the supplier is operating on a fixed-price basis, it makes more sense for him to internalize the innovation because the more the supplier can control costs, the greater will be his profit.[21]

The 1984 Congressional Budget Office study "U.S. Shipping and Shipbuilding: Trends and Policy Choices" summarized the supplier productivity issue when it stated:

> . . . even if manufacturing costs were halved through productivity improvements, which would be a great industrial achievement, the total cost of the ship would be reduced by only about 4 or 5 percent. Shipyard manufacturing productivity improvements, however important they may be in other respects, are not the key to substantial reductions in warship costs. For that, it would be better to look at combat systems which represent a much larger portion of the total cost.[22]

Options to Increase Productivity and Lower Costs

In 1981, the Shipbuilders Council of America contrasted the costs of building a generic merchant vessel (500 man-years of labor) in the United States and Japan. One purpose of the study was to determine the limits of increased efficiency in U.S. shipyards. Assuming the total hourly compensation of workers to be $12.78 in the United States and $7.84 in Japan, it was calculated that if a U.S. shipyard (1) utilized Japanese technology and (2) built a series of 10 ships, the cost of a $36 million U.S.-built ship could be reduced to approximately $30 million. Under the same circumstances (i.e., a 10-ship order), the Japanese cost would be approximately $20 million. The analysis found that labor and overhead costs did not account for most of the difference, but rather the cost difference was attributable to materials—that is, a Japanese material cost of $7.8 million versus a U.S. cost of $18 million.[23]

Using Japanese technology reduced U.S. costs by 20 percent, while the series build was assumed to reduce labor and overhead costs by 15 percent.[24] However, with respect to series building, one authority questioned its long-term impact when he noted, "I sincerely believe that series construction would just sustain our industry for a little while; it would do nothing really to improve its productivity, particularly if it's for ordinary merchant ships."[25]

It was previously stated that by adapting Japanese manufacturing technology, a U.S. shipyard could reduce labor costs by 20 percent. While the assertion is generally true, two points need be made.

First, much of the basic underlying technology that foreign yards utilize so efficiently was developed in the United States, including prefabrication, subassembly of components, steel fabrication, systems management techniques, and quality control. As a matter of record, the United States is the most accomplished builder of ships in series the world has ever known. Witness the some 2,700 Liberty ships constructed in World War II and to a lesser extent the series builds during and after World War I. In this respect, it has been fairly noted that the "United States lags in the application of its own research and the effective introduction of innovation based on scientific and technological discoveries."[26]

The second point is that a number of U.S. shipyards have already invested in modular construction (building in separate sections to be joined later), zone outfitting (preassembling components of a major unit and testing it before installing it in the hull), developing group technology skills (ability to utilize labor at diversified tasks), which in turn leads to a flexible manufacturing capability, and expanding the physical area of assembly areas so that process lanes (production lines) can be used to maximum efficiency. In a recent congressional hearing, one U.S. shipyard was complimented on implementing some of these technologies. Congressional compliments notwithstanding, the important point brought out was that this particular yard submitted a bid for a naval dock landing ship (LSD) 50 percent below the bid cost of prior vessels of the same class.[27]

Another area in which shipyard profitability, not necessarily productivity, could be improved is product diversification. The National Research Council study *Toward More Productive Naval Shipbuilding* noted:

> In May 1984, for example, one large Japanese shipbuilder was producing a mix of products, including commercial car carriers, bulk product carriers, submarines for the Japanese defense force, large slow-speed diesel engines, large steel structures such as bridge sections and land based nuclear power plant containment vessels, and simultaneously carrying out ship repairs for both commercial and naval vessels.[28]

Product areas outside of shipbuilding/repair in which U.S. yards might compete were noted to be bridges, piping, warehouses, sewer pipe, prefabricated buildings, oil rigs, and trash incinerators.

As pointed out earlier in this chapter, U.S. shipyard competitiveness improves as builds become more technologically complex, and in general the most technologically complex vessels are naval combatants.[29] In this regard, suggestions have been made over the years that U.S. yards participate in a naval building export market estimated at over $3 billion annually.[30]

Building naval vessels for foreign account became an issue when Congress was considering the FY 1985 Defense Appropriations Bill. The Senate Armed Services Committee in its report on the bill requested DoD to prepare a report on guidelines for U.S. yards to use in building foreign-designed diesel-electric submarines for allied or friendly nations. Historically, the Navy has opposed U.S. yards' building submarines for anyone but the U.S. Navy. Many and varied reasons are cited, but as one observer commented:

> ... the Navy is afraid that U.S. yards could build diesel subs so cheaply that members of the Senate and House Armed Services Committees would say, "Hey, why aren't we doing that?" They might even insist on the ultimate heresy, that some of our missile subs could be built far more cheaply with diesel propulsion.[31]

Another option to increase American shipyard profitability is for the industry to utilize foreign-built subassemblies up to and including entire power plants (i.e., diesel engines). However, the extent to which U.S. yards can use foreign-built components is directly related to the extent that government participates in ship financing. At one end, with no government participation, probably the only requirement for a ship to be considered "American-built" would be that the hull and superstructure be constructed in the United States. With construction subsidies a dead letter for the moment, the major government financing program is Title XI (Merchant Marine Act of 1936, as amended), under which the federal government guarantees the loan that finances vessel construction. (See footnote "c" in Table 4.1.) Under current regulations, only American material and supplies may be used in constructing Title XI vessels unless a waiver is granted by the Maritime Administration. In March 1985, the Maritime Administration published a notice in the *Federal Register* that it proposed to amend the rule to allow shipyards to purchase less costly foreign components, up to and including main propulsion diesel plants.

Assuming the proposed rule goes into effect, it does not mean there will be a quantum leap in the use of foreign components. Still to be negotiated are price, terms of sale, interest charges, and delivery schedules, not to mention the priority, or lack of priority, a foreign supplier is likely to give a U.S. shipyard.

Conclusion

At present there are four classes of major shipyards in the United States:

1. Yards capable of building technologically complex naval vessels that have invested in productivity-increasing manufacturing methods and management techniques.
2. Yards capable of repairing/overhauling complex naval vessels that have invested in productivity-increasing manufacturing methods.
3. Build-capable yards that are noncompetitive with respect to building complex naval vessels but can build merchant and naval auxiliary vessels if the orders are there.
4. Repair/overhaul-capable yards that are noncompetitive with respect to repairing technologically complex vessels but can repair/overhaul merchant vessels and less sophisticated naval vessels.

The current situation as seen by most observers is that yards in categories (1) and (2) will survive even under the worse possible economic conditions. However, these yards account for only 15 percent of the total number of major shipyards but do 80 percent of the naval work.

Yards in categories (3) and (4) will have a much more difficult time, and their numbers can be expected to diminish unless there is a government-induced demand for merchant vessel construction. Truly they are prisoners of the axiom that "There is no reason to build ships without cargo."

As noted above, even under optimum conditions—adopting foreign technologies and techniques and building in series—U.S. shipyards would still suffer a significant cost disadvantage, particularly with "new" shipbuilding nations such as South Korea and China. While still greater capital investment might reduce labor and overhead costs still further, the incentive to invest beyond that required for the U.S. naval market simply does not exist.

However, some innovative policy combinations to ensure a sufficient shipyard mobilization base are possible. Three initiatives that might be combined include: (1) construction differential subsidies in conjunction with unlimited use of foreign-built components; (2) a modest cargo reservation policy for non-government-impelled cargoes; (3) encouragement of foreign investment in U.S. shipyards competing in non–U.S. naval markets, particularly in repairs to commercial vessels and building bulk carriers. The cargo preference and construction initiatives will be examined in Chapter 11.

10 World Shipbuilding and Ship Repair

OF THE 18.3 MILLION gross tons of new ships built worldwide in 1984, Japan, South Korea, and China (including Taiwan)* accounted for two-thirds of the total. Japan, alone, built 53 percent.[1]

Percentages, however, can be misleading, for while Japan maintained its dominant position in shipbuilding, it was a dominant position in a declining market. Worldwide orders placed in 1983 were 19.5 million gross tons; in 1984, the total was 16 million, and the figure was expected to fall still further in 1985.[2]

All too often it becomes easy to believe (with all the attention focused on the subject) that the United States stands alone with its shipyard problems. This is patently not the case, if events during the first quarter of 1985 were an indication:

CANADIAN GROUP DETAILS PLANS FOR SHIPBUILDING

The shipbuilding/repair labor force in Canada decreased from 14,000 in 1982 to 8,000 in 1985. Duties on foreign built vessels and increased government subsidies were proposed.[3]

NEW YARD GROUP FORMED IN INDIA

An Indian Shipbuilders Association (ISBA) made up of 7 large public yards and 28 smaller ones was created to share technical information and formulate proposals for government aid. All of the large public yards were in need of financial assistance.[4]

UK SHIPBUILDERS FACING ORDER LOSS

Approximately 1,900 jobs will be lost in the second quarter of 1985 if no additional orders are forthcoming for UK shipbuilders.[5]

DUTCH SHIPYARDS SEEK GOVERNMENT ASSISTANCE

Twenty eight small to medium size yards requested 82 million guilders (3.75 guilders to $1). It is estimated that 250 million guilders would be needed and even then jobs would be lost.[6]

*Lloyds Shipping Register combines the tonnages of the two Chinas and reports the total as one figure.

SINGAPORE SHIPYARDS GAIN BUT JOBS STILL BEING CUT

One of the nation's largest yards had after tax losses of $3.1 million. The nation's largest yard, Hitachi Zosen, laid off 200 workers.[7]

NIARCHOS SHUTS DOWN HELLENIC SHIPYARD

The Hellenic shipyard at Skaramansa is being closed by its owner as a result of continuous losses caused by continuing labor disputes.[8]

Perhaps the most direct approach to maintaining shipyard jobs was taken by the Australian Council of Trade Unions:

> The unions are demanding that ships regularly visiting Australia have at least some of their repairs carried out in Australia . . . . [They] claim that the Australian ship repair industry is in a desperate condition, and that it will not survive unless supported by foreign ships visiting Australia. Over the past couple of years, a large proportion of workers within the industry have lost their jobs . . . . The unions have alleged that shipowners are ignoring repair facilities available in Australia. They have stated that shipowners have repeatedly elected to have repair carried out in their homeports or in Asian ports where labor costs are must lower . . . . Waterfront unions are now refusing to allow many foreign ships to leave until obvious repairs are carried out . . . . Selected ships are inspected by members of the Shipbuilding and Shiprepairing Subcommittee of the Australian Council of Trade Unions. Owners receive a list of repairs which must be affected before clearance is given for the ships to leave port.[9]

In 1985, the maritime world entered the fifth year of a general shipping recession. Millions of tons were idle. And even an increasing amount of tonnage going to the shipbreakers did little to improve the long-term economic outlook for shipbuilders and ship repairers. By mid-1985, Japan, the dean of world shipbuilders, was looking to a 10 percent reduction in shipyard capacity. And while South Korea was still the world's low-cost shipbuilder, it was increasingly clear that the South Korean government was heavily subsidizing its shipyards in order to maintain their market share.

Long-Run Equilibrium

"When there is a balance—an equilibrium—the tendency for change is absent. Before a market equilibrium can be attained, the decisions of consumers [shipowners] and producers [shipbuilders] must be brought into harmony with one another."[10]

Economists speak of short-run equilibrium and long-run equilibrium. A short-run equilibrium period is one in which there is insufficient time for buyers and sellers to adjust to changing market forces. Essentially, both buyer and seller contract (set a price) on the basis of current information, including price, quality, quantity, and delivery dates. The agreed-upon price could be called a short-run equilibrium price. If nothing changes—that is, no new producers enter the market, there is no change in demand, product preferences stay about the same, the ability of a customer to buy a product (his income) remains constant, and purchasing power is constant—then contract terms will remain essentially unchanged from one time period to the next. This economic environment would be defined as a long-run equilibrium condition for the industry.

With respect to world shipbuilding in the period 1980–86, there has been anything but long-run equilibrium conditions. New producers have aggresively increased their market share, while some traditional shipbuilding nations have fallen upon hard times. Slow-speed diesel main plants continued to increase their market share in all vessel classes— tankers, dry bulk, and general cargo. Subsidized U.S. shipowners entered the world market for the first time in half a century and demonstrated that they have an eye for price and delivery times like any of their competitors. And with price, price, and nothing but price the bottom line, governments have moved to maintain their shipbuilding/repair industries with greater direct and indirect subsidies.

While it is often difficult to disentangle government programs primarily in support of shipbuilding and ship repair from those supporting shipping companies, it is generally agreed that construction subsidies are basically a mechanism to support shipyards. Table 10.1 lists those nations that utilize construction subsidies in this regard. (Chapter 11 examines the U.S. construction subsidy experience as well as other indirect aids to shipbuilding.)

What is the likelihood of a long-run equilibrium in world shipbuilding/ repair, say, from 1986 to 1990? By any measure, the answer must be hardly any at all. Some factors that will continue to work against any movement toward an equilibrium include:

- The tendency of supplier nations to engage in intermediate processing of their raw materials. Examples include the building of refineries in petroleum-producing nations (e.g., Persian Gulf), the processing of iron ore into pellets at supply sources, and the milling and planing of lumber in Africa and South America (e.g., mahogany). This trend toward domestic processing of raw materials will have a considerable impact on the type and amount of tonnages required over the next decade. In the United States, tanker and coal carriers will be directly affected by oil, and possibly coal slurry, pipeline competition.
- The ability or inability of the Organization of Petroleum Exporting Countries (OPEC) cartel to maintain relatively high crude oil prices.

Table 10.1. Countries supporting their shipbuilding infrastructure with construction subsidies, 1982.

Country	Comment[a]
Argentina	Subsidies that cannot exceed difference between construction cost in a domestic shipyard and the international cost.
Australia	Subsidies for fishing vessels having a designed load waterline of more than 21 meters, and other vessels having a gross construction tonnage of more than 150 tons, built in registered Australian shipyards for use in Australian waters.
Brazil	Merchant marine financing fund that absorbs the cost difference between Western European prices and higher Brazilian prices, for ships constructed in Brazil and engaged in international trade.
Canada	A 35 percent subsidy provided for fishing vessels and 17 percent subsidy for commercial vessels built for Canadian ownership.
France	A 10 percent export building subsidy for small yards. Only when a price difference of 10 percent exists can French orders be placed abroad. Direct subsidies are available for domestic ships and ships for export based upon percentage of cost.
German Federal Republic	Grants that may amount to 12.5 percent of the construction cost in either German or foreign shipyards.
India	Subsidies that vary according to cost. Until 1976 it was 5 percent of the international price of the ships fixed at the average of the valuation received from reliable foreign ship valuers in three or four leading shipbuilding countries.
Ireland	State subsidies payable for ships built in Irish yards.
Italy	Construction subsidy law expired 31 December 1980. New construction subsidy law under consideration.
Japan	Subsidies for shipbuilders scrapping uneconomical oceangoing vessels.
Netherlands	Dutch owners eligible for 12 percent fiscal subsidy for purchase of new and existing ships.

Table 10.1. (cont.)

Country	Comment[a]
Pakistan	A government-granted construction differential subsidy of up to 40 percent of building cost for ships built by the Karachi Shipyard and Engineering Works, the only national shipbuilding yard.
South Africa	A fixed rate of 25 percent of the contract price for ships between 500 and 6,000 tons; 10 percent for ships between 200 and 500 tons. Assistance for foreign contracts will be considered but must be approved by the Treasury.
Spain	Subsidy of 5.5 percent of the official valuation for all ships whose construction was authorized in 1979. An additional subsidy of up to 9.5 percent is available to assist in financing export operations that are judged necessary to guarantee an adequate workload for the shipyards.
Taiwan	Subsidies granted only in special cases. Ships must be registered in Taiwan and ordered from a domestic shipyard.
United Kingdom	Aid for shipbuilding industry must be approved by European Economic Community. Fund established to subsidize U.K. shipbuilders in 1977; fund is being gradually reduced.

SOURCE: U.S., Department of Transportation, Maritime Administration, *Maritime Subsidies*, pp. 1–165.

[a]Defining a construction subsidy is difficult at best. In many countries guaranteed loans at low interest rates are considered "construction subsidies" and reported as such. Construction aids that were more in the nature of a loan to the shipowner than a payment to a shipyard were not included in this table.

While many maritime nations do not support their shipbuilding/repair industry with direct grants, indirect and direct aids to shipowners and shipyards are part of a conscious policy designed to support shipyards. Foreign government aids to their maritime industry noted by the Maritime Administration include operating subsidies, construction subsidies, trade-in allowances, official low-interest loans, interest subsidies, official loan guarantees, accelerated depreciation, tax-free reserve funds, duty-free imports of material needed for ship construction, cargo preference schemes, and cabotage restrictions.

Examples of assistance not catalogued by the Maritime Administration include schools for training merchant seamen, hospital and medical care for seamen, social security family payment to seamen, laws requiring the construction of national flag ships only in domestic shipyards for operation in a nation's foreign and domestic commerce, and requirements that materials for ship construction, maintenance and repairs, and ship stores and subsistence be purchased domestically.

To the extent that they are successful, then to that extent will coal shipments be an important commodity in world trade, which in turn will affect the demand for large coal carriers. The relative price of the two fuels will also determine the long-term viability of coal-fired ships.[11]

- The Navy's decisions about a shipyard mobilization base. The Navy is now responsible for approximately 80 percent of American shipyard revenues. When the present ship buildup ends (550–600 ships), the U.S. government will face some hard choices with respect to maintaining a shipyard mobilization base. To the extent that it responds positively, then to that extent will American yards be factors in the "game of world shipbuilding."
- Co-production shipbuilding. Several studies have recommended that a co-production shipbuilding scheme be written into U.S. law. Under this scheme, a U.S. operator would earn "credits" for orders placed in U.S. shipyards. These credits could then be used to build an equal dollar amount of construction in foreign yards. Such foreign-built vessels, for purposes of registry and participation in preference cargo movements, would be considered American-built. This proposal was made by the National Advisory Commission on Oceans and Atmosphere in a 1985 report to the president and Congress with respect to Jones Act shipping. An earlier, and essentially similar, proposal was made by W. James Amoss, president of Lykes Lines, with respect to vessels in foreign trade.[12]
- Whether, and to what extent, foreign capital might be willing to invest in commercial U.S. repair facilities.
- The extent to which traditional European shipbuilding nations will subsidize their shipyards as Far Eastern shipyards continue to increase their market share by severe price cutting. In 1984, West Germany fell from third to fourth in world shipbuilding orders placed.
- Whether Western investment capital (North America and Europe) will be willing to build new shipyards from the ground up. The technologies cited in Chapter 9—module construction, prefabrication, assembly lines—all require large amounts of physical space, a commodity in very short supply and one difficult to create in older yards. For many U.S. and Western European yards, absent government financial support, the only real long-term option is to start over or go out of business.
- Whether developing nations with a growing number of ships registered under their flags will also opt to become shipbuilding countries. The trend, although slowly, has been in this direction.

• The amount by which world trade will increase over the next decade, which in turn determines the demand for tonnage. In 1982, the Shipbuilders Association of Japan estimated an annual demand of around 20 million gross tons in 1990. The Association of Western European Shipbuilders was somewhat more pessimistic and forecast an annual demand on the order of 14 million gross tons.[13] Both forecasts include the assumption of a relatively high continuous scrapping of older ships, an assumption that may not be a firm one.

Geographic Location of Major World Shipyards

Table 10.2 lists the major shipbuilding countries, the number of shipyards in each, and orders for ships of 1,000 gross tons and over as of 15 April 1985. Figures 10.1 through 10.7 show the geographic location of the most important yards. And while it is fair to conclude that shipbuilding is a pervasive industry worldwide (Table 10.2 shows 41 nations currently building ships), ship repair facilities are even more widespread. Appendix G lists those countries having ship repair capability.

Conclusion

In 1984, in terms of new commercial ship orders placed, three economies dominated the industry: Japan with 55.9 percent of new orders, South Korea with 17.4 percent, and Western Europe with 10.6. The rest of the world, including the United States, accounted for about 16 percent.[14] Plainly, it was Japan and South Korea against the world, with China, including Taiwan, moving up fast. For the foreseeable future it seems clear that South Korea and possibly the People's Republic of China will be the world's low-cost producers.

Of most interest to the United States, however, is the response of the Western European countries to the growing dominance of Far Eastern shipbuilders, particularly since the Europeans, like Japan and South Korea, depend heavily on export orders. In terms of labor, both U.S. and Western European costs are high when compared to the Far East. In terms of modern technology and management practices, the biggest and best European yards are competitive with Japan and South Korea. As the shakeout of marginal shipbuilding firms and the consolidation of the better ones continue, European yards should ultimately be on a technological par with Far Eastern competitors. Figure 10.8 shows the layout of an advanced Netherlands shipyard utilizing the most modern shipyard construction techniques (e.g., preassembly and modular construction).

However, until a long-run equilibrium is reached in world shipbuilding, Western Europe and the rest of the world must scramble to survive in what has become a price war of major proportions. Western European

Table 10.2. World shipyard orders, 1985.

Country	Number of firms/yards with orders	Number of ships on order[a]	Gross tons
Argentina	6	20	336,000
Australia	1	1	1,000
Belgium	5	11	217,000
Brazil	7	47	1,369,000
Bulgaria	1	6	93,000
Canada	12	17	123,000
China, People's Republic	8	44	567,000
Denmark	8	45	749,000
Egypt	3	6	58,000
Finland	8	44	598,000
France	8	19	363,000
German Democratic Republic	4	30	425,000
German Federal Republic	21	79	623,000
Greece	7	15	79,000
India	7	33	353,000
Indonesia	5	7	14,000
Iran	1	1	2,000
Italy	12	26	98,000
Japan	75	476	11,437,000
Korea, South	10	174	5,551,000
Malaysia	2	3	6,000
Malta	1	2	3,000
Mexico	3	19	90,000
Netherlands	22	39	194,000
New Zealand	1	1	1,000
Norway	16	26	112,000
Peru	2	5	51,000
Philippines	2	13	6,000
Poland	4	123	1,269,000
Portugal	3	12	109,000
Romania	5	28	471,000
Singapore	7	12	20,000
Spain	20	53	820,000
Sweden	3	8	267,000
Taiwan	3	21	1,250,000
Turkey	17	41	143,000
U.S.S.R.	2	2	73,000
United Kingdom	11	31	413,000
United States	12	26	533,000
Venezuela	1	1	4,000
Yugoslavia	3	44	577,000
	349	1,601	29,462,514

SOURCE: "World Orderbook for Ships 1,000 GT and Above as of April 15, 1985," *Marine Engineering/Log*, June 1985, pp. 64–88.

[a] Does not include naval construction.

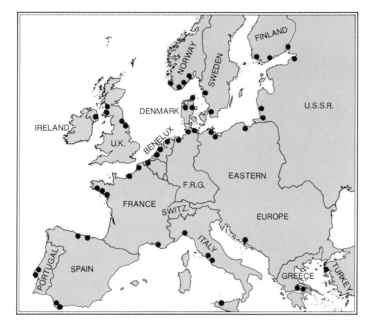

Figure 10.1. Major European shipyards.

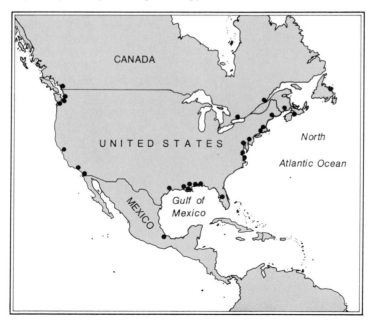

Figure 10.2. Major North American shipyards (U.S. yards are those in the active shipbuilding industrial base).

Figure 10.3. Major South American shipyards.

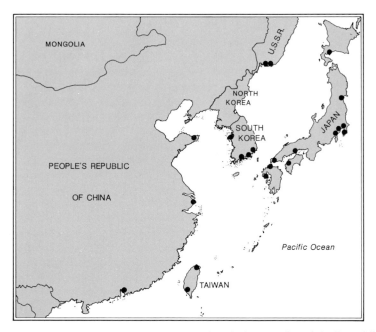

Figure 10.5. Major shipyards in Japan, South Korea, People's Republic of China, and Taiwan.

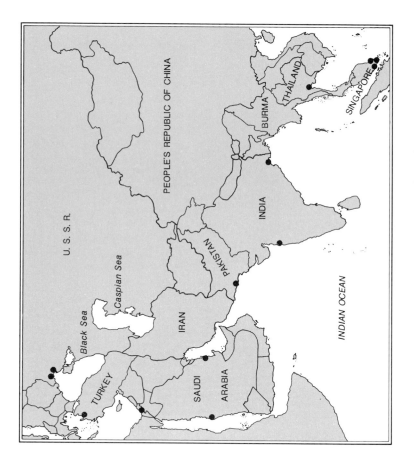

Figure 10.6. Major Middle Eastern and Asian shipyards.

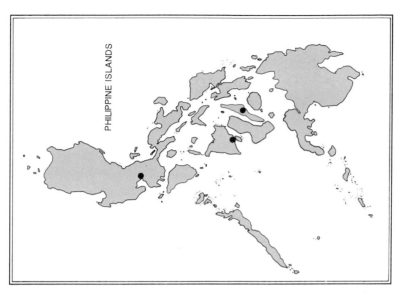

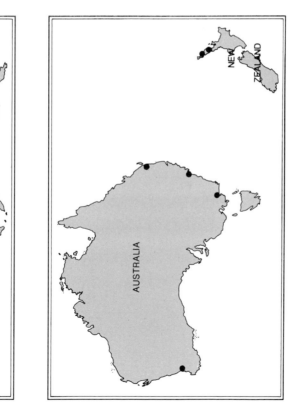

Figure 10.7. Major shipyards in Indonesia, Philippine Islands, Australia, and New Zealand.

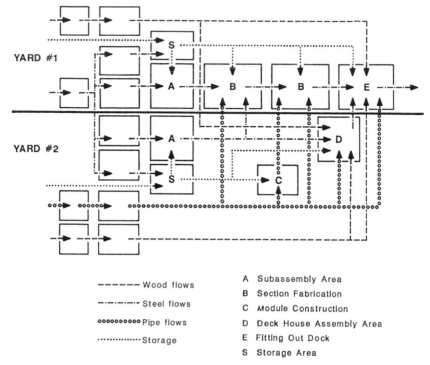

```
                                    A  Subassembly Area
------- Wood flows                  B  Section Fabrication
                                    C  Module Construction
-·-·-·-· Steel flows                D  Deck House Assembly Area
ooooooooo Pipe flows                E  Fitting Out Dock
                                    S  Storage Area
·············· Storage
```

Figure 10.8. Production flows at twin yards of van der Glessen-de Noored in the Netherlands. Adapted from drawing published by *Marine Engineering/Log* (October 1983) and used by permission.

Yard #1: section fabrication and assembly up to 240 tons, with hull assembly on the berth and fitting out alongside the dock being the main activities.

Yard #2: section fabrication up to 60 tons, deck houses construction, pipe work and machining for supplying construction shed at Yard #1.

survival strategies include consolidating the most economically efficient yards (Spain, Great Britain, France, Sweden) and providing government support in the form of low-interest loans for the export sector (Norway, France, Great Britain, West Germany). Other strategies include emphasizing repair and overhaul work (Portugal, Netherlands) and increasing government subsidies of all kinds (all countries).[15]

In terms of naval shipbuilding, particularly in building technologically complex vessels, the advantage remains with countries in the NATO Alliance and the Soviet Union.[16] In the United States, Great Britain, and France, domestic shipyards will continue to be monopolies with respect to naval construction. This same tendency can also be found with respect to shipbuilding countries that maintain moderate-size naval forces (e.g., Spain, West Germany, and Sweden).

While both the United States and Western Europe suffer significant cost disadvantages when competing with the Far East for commercial ship contracts, their approaches to the problem are markedly different. The U.S. government has virtually written off its commercial shipbuilders as being forever high-cost and noncompetitive, instead relying principally on naval work to maintain a shipyard mobilization base. Western Europe, on the other hand, has not "thrown in the towel." In general, those countries have increased government support for their shipbuilding/ship repair industries, accepting the fact that while they may never again attain their preeminent rank, they can still remain significant producers. Unlike the United States, the Europeans share the long-term view of economists, who do not easily accept the permanence of economic institutions, whether they be national economies, shipyard industries, or individual firms.

11 Shipyard Support Options

DURING THE MID-1980s, numerous studies, sponsored by a variety of agencies, public and private, have examined the question of *how many* active shipyards are needed to constitute an adequate shipbuilding/ship repair mobilization base. Considerations included numbers (how many?), yard capability, geographic location, and manpower requirements. These questions of size and the necessary constituent parts of an adequate base have been examined and commented upon in several chapters of this book.

This chapter, however, is not concerned with the question of how many shipyards are enough, but starts with the assumption that whatever the final requirements are held to be, federal support, in addition to programs already in place, will be needed.[1]

A list of major federal government support options, not including those cited in footnote 1 of this chapter, are:

1. Unilateral, foreign-trade cargo reservation (i.e., reserving certain types or a percentage of certain types of cargo) to U.S.-flag, U.S.-built ships; or reserving a percent of all U.S.-originated cargo to U.S.-flag/built ships.
2. Continuing to reserve domestic-trade ocean shipping cargoes to U.S.-flag/built ships.
3. Building a specified number of merchant type ships for government account, such tonnage either being leased to the private sector, operated by a government agency, or put into the National Defense Reserve Fleet.
4. Allowing U.S.-flag operators the option of building some ships in foreign yards in return for an agreement to construct some of their tonnage in U.S. yards. With respect to government support programs (e.g., mortgage guarantees), such foreign-built ships would be considered as built in the United States. The necessary workload

to maintain a shipyard mobilization base would determine the ratio between U.S. and foreign-built vessels (i.e., one for one, one for two, etc.).

5. Maintaining a navy, including Military Sealift Command tonnage, of such a size that normal replacement and repair work for this fleet would sustain an adequate mobilization base.

6. Accepting as an adequate mobilization base the number of ship-yards that can be supported by long-term naval work, reserving domestic ocean commerce to U.S.-built ships, and keeping the indirect shipyard suport programs already in place (e.g., reserving military cargoes to U.S.-flag, U.S.-built ships).

7. Renewing the construction differential subsidy program.

8. Mandated cargo sharing between trading partners, through either bilateral agreements or adherence to a blanket cargo sharing arrangement such as the UNCTAD Code of Conduct for Liner Conferences.

In evaluating the above options, the chief consideration must be that the option is long-term in character and politically stable, that is, unlikely to be significantly modified by succeeding Congresses or administrations. Other criteria would include ensuring that the type of ship built in U.S. yards for U.S.-flag operation have a national defense/national security value, and finally that the option be relatively easy to administer—in other words, that transaction and administrative costs not be prohibitive.

We shall consider the options in order.

1. At present the United States reserves military cargo and a percen-tage of government-impelled cargo to U.S.-flag/built vessels. The great drawback to expanding the option of cargo reservation is that it would be a *unilateral* action and hence almost certain to invite foreign retaliation. The added cost of shipping in U.S.-built/flag vessels, however, is not a consideration, a point that will be developed later.

2. The option of reserving the domestic trades to U.S.-built ships is already in place. The drawback here is that while construction for this trade is important at the margin for many yards in the mid-1980s, in the long run its contribution to shipyard order books will significantly de-crease. Several reasons support the assertion. First, with the exception of the noncontiguous trades, domestic ocean transportation must compete with increasingly efficient land transportation systems (e.g., pipelines in the case of Gulf coast–east coast petroleum shipments). Second, the trade that has primarily driven new Jones Act construction is Alaska–lower 48 state petroleum shipments. Tonnage on this route is ap-proaching saturation levels, and always in the background there is the possibility of allowing existing construction differential subsidy (CDS)–

built tankers—through paybacks—to enter the trade. Third, unless new fields are discovered/opened on Alaska's North Slope, at some time in the future present wells will play out. Fourth, in the last three years a number of proposals to loosen Jones Act restrictions have been made. And although the Reagan administration remains committed to a policy of maintaining Jones Act integrity, it seems better than an even bet that some modifications will be made in the legislation that would allow foreign-built vessel participation.

3. The option of building merchant ships for government account fails for two reasons. First, it is a short-term approach, not one on which an enduring shipyard support policy could be built. Second, the most likely resting place for such ships would be the National Defense Reserve Fleet, a fleet that is already programmed to include upwards of 100 ships being maintained in a fast breakout status.

4. The option of an operator constructing part of his fleet in the United States and part overseas is flawed primarily because of its built-in uncertainty. For example, if a 2 by 3 agreement were in place (i.e., build two in the United States and three foreign), would the requirement be that all five orders be placed simultaneously (rather unlikely), and, if not, which order(s) would come first? And more important, what if trade conditions change over the building period? Is the operator still committed to invest irrespective of the demand for new tonnage? A second problem concerns the type of ship that would be built. To avail himself of the foreign build option, would an operator be committed to building a militarily useful ship and/or employing his vessel on trades that enhanced national security (e.g., on strategic import trades)?[2]

5. The option of supporting a shipyard mobilization base by maintaining a relatively large navy fails primarily because reasonable persons (and political administrations and Congresses) will disagree on what size navy is needed. Moreover, all top-ranking naval authorities, including the present secretary of the navy, John Lehman, have stated that naval work alone is insufficient to support the needed number of shipyards—and this at a time when naval budgets are at an all-time peacetime high.

6. The option of accepting a shipyard mobilization base that relies entirely on naval work and Jones Act construction entails an unacceptable degree of risk. The statistic that most strongly supports this conclusion is the number of commercial shipyards that closed in the five-year period 1979–84. There were 29 with perhaps an additional 8 or 9 in financial difficulty.[3]

What is left? The option of renewing the CDS program (7, above) and/or bilateral or multilateral cargo-sharing agreements (8). By their nature and by definition, both are long-term options. Also neither is likely to provoke retaliation by foreign governments. In this respect, note that a U.S. CDS program was in place from 1937 to 1981 and that bilateral and multilateral cargo-sharing arrangements have long been acceptable mechanisms for rationalization of particular trades.

The chief criticism of the options is their alleged high cost—to the federal treasury, the shipper, and the consumer.

The Cost of the CDS Option

The CDS cost figure most often cited is the outlay by the federal government between 1936 and 1983 for construction and reconstruction differential subsidies. It was $3.8 billion, an amount that critics considered too great for what was received.[4] What was received was a presumably acceptable shipyard mobilization base, and one considerably less dependent upon naval work than the current one.

As a general rule, critics of CDS do not attack the $3.8 billion figure head-on. (Over a 40-year period it amounted to little more than the cost, in 1986, of two ballistic missile submarines.) Rather, criticism has focused on the difference in cost in building a particular ship in the United States as compared to overseas. As this differential has increased to 50 percent and more, so has criticism mounted. Fairly or not, critics have generally focused on poor shipyard productivity, occasioned by high American wage rates and a slowness and/or unwillingness to invest in and adopt new production and management techniques. Ship cost differential alone has provided the underlying argument for deeming the CDS program a failure and hence for its abandonment. It is truly a case of not seeing the forest for the trees.[5]

In analyzing the CDS option, the assumption is made here that federal expenditures to maintain an adequate shipyard mobilization base are, in fact, defense expenditures. This has never been stated categorically, for a number of fairly obvious reasons. Mainly, if the cost to maintain a sufficient maritime security posture were contrasted with numerous *other* items in the defense budget, the latter would fare poorly when subjected to even the most rudimentary cost–benefit type of analysis.

Secretary of Defense Caspar Weinberger came as close to defining maritime expenditures as defense expenditures as anyone is likely to do, in a letter to the chairman of the board of the Shipbuilders Council of America. Weinberger stated:

> We in Defense agree that the Nation must take steps to revitalize our maritime industry if we are to have sufficient capacity and capability to meet our mobilization requirements. . . .
>
> The department [of Defense] has supported legislation and policy initiatives proposed from time to time on behalf of the Merchant Marine that would foster stability in our merchant fleet and shipbuilding industrial base. Unfortunately, we have not been entirely successful.[6]

Tables 11.1, 11.2, and 11.3 list the unit cost for a number of military hardware items scheduled for funding in the FY 1985–87 period, as well as the planned production of these items and the number that would have to be given up (forgone) to construct a 35,000-dwt dry bulk carrier in a U.S. shipyard under a construction differential subsidy program. The total cost of such a vessel is approximated at $40 million with a CDS payment of 50 percent, or $20 million.[7]

What do these tables show? Essentially, the figures indicate that by giving up relatively little in terms of some classic defense hardware items, the United States could fund the building, under a 50 percent CDS program, of 10 handy-size bulk carriers. To achieve this total, the Army would, for example, give up seven main battle tanks out of a planned production of 840 and two AH-64 helicopters out of 144, while the Navy would give up three air cushion landing craft out of 12, one anti-submarine helicopter out of 18, and two F-18 fighters out of 84.

Or if the Navy gave up a dock landing ship, LSD-41, a 10-ship-a-year building program could be funded for two years, while giving up one DDG-51 destroyer would fund the hypothetical CDS program for five years.

And when the Air Force is factored into the equation, two fewer B-1 bombers would more than fund a 10-bulk-carrier building program for one year.

The point is quite simple: if a defined number of shipyards are considered vital to our national defense posture, and the cost of maintaining them in place is viewed as a "national defense expenditure," then that cost is relatively little compared to the total defense budget. In other words, defense expenditures should be compared with defense expenditures, in efforts to maximize the utility of national defense dollars.

Critics of the CDS program emphasized that the cost differential between American and foreign yards was increasing, and that even a 50 percent CDS payment would not equalize costs. However, in abandoning the CDS program, little, if any, thought was given to ways in which CDS costs might be reduced.

One after-the-fact approach that seems to have tacit Reagan administration approval is to utilize foreign components, including diesel engines, to the greatest extent possible. In an extreme case, only the hull and superstructure would be U.S.-built.[8] In essence, do in shipbuilding what automobile makers have long done in their industry—utilize cheaper foreign components in the products.

In Chapter 9, reference was made to a study by the Shipbuilders Council of America which concluded that, under the best of conditions, a ship with wide general application (generic) could be built in the United States for $30 million versus a Japanese cost of $20 million. If this figure is

Table 11.1. Selected army defense expenditures contrasted with CDS cost of constructing a 35,000-dwt bulk carrier ($ millions).

Item	Planned production/funding request (FY)		Unit cost	Number forgone to construct a bulk carrier under 50% CDS program
M-1, main battle tank	$2,285.7	840	FY '86	$2.720	7
Assault amphibious vehicle	107.2	248	FY '85[a]	.432	46
Light armored vehicle	249.7	292	FY '85	.855	23
Attack helicopter, AH-64	1,376.3	144	FY '86	9.560	2
Assault support helicopter, UH-60	486.2	78	FY '86	6.200	3
Assault support helicopter, CH-53E	101.0	4	FY '86	25.200	0.8
Hawk anti-aircraft missile	140.1	550	FY '86	.254	79
Field artillery ammo support vehicle	101.5	212	FY '86	.478	42

SOURCES: Department of Defense *Annual Report To Congress, FY 1986*, pp. 140, 143, 145 and Maritime Administration, *MARAD '82*, p. 3. Bulk carrier used as example was scheduled for delivery in December 1982. It was the last bulk carrier built under the CDS program.
[a]Includes new and rebuilt vehicles.

Table 11.2. Selected naval defense expenditures contrasted with CDS cost of constructing a 35,000-dwt bulk carrier ($ millions).

Item	Planned production	Funding request	(FY)	Unit cost	Number forgone to construct a bulk carrier under 50% CDS program
Amphibious assault ship, LHD-1	$1,365.7	1	FY '84	$1,365.70	.015
Dock landing ship, LSD-41	396.6	1	FY '84	396.60	.050
Air cushion landing craft, LCAC	316.2	12	FY '86	26.30	.760
Battleship reactivation	473.1	1	FY '84	473.10	.040
Guided missile cruiser, CG-47	2,834.8	3	FY '86	945.00	.020
Destroyer, DDG-51	2,246.8	2	FY '87	1,120.0	.020
Attack submarine, SSN-688	2,770.3	4	FY '86	693.00	.030
Maritime patrol aircraft	496.5	9	FY '86	55.20	.360
Anti-submarine helicopter, SH-60B	378.8	18	FY '86	21.00	.950
Fleet oiler, TAO-187	330.5	2	FY '86	165.20	.120
Mine counter-measure ship, MCM-1	371.1	4	FY '86	92.8	.220
F-14 fighter	812.4	18	FY '86	45.00	.44
F-18 fighter	2,849.6	84	FY '86	33.90	.59
Airborne early warning aircraft, E-2C	390.3	6	FY '86	65.00	.31
Recon aircraft, TR-1	363.6	8	FY '86	45.50	.44
Trident submarine	1,546.4	1	FY '86	1,546.40	.01
Trident II missile	1,865.5	27	FY '87	69.00	.29

SOURCES: Department of Defense, *Annual Report to Congress, FY 1986*, pp. 161, 162, 166, 172 and Maritime Administration, *MARAD '82*, p. 3. See source note Table 11.1. Secondary source for DoD expenditures, *Seapower*, June 1985, pp. 42, 43.

Table 11.3. Selected Air Force defense expenditures contrasted with CDS cost of constructing a 35,000-dwt bulk carrier ($ millions).

Item	Planned production	Funding request	(FY)	Unit cost	Number forgone to construct a bulk carrier under 50% CDS program
F-15 fighter	$2,209.1	48	FY '86	$46	.43
F-16 fighter	3,708.7	180	FY '86	20.6	1.00
Cargo plane, MC-130H	83.3	1	FY '86	83.3	.24
Bomber, B-1	5,624	48	FY '86	117.0	.17
MX missile	1,000	21	FY '85	47.6	.42
Cargo plane, C-5B	2,380	16	FY '86	149.0	.13
Tanker, KC-10	519	12	FY '86	43.2	.46

SOURCE: Department of Defense, *Annual Report to Congress, FY 1986*, pp. 184, 186, 212.

even reasonably close for a moderate-size bulk carrier, a CDS payment of 35 percent becomes a meaningful figure.[9] If a $10 million per ship CDS payment is a possibility, then the hardware that would have to be forgone by the armed services, as outlined above, could be halved (e.g., by giving up one DDG-51 destroyer at $1.12 billion a copy, we could fund a 10-ship-per-year build program for 10 years).

Bilateral/Multilateral Shipping Agreements

It has been often and correctly noted that cargo must drive any increase in (world) new construction, and that a *guarantee of cargo* for higher-cost U.S.-flag/U.S.-built ships must precede any new building in U.S. shipyards.

In theory, two somewhat similar, though different, approaches (policies) can effectively guarantee U.S.-built/flag ships a share of the nation's bulk foreign trade.[10] One is cargo reservation; under this approach a certain percent of cargo over which the United States has jurisdiction is reserved for U.S.-flag ships, either because the cargo is publicly financed, or the government uses its sovereign power coercively. The "public finance" rationale for cargo reservation programs is the most common in the United States and dates back to 1904, when all military cargo was required to be moved in U.S.-flag vessels. In 1954 the concept was extended to include 50 percent of all government-impelled cargo (Public Law 664).

The proposed "Competitive Shipping and Shipbuilding Act of 1983" (HR 1242) is an example of government using its sovereign power to coerce shippers into using American ships. The bill would initially require all U.S. importers and exporters to ship 5 percent of their bulk cargo in U.S. ships, and that this amount be increased incrementally by 1 percent a year until a 20 percent share was obtained. Essentially similar bills were introduced with respect to oil imports in 1975 and 1977. Both failed to become law.

The second approach is to negotiate a cargo-sharing agreement with a trading partner (bilateral agreement) or subscribe to a multilateral agreement such as the UN-ratified Code of Conduct for Liner Conferences.[11] The U.S. position on agreements with trading partners has been ambivalent. On the one hand, the United States vigorously opposes the Code of Conduct for Liner Conferences; on the other, it has signed bilateral agreements in the past with the Soviet Union and the People's Republic of China, and in 1986 it had cargo-sharing arrangements with Brazil and Argentina.[12]

The main U.S. objections to strictly cargo preference legislation are: (1) the additional costs imposed on shippers, (2) the possible impairment of U.S. bulk exports, and (3) the adverse impact on foreign relations.

Essentially the same objections are raised against bilaterals, even though the cost arguments cited are considerably weaker and the foreign relations caveat is rejected entirely.

The costs of cargo preference have been analyzed perhaps more than any other single maritime issue. When the U.S. domestic trades are analyzed, one conclusion is that in the case of general cargo on the U.S.–Hawaii route, the increased cost of using American ships is relatively small, but on oil shipments from Alaska to the lower 48 states it is relatively large.

In a 1984 Report to Congress, the U.S. General Accounting Office noted that 2.3 million tons of cargo moved in U.S.-flag vessels because of cargo preference legislation in 1980, and that this movement gave employment to an additional 21 to 33 U.S.-flag ships, and increased seafaring employment by between 1,400 and 2,200 workers. The increased transportation cost was estimated to be between $71.4 million and 78.6 million.[13]

Another report on the overall impact of cargo preference was done by the Center for Naval Analyses (CNA). The analysis was requested by the Navy and specifically addressed the economic and defense aspects of the proposed 1983 Competitive Shipping and Shipbuilding Act (HR 1242). The report estimated that when the U.S. share of its bulk trades reached 20 percent, 329 new bulk ships would be initially added to the U.S. merchant fleet.[14]

Table 11.4 breaks down these 329 ships by vessel type and deadweight tonnage.

The aggregate annual additional transport cost of HR 1242 was estimated to be $1.64 billion, or about 1 percent of the landed value of total

Table 11.4. Estimated additional U.S.-flag shipping if 20 percent share of U.S. bulk trade reserved to U.S.-flag/built ships.

Vessel type	Deadweight tonnage	Number
Dry bulk, geared[a]	20,000– 35,000 dwt	214
Dry bulk, gearless	40,000– 60,000 dwt	53
Ore-bulk-oil	60,000–120,000 dwt	50
Tankers	50,000– 80,000 dwt	12
		329

SOURCE: Center for Naval Analyses, *Defense and Economic Aspects of HR 1242 (Competitive Shipping and Shipbuilding Act of 1983)*, pp. 1–5.

[a]Geared dry bulk carriers generally have cranes with 10–25-ton lift capability.

[b]Approximately 25 ships should be subtracted from the initial build estimate because of reductions in demand for U.S. exports due to higher U.S. shipping costs.

Additional shipping hypothesized would come on line over an approximately 15-year period.

U.S. trade.[15] This cost would be borne by U.S. importers and exporters.

Citing earlier studies, the CNA report noted that with a 10 percent increase in U.S. transport costs (the transport cost differential between a U.S. and foreign-flag 35,000-dwt bulk carrier), wheat exports, for example, might decrease by 7 percent to Europe, and by 3.4 percent to Japan. Coal exports were assumed to decrease by 9.6 percent.[16] However, the overall decrease in bulk commodity shipments would, of necessity, cause a decrease in the number of U.S.-flag ships employed. This loss was estimated to be between 21 and 32 ships out of the 329 cited above.

In summary, a cargo preference policy imposes a cost on the shipper that ultimately translates into higher consumer prices (imports) or loss of revenues for exporters. It does not directly impact on the federal treasury.

In October 1984 there were 106.2 million civilians employed in the United States with another 1.7 million in the armed services.[17] On an *annual* basis, the cost of a cargo preference policy could be viewed as a net $15.00 loss in income for all employed persons in the United States. Or looking at the cost in terms of forgone defense hardware, the real cost of a 20 percent share in our bulk trades can be calculated by subtracting out various combinations of defense hardware items (e.g., one less DDG-51 destroyer and five fewer B-1 bombers).

Conclusion

Under the most optimistic scenario, a renewed CDS program would certainly cost the taxpayer. To fund construction subsidies for 100 35,000-dwt bulk carriers, under a 35 percent CDS program, would cost $1 billion. On its face this seems to be a large expenditure until what is received is contrasted with other defense purchases. In this context, as noted above, the figure is considerably less imposing.

A cargo preference policy also has some seemingly large costs until these costs are contrasted with the gross national product or the cost imposed on the individual wage earner. Moreover, the cost to the taxpayer with respect to cargo preference would be phased in. The cost of adding some 300 bulk carriers to the U.S. merchant marine under the CNA study assumptions would not reach a maximum until 16 years after the policy was put in place, or until the last ship built because of cargo preference joined the fleet.

As a general rule, the Reagan administration has opposed a unilateral cargo preference option, for example, HR 1242, and the UNCTAD Code. It has, however, been party to certain bilateral agreements in the past and is being pressed to consider such agreements with Venezuela, South Korea, and the Philippines.[18] Moreover, the jury is still out with respect to the added cost of bilaterals. Studies in 1979 and 1983 reached opposite conclusions about the cost of the Brazil–United States bilateral agreement. One concluded that it did not adversely affect trade flow, costs, or service. The other study concluded that shipping rates were much higher in the U.S.–Brazil trades than in other U.S. trades.[19]

On the other hand, bilateral agreements and a disciplined CDS program have substantial benefits. In this respect, funding a 150-ship bulk carrier fleet would provide some minimum of long-term support for private shipyards in a period when naval work will be tapering off. Moreover, the cost of such bilateral agreements should not be prohibitive.

If the added shipping costs to support 300 U.S.-flag bulk carriers is estimated to be $1.64 billion annually, then halving that fleet to a more modest 150 ships should reduce the cost by at least 50 percent. Finally, as mentioned earlier, bilaterals do not trigger retaliation by one's trading partners.[20]

In times past, bulk carriers were thought to have little value in wartime as logistics support vessels. This view has changed. The Navy now recognizes that bulk vessels can be useful in logistics support roles when national defense features are added.

Table 11.5 lists four levels of national defense features together with their associated costs.

Numerous studies have cited American dependence on foreign-flag shipping for strategic bulk imports. In 1985 there were only 10 dry bulk carriers (including tug barges) and 16 tankers engaged in U.S. foreign trade.[21] This deficiency cannot be rationalized away by citing U.S.-owned, foreign-flag shipping. Far too many studies have examined any purported defense role for "flag of convenience" shipping and found it wanting. The above-cited CNA study is now added to that list.[22] It states:

> The EUSC fleet has a significant number of ships, but most of them are either tankers (62 percent) or gearless ships (24 percent), both of which are of limited utility for military sealift augmentation. Moreover, questions have been raised about the wisdom of relying on the EUSC fleet. The understandings between the U.S. and the three flag of convenience countries are based on agreements, not treaties, and effective during friendly relations only. In the past 10 years, anti-U.S. feeling and waves of nationalism have swept through Third World countries. Sympathy for U.S. policies and goals is questionable.
>
> In addition, all these ships are manned by foreign crews of mixed nationality, some of whom may not be sympathetic to the United States or its policies and might not sail for U.S. military support. EUSC doctrine has never been envoked.[23]

Table 11.5. Cost of national defense features in selected bulk carriers when feature added during initial construction (thousands of 1983 dollars).

Vessel type	NDF Cost[a]			
	Level #1	Level #2	Level #3	Level #4
Dry bulk, geared, 35,000 dwt	704	175	51	10
Ore-bulk-oil, gearless, 60,000 dwt	1,090	131	316	74
Tanker, 80,000 dwt	78	52	58	NA

SOURCE: Center for Naval Analyses, *Defense and Economic Aspects of HR 1242 (Competitive Shipping and Shipbuilding Act of 1983)*, pp. 4–9.

[a]Does not include any additions to vessel operating costs occasioned by incorporating NFDs into vessel design.

Level #1—For dry bulk and OBO, carry breakbulk cargoes on existing deck structure. For tanker, carry a mix of petroleum products. All have Navy-compatible communcations systems. Eliminate shock-failure–prone gray cast iron from vital systems. Have water washdown clips.

Level #2—For dry bulk and OBO, have breakbulk storage capability on tween-deck levels. For tanker, have astern refueling system.

Level #3—For dry bulk, carry lighters alongside. For OBO, have cargo gear for self-sustaining operations. For tanker, have multiple stations for transfer of fuel.

Level #4—For dry bulk, and OBO, have capability to replenish naval auxiliary under way. For dry bulk, receive fuel under way. For OBO, provide and receive fuel under way; have astern refueling system.

If the lack of bulk shipping under the American flag is an issue now, the question may become even more important in coming years. As recently as 1971 the underdeveloped nations put forth their concept with respect to general cargo sharing on a multinational basis—the Code of Conduct for Liner Conferences. The major maritime nations of the world paid scant attention at the time. Yet in 1984 the Code was ratified by the necessary number of nations, and it has, for what it's worth, UN sanction. A code of conduct for bulk shipping has been proposed, and like the earlier liner code it was initially opposed by the Organization for Economic Cooperation and Development (OECD) as well as the United States. In this environment, the chances of a bulk carrier code receiving UN sanction seem remote. However, no one is certain of that.

Since 1981 it has become fashionable to disparage construction differential subsidies as a way of ensuring a U.S. shipyard and shipping capability. This derision is second only to the paranoia that is evoked when cargo preference legislation is discussed. However, these are really the only games in town for determining ways to ensure the survival of high-cost U.S. ships and shipyards.

In framing a reasonable U.S. shipyard policy, initial guidelines for policymakers might be:

- A CDS program for bulk carriers would be reinstated, with differential payments limited to 35 percent. National defense features for these vessels would be required, and they would be Department of Defense–funded. The goal of adding 150 dry bulk carriers and tankers to the foreign trade fleet would be made explicit.
- Liner firms would continue to have the option of building foreign.
- Reaching bilateral agreements with nations that supply our strategic imports would be established U.S. policy.

What we would get and what we would give up to achieve a modest tanker and dry bulk capability in our foreign trades, and to some extent to ensure an adequate shipyard mobilization base, have been explained in this chapter. The cost is relatively small in terms of the benefits received.

12 Shipyards and National Security

> Our economic vitality, national defense, and foreign policy options will depend increasingly on the use we make of the sea during the remainder of this century . . . .
>
> A specific naval-maritime program must be developed that will . . . insure that our vital shipbuilding mobilization base is preserved. It is essential that sufficient naval and commercial shipbuilding be undertaken to maintain the irreplaceable shipbuilding mobilization base. Without this nucleus of trained workers and established production facilities, we can never hope to meet any future challenge to our security.[1]

THE INTRODUCTORY REMARKS, with suitable period embellishments, could have been made on the eve of the birth of this nation, as well as in the major wars in our history. They remain timely and valid today, even as debate intensifies over what constitutes the "vital" and "sufficient" resources of the "irreplaceable" mobilization base.

For New York in 1775, the award of two frigates from the Continental Congress's 13-frigate shipbuilding program impelled a scramble for a site, suppliers, and craftsmen. New production methods had to be devised. Men and material were diverted to meet higher-priority requirements that developed after the keels were laid. The threat of British attacks up the Hudson River diverted resources to defensive fortifications. Weather slowed progress prior to launching and during fitting out. Finally, after nearly two years of effort, and without firing a shot, the ships were burned to keep them out of the advancing enemy's hands.[2] Was the building of the site near Poughkeepsie vital? Were resources sufficient and timely? Was the output required for the war effort?

In 1861, Secretary of the Navy Gideon Welles ordered an inland navy of ironclad gunboats to control the Mississippi River and split the Confederacy. Seven gunboats were laid down at shipyards in St. Louis and Mound City, Illinois. Four thousand men were mobilized to work seven days a week for two months to launch the ironclads. The craft were indispensable to the Union strategy. Jefferson Davis observed after the South's defeat: ". . . we required vessels like theirs, or the means of constructing them. We had neither."[3] Were the yards strategically located? Was there a nucleus of trained workers?

In World War I the U.S. shipbuilding industry was not ready to respond rapidly to surge demand, despite the country's late entry. Poor planning, long lead times, and inadequate national control mechanisms affected all areas of mobilization. Only 107 of 1,741 new ships were completed before the Armistice. Despite some policy changes during the aftermath, no approved industrial preparedness plan existed by the late 1930s. The commercial arms production base was dismantled, leaving only government-owned facilities.[4] Was the civil sector irreplaceable?

A 10-year shipbuilding program to renovate the U.S.-flag fleet as well as large orders from U.S. allies during the two years prior to U.S. entry into World War II served to stimulate defense industry production, but high levels of output were not reached for three to four years. The 10 major private shipyards that existed in 1937 were increased to 40 by 1941 and 80 by 1945. After the war, the oversupply of merchant ships was the key factor causing several yards to close. A postwar commission stated: "What is needed is a group of shipyards engaged in building merchant ships, whose workers are skilled in their trades, whose methods are progressive. In time of emergency the knowledge and skill of this group can be expanded to meet the inflated demands of war . . . ."[5]

Though eventually adequate during the Korean conflict, shipyard production output was again slow to increase. Perhaps the most important result of the experience was emergence of a new national view of the mobilization base. The concept included the necessary industrial planning to determine requirements, develop available capacity to expand military and essential civilian production rapidly to high output levels, and maintain the facilities in a ready state to reduce delays. Direct links were forged between national security and industrial preparedness through construction appropriations, tax incentives, and stockpile formation. Still the readiness of the defense industrial base suffered under varying service policies, inadequate peacetime funding, the long-war versus short-war debate, and the leisurely pace of the Vietnam conflict. In 1976, the Defense Science Board declared that the defense industrial base was in a state of deterioration.[6]

Current Mobilization Policy

National Security Decision Directive 47 (NSDD-47) was issued on 22 July 1982. It states that the policy of the United States is "to have an emergency mobilization capability that will insure that government, at all levels, in partnership with the private sector and the American people, can respond decisively and effectively to any major national emergency."[7] This process of mobilizing the resources of the country includes marshaling the industrial sector to produce goods and services, including construction, that are required to support military operations during national security emergencies. It may involve a mix of short-lead-time surge production and longer-term expansion of productive capacity.

"Within the Department of Defense, mobilization planning and preparedness is the Department's *principal responsibility* [emphasis added] in peacetime, crises, and situations short of war."[8] It includes a range of phased, incremental improvements in force readiness, deployment capability, and sustainability, that are to be taken as the nation moves from peacetime to a war-fighting capability and, therefore, as a deterrent element of national strategy. To support the strategy, the industrial base must:

• Provide efficient, competitive peacetime production.
• Maintain "warm" production base capabilities.
• Have the capability to accelerate output through surge capability and reduced manufacturing lead times.
• Be prepared to indefinitely sustain combat forces and essential functions of the economy.
• Reduce dependency on imported raw materials.
• Reduce unacceptable dependency on unreliable foreign sources of military weapon systems.[9]

Also, the Department of Transportation conducts annual surveys of the shipbuilding and ship repair industry to determine whether an adequate mobilization base exists for national defense and for use in a national emergency. This responsibility is mandated under the Merchant Marine Act, 1936, as amended, and includes an evaluation of the adequacy and efficiency of facilities and skilled personnel, the strategic location of facilities, the ability to construct and repair merchant ships, and the capability to reactivate the reserve fleets.

Since about 1977 the Navy and the Maritime Administration have collaborated on three major, classified studies of the shipyard mobilization base. None of the studies has been published, but all have been accorded the status of final draft internal working reports. Selected results have been briefed to various government organizations and government-sponsored symposia. Unclassified portions have been quoted and referred to in the open literature.[10]

The Reagan administration has declared its full commitment to achieving global maritime strength, but has recognized the tension that exists between the requirements of national security interests and the

This destroyer section has reached modular size, still providing open access to every level. Much of the ship's own equipment, including her lighting, is already in use. (Courtesy Shipbuilders Council of America and Ingalls Shipbuilding Corporation)

economics of maintaining broad-based domestic maritime industries. Those who formulate policy in this area understand that the national security/national defense rationale is a blend of quantitative and qualitative analysis, and is difficult to equate with economic projections based on a different rationale and derived from different views of the world. A clear understanding of a particular viewpoint is often rendered difficult by the way the term "national security" is used to describe objectives that derive from both defense requirements and the global economic and political status of the nation.

National defense interests require continuous assessment of a wide range of conditions that define the time-phased requirements for personnel and material in various conflict or crisis situations. These considerations include battle fleet deployment and readiness; strategic sealift quantity, capability, and availability; and the sustaining logistic support provided by the industrial mobilization base and mobile logistic support forces. The private and public shipyards, together with many tiers of suppliers, must be able to provide the requisite support to naval forces and sealift shipping in peacetime and across a broad spectrum of mobilization and war scenarios. Figure 12.1 indicates the major U.S. embarkation ports.

Generally accepted criteria currently used to assess the "adequacy" of the available facilities and projected resources to provide this support include:

- Geographical dispersion.
- Proximity of combatant repair yards to naval bases and home ports.
- Availability of commercial repair facilities near sealift ports of embarkation (see Figure 12.1).
- Proximity of activation capability to reserve fleet layup sites (currently James River, Virginia; Suisun Bay, California; and Beaumont, Texas).
- New construction capability to efficiently sustain or expand existing fleets, replace combat losses, and expand wartime capability to a level required to execute, with reasonable assurance of success, the national military strategy.
- Availability of a workforce capable of short-term increased output and of a proper skill mix to act as the nucleus for rapid expansion.
- Ability of the supplier/subcontractor base to provide material, components, and systems when needed in the construction and repair/overhaul sequences.

Figure 12.1. Major U.S. embarkation ports.

Wartime Role of Shipyards

The national security argument for the maintenance of some, usually unspecified, mobilization base of shipyards ultimately depends on three major factors: (1) the premobilization state of the industry, (2) the projected sequence of mobilization events (scenario), and (3) the projected workload associated with the event schedules.

The premobilization state of the industry is subject to a variety of interpretations. The usual forecasting procedure is for the Maritime Administration and the Naval Sea Systems Command periodically to issue estimates of total employment for the industry or selected slices of it, such as yards that actively build ships or have naval contracts. Sources of data include the Bureau of Labor Statistics, agency surveys, and projections of labor required to accomplish approved or anticipated work. Few forecasts of yards expected to close in the future are available, because of the self-fulfilling nature of such forecasts and the lack of clear indicators for projecting individual yard financial health. Additionally, parent conglomerates have sometimes used a subsidiary shipyard's losses to offset taxable gains from other subsidiaries.[11]

The projected sequence of mobilization events strongly influences requirements and the resulting judgments about adequacy of the base. Generally, one must also include some threat assessments and assumptions about participating allies and the nature of the crisis decision-making process. The Reagan administration has been using several similar variants of a three-year global war scenario that was developed by the Joint Chiefs of Staff for the Military Mobilization Working Group of the Emergency Mobilization Preparedness Board in September 1982. The details are classified, but the scenario variants have been used extensively for mobilization and program planning. Elements are included that permit assessment of difficult unilateral military operations and complex joint and combined campaigns.

Finally, the projected workload must be identified from a combined consideration of scenario events, existing resources, and projected surge and sustaining actions. The tasks to be accomplished fall into three general categories:

• Existing work—ships in yards at the start of mobilization that would be completed according to some priority scheme for resource use. Categories include new construction, conversion, maintenance and modernization (scheduled), and repair (unscheduled). Some total capacity may also be engaged in nonship work such as drill rigs, smaller craft and barge construction, and general manufacturing of such items as boilers and propellers.
• Activation work—restoring ships in reserve or idle status to wartime

utility. The degrees of utility may vary as well as the readiness condition, which specifies the allowable delay in making the ship ready for sea. Such work may also include planned modifications or enhancements, for selected reserve or active ships, which are designed to optimize commercial ships for strategic sealift or support roles, or provide compatible modern systems for inactive combatants.

- Induced work—work derived from the continuation and progress of the emergency situation. Actions include battle damage repair, earlier overhaul dates due to an increased operational tempo, and wartime new construction for attrition replacement or fleet expansion.

Thus, the national defense requirement for the shipbuilding and ship repair industry derives from the continuing peacetime activity necessary to achieve and maintain approved levels of ships for the Navy, the Coast Guard, and the merchant marine; the known activation workload to augment sealift and combat ship inventories; and sustaining or expansion activity for the sealift and combatant fleets. Each scenario will imply an ordering of tasks by priority within and among these work groupings. Priorities may change over time, vary among geographic regions, or be unique to either the public or private yard sectors. The expected duration of an emergency will also affect work priorities, particularly during the early phases of mobilization.

During mobilization, existing and additional resources would be biased toward providing the precise types and numbers of ships required. Priorities would be established in accordance with the following scheme:

- Relative positions are assigned on the Department of Defense Master Urgency List (MUL).[12]
- Commander, Naval Sea Systems Command functions as Coordinator of Shipbuilding, Conversion and Repair for Navy and DoD, and, in addition, does peacetime planning as Coordinator of Ship Repair and Conversion for DoD and DoT. A private sector maritime official would be appointed during mobilization to coordinate the DoD/DoT repair and conversion in wartime.
- The maritime administrator coordinates merchant shipbuilding.
- Fleet commanders assess each ship undergoing depot level maintenance in shipyards and establish the priority of effort by balancing the achievable level of logistics, operational, and combat capabilities against the desired date of return to service.

Resource and readiness planners must establish capability or output goals to guide peacetime preparations for mobilization. These goals are understood to be surrogates for the actual case-by-case determinations that would be made in a crisis or during a war. Some shipyard output goals that have been used for planning include: double production output in six months, complete yard work packages in one-half or two-thirds the scheduled time remaining, expand the fleet to achieve the current Planning Force defined by the Joint Chiefs, and build 250 new sealift ships as soon as possible. Since the duration of the crisis will be unknown at the onset, and since the industrial production base will require time to expand, the goals usually assume a long-war scenario. Several valid reasons underlie this assumption:

- A short-war mentality runs the risk of being self-fulfilling, but with an unfavorable outcome if the enemy believes it could last a bit longer, and does.
- A short-war approach fails to use one of the nation's strengths, its industrial capacity.
- Some warning time to surge production has always been available in large, extended conflicts (World Wars I and II).
- Conflicts not involving NATO or direct Soviet confrontation could develop slowly and require gradually increasing levels of material (Korea and Vietnam).[13]

Defining the Base

Several metrics have been devised for tracking the "shipyard mobilization base." Each responds to a particular view of the base, the data that are available, or the analytical methods in hand. All are individually incomplete measures of mobilization capability, but each is useful in defining a portion of the base.

The Maritime Administration conducts an annual survey of the shipbuilding and ship repair industry, primarily to determine whether an adequate mobilization base exists. The survey for 1984[14] provided data in the following categories of private yards:

- 138 *topside repair facilities* for ships at least 300 feet in length (named only).
- 86 *major facilities* capable of building ships at least 475 feet in length by 68 feet wide or drydocking ships at least 300 feet in length (abstracts of data).
- 29 *major shipbuilding yards*, which are a subset of the previous category (a facility plan and narrative description of the yard's activity or capabilities is provided).
- 23 *active shipbuilding base yards* that are open and currently engaged in or seeking contracts for the construction of major oceangoing or

Great Lakes ships 1,000 gross tons or over (a subset of the major yard list—includes orderbook and employment projection).

Recent history of the ASB shows fluctuations in the number of yards included:

1959–73: 19–21	1977–83: 27
1974: 25	1984: 25
1975–76: 24	1985: 23

Figure 12.2 illustrates the recent production worker employment history of the ASB yards. Fifteen of these yards were engaged in naval construction in 1984.

The Coordinator of Shipbuilding, Conversion and Repair, Department of Defense, issues an annual report on the status of the industry.[15] The report for 1983 provided an overview of major shipbuilding programs, ship conversions and modernizations, shipyard improvements,

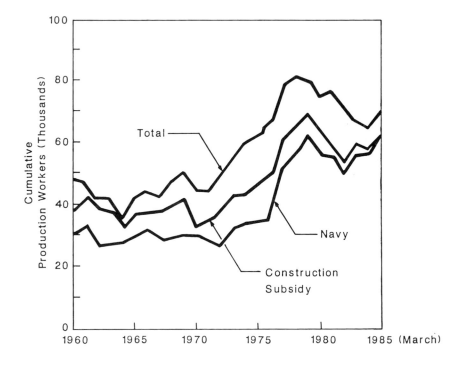

Figure 12.2. Production workers engaged in ship repair, construction, and conversion work at shipyard in the active shipbuilding base. Source: Office of Assistant Secretary of the Navy (Shipbuilding and Logistics).

and research and development programs. It also included a summary status of worldwide shipbuilding, with a special section on the U.S.S.R. Extensive data and descriptions were provided for the U.S. private yards and the nine public yards. A much shorter version of the report was completed for 1984.

In 1984, 142 facilities held *master ship repair contracts* with the Navy, but only 48 yards actually were awarded naval ship overhaul and repair work. Only five private yards were certified as *master ordnance repair* contractors for naval surface ships. Fifty-seven yards were engaged in some form of naval work during 1984.[16] Those yards are classified by ability to overhaul ships in three categories:[17]

- Complex—nuclear-powered ships, carriers, guided missile cruisers and destroyers, command ships (AGF, LCC), submarine rescue ships, and amphibious assault ships.
- Moderately complex—battleships, guided missile frigates, destroyers, and submarine tenders.
- Noncomplex—all other ships.

The Navy/Maritime Administration Shipyard Mobilization Base Study (SYMBA) cataloged potential mobilization base yards, in existence on 1 October 1982, according to ability to build or repair ships over 400 feet in length. This size cutoff includes all classes of ships except attack submarines, minesweepers, and cutters. Yards that handle such ships do meet the larger size criteria, however. SYMBA listed all 9 public yards and 110 private yards. Appendix H is a listing of yards that qualified at the end of 1984. The SYMBA yards contained over 90 percent of the workers and all of the major docks, basins, and ways. Figure 12.2 breaks down production workers with respect to naval and private contract work. The SYMBA study derived mobilization requirements for a late 1988 global war scenario of three years' duration and modeled a relatively efficient set of schedules for doing the work in a large portion of the 119 yards. Resource requirements were measured in terms of average production workforce per month, tons of steel for new construction per month, and utilization of building and repair facilities. Major findings of the study included the following:

1. Naval work alone will not sustain an adequately diversified base because such work tends to be concentrated in a few yards.
2. Twenty-four of the 110 private yards were used only for activations, 28 were not needed after the initial phase of mobilization, and 7 of the yards were not used at all.
3. For the first year of mobilization, 51 building positions and 97 drydocks/basins were the minimum facilities required.

4. For the first year, the number of production workers rose from an estimated starting workforce of about 165,000 to about 190,000, a 15 percent increase.
5. Early production bottlenecks could be caused by long lead times to deliver nuclear reactors, gas turbine engines, reduction gears, and selected weapons systems to the yards.[18]

The SYMBA Study focused on careful documentation, definition of the potential base, and analytical compatibility with other ongoing mobilization studies.[19] Not all of its results were accepted uncritically, and several factors suggested the need for a follow-on study. The MarAd simulation model imposed certain limitations on realistic modeling of production work, and several changes were made to the mobilization module. Government policy changes affected several key assumptions even as preliminary results became available in 1983. Results of the DoD Sealift Study then affected the 1985–90 Five-Year Defense Plan and changed the mobilization task projections for 1988. Sixteen yards from the 110 private yard list closed between 1982 and 1984; one new yard was added. Finally, assumptions about the rate at which private yards could add newly hired workers and the way in which high-priority work could be accommodated as the workforce was growing were significantly modified. For these reasons, the National Defense Shipyard Study (NADES) was initiated in late 1983 and completed in February 1985.

The NADES study projected a continued decline in the number of open yards from 1982 to 1988 as a worst case. The 9 public yards and a 57-yard subset of the SYMBA list were assumed to be the only yards available for mobilization. The projected peacetime workload was then imposed on these 66 yards. Major changes to previous assumptions included more time between the start of mobilization and the start of conflict (D day) to more closely match current planning scenarios, better peacetime readiness of some active and reserve sealift ships, an earlier start on 40 percent overtime for workers on high-priority tasks, temporary suspension of low-priority work to remain within workforce constraints, and an either-month analysis horizon designed to focus on initial mobilization tasks. Major findings of the study included the following:

1. Dispersing the layup sites of Ready Reserve Force strategic sealift ships may be required to avoid breakout and towing delays.
2. Sealift enhancement modifications such as refueling, communications, and cargo space features should be accomplished in peacetime to avoid delaying ships required early in the deployment of combat equipment overseas.
3. The rate at which newly hired labor can be assimilated into the productive workforce significantly affects the ability to do the early

mobilization work without delaying necessary but lower-priority work.[20]

4. If the workforce can be moved freely to where work is being done, the minimum production workforce would have to increase only 10 percent above an estimated initial requirement for about 142,000 workers. Figure 12.3 shows NADES production workforce requirements.

5. If workers do *not* move freely, but are retained where initially required (and hired), aggregate requirements would increase to nearly 194,000 workers—37,000 more than the minimum case.

6. Minimum facilities required to accomplish initial mobilization tasks are 49 building positions and 123 docks/basins. In the study, these facilities were distributed among 9 public and 55 private yards.

7. The anticipated workload for a late-1990s mobilization derives from:
   - 155 government ships in maintenance, modernization, and repair at the onset.
   - 89 government ships under construction from the peacetime authorized building programs.
   - 208 activations, plus the number of Victory ships remaining and required.
   - Over 400 sealift enhancement modifications requiring from 5 to 12 days to complete; 145 of the ships are in the reserve fleets. Additional peacetime funding is planned to reduce this requirement.

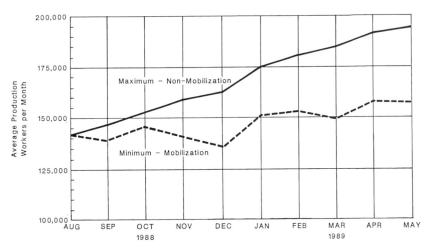

Figure 12.3. National Defense Shipyard Study (NADES) production workforce requirements.

- Over 760 ships inducted after D day for maintenance, modernization, and repair; includes about 460 merchant ships.

The basic conclusions derived from the NADES Study are: (1) the shipbuilding and ship repair industry of the United States has adequate capacity and capability to accomplish present and planned programs of the Department of Defense; and (2) though naval work alone is unlikely to sustain the entire nation's shipbuilding base for mobilization (Figure 12.4 indicates shipyard employment trends, 1975–90), little government intervention is required in the mid-1980s to have a reasonable assurance that the initial mobilization requirements can be met through 1990. Though the manpower situation has been of concern, a recent National Defense University report examined the manpower requirements for mobilizing the nation's shipyards and concluded that, at least for the next five years, "manpower would not be a major constraint." However, it warned that "the requirement for crew supervisors will be a key weak point" and that "the manpower base may become too small to support further expansion at needed speed" if the base continues to decline in size and manning.[21]

Whatever metric is used to define requirements and assess capability, both defense and economic interests will need to be considered in determining the adequacy of future maritime policies. In partial amplification of this view, Secretary of the Navy John Lehman told Congress, in

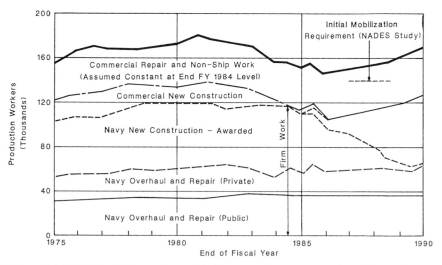

Figure 12.4. Shipbuilding and repair industry employment trends and peacetime forecast. Source: Office of Assistant Secretary of the Navy (Shipbuilding and Logistics).

response to concerns about the geographic distribution of shipbuilding yards:

> . . . building a given combatant, as a generalization, [is] much more expensive on the West Coast. Now the West Coast yards have taken major steps to make themselves more competitive and it is essential for mobilization that we keep a ship repair industry. I think it is less essential that we keep a shipbuilding industry on the West Coast as opposed to our other coasts. I could not foresee accepting the disappearance or the major reduction of our ship overhaul and repair base on the West Coast, regardless of what the [wage] differential is.[22]

Shortly after this statement was made, the lead contract for the Aegis guided missile destroyer, *Arleigh Burke* class (DDG-51), was awarded competitively, on the basis of cost alone, to an east coast yard.

Reliance on Foreign Yards and Suppliers

In 1980, the Defense Industrial Base Panel of the House Armed Services Committee reported that the United States was becoming increasingly dependent on foreign sources for critical raw materials and for some specialized components for military equipment. Concern was also noted about a dependence on overseas labor for assembly of critical, defense-related components. Imports in several industrial sectors were highlighted in questioning the acceptable degree of dependence. The situation would be of concern during mobilization because foreign sources might be captured, destroyed, or denied by blockade or political action. In addition, even reliable and accessible foreign sources might be unable or unwilling to expand production in precise accord with U.S. requirements.

In the tradition of free trade and open markets, the Reagan administration has taken the view that government roles, rules, and regulations must be reduced, and that the expansion of the basic economy serves as a foundation for strength. Competition has been exalted as the way to acquire adequate defense capability with the least drain on the treasury. An inevitable fallout from this policy has been increasing pressure on the domestic industries from foreign producers and suppliers. Domestic firms have struggled to remain competitive worldwide by reducing capital expenses, purchasing abroad, and lobbying for protectionist laws mirroring some foreign governments' policies.

The size of the U.S. merchant marine has been decreasing as older ships have been retired, sometimes to be replaced by newer cargo carriers; foreign-flag carriers have undercut shipping rates; and construction subsidies for U.S.-flag ships have disappeared. The recent output of commercial ships from U.S. yards has been insufficient to support competitive sources of material and components. Figure 12.5 and Table 12.1 show the present and projected state of the U.S.-flag merchant marine.

Denied the option of purchasing from foreign suppliers by U.S. government policy, shipbuilders who were receiving financing under Title XI of the Merchant Marine Act, 1936 (as amended), saw costs increase beyond economical limits. Buyers began turning to foreign sources and flags of convenience. In an attempt to reverse this cycle, the Maritime Administration unsuccessfully sought in 1983 to change the Title XI policy and make it similar to requirements imposed on the Navy and on ships built for the domestic (Jones Act) trades.[23] They tried again in 1985.[24]

For naval ships, amendments to the annual appropriations bills prohibit ships and integral parts of hulls and superstructures from being built in foreign shipyards. However, foreign main propulsion machinery is permitted, and up to 50 percent of the costs for other components can be for foreign material. Ship contract clauses regarding availability of spare parts tend to encourage American sources and discourage use of foreign proprietary equipment which may not be built in the United States under license. Jones Act construction may use foreign main propulsion machinery, unimproved steel plates or shapes, and up to 50 percent by cost of other components.

During peacetime, there may be sufficient political and economic

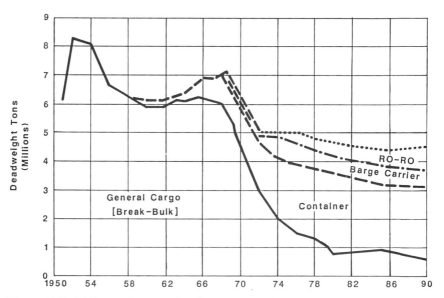

Figure 12.5. U.S. merchant marine dry cargo trends by ship type. Source: U.S., Department of Transportation, Maritime Administration.

Table 12.1. U.S. petroleum ship resources (in number of militarily useful hulls).

Type	1985		1990–91	
	Number	Deadweight tons	Number	Deadweight tons
Coated	113	5,331,748	92	4,786,908
Tug/barge	15	569,266	15	569,734
Military Sealift Command charter	29	931,463	19	576,303
Military Sealift Command owned	2	53,818	0	—
	159	6,886,295	126	5,932,945

SOURCE: U.S., Department of Transportation, Maritime Administration-373, 29 April 1985.

reasons for reliance on foreign suppliers. However, a prudent-risk approach suggests that contingency provisions be made for the domestic wartime support of all foreign-supplied defense resources and for sufficient capability to expand or replace forces destroyed in battle without having to rely on foreign sources. Defense Department policy is moving in that direction, but peacetime funding constraints have restricted goals only to reducing unacceptable dependency on unreliable foreign sources. Some observers have suggested that we may have reached the point at which the marginal cost of nonproductive environmental protection and safety measures would yield a greater return if applied to improved capital recovery in support of national defense goals, which are also protection and safety measures.[25]

Nothing in the preceding discussion has addressed the realities and practicalities of global coalition war. While the United States should retain the option and capability of unilateral action in its own interest, large-scale wars of long duration surely would involve interlocking resources among allies. Illustrative of the multilateral planning that would then be necessary, the SYMBA study listed 49 overseas facilities capable of drydocking or repairing most merchant ships and many combatants.

Ship Construction in Naval Shipyards[26]

Naval shipyards were first established with the basic mission of "repair and upkeep" of the fleet. This mission was subsequently expanded to include new construction and conversion. This role was legislated by Congress in the provision of the Vinson-Trammel Act of 1934 that required the lead ship of each new class and every other follow-ship to be built in a naval shipyard.

During World War II, naval shipyards accomplished considerable new construction to fully utilize the capacity that was available. For some 20 years after World War II, naval shipyards continued to design and build ships at reduced rates to retain the capability, to keep pace with the rapid advance of technology, and to maintain a "benchmark" standard against which the performance of private shipbuilders could be measured. Since 1968 the Vinson-Trammel Act provisions have been waived in all cases.

Collectively, the eight naval shipyards constitute the nation's naval arsenal for continuous and immediate industrial support of the active fleet. Six of the yards are qualified to provide support to nuclear-powered ships.

Nuclear-powered naval ship construction in wartime may not be able to be fitted into existing private yards qualified to perform such work (Newport News and Electric Boat). Since unused capacity would be unlikely to be maintained in those yards without direct subsidies, and because it could be difficult to obtain licensing and public acceptance for additional nuclear construction sites, contingency plans for using the naval shipyards should be formulated. Three of the yards—Puget Sound, Mare Island, and Portsmouth—have the technical capability and special qualifications necessary to commence nuclear ship construction. Some facilities improvements and higher manpower ceilings would be required first, however, and some of the current overhauls would have to be shifted to the private sector.

The SYMBA study anticipated a contingency requirement to build a conventionally powered aircraft carrier in a naval shipyard. However, the best estimates available in 1983 led to the conclusion that it might be two and one-half years before significant work could start if the yard were in its current state.

Soviet Shipbuilding[27]

The Soviet Union has several hundred ship construction and repair yards, although only 13 are known to be involved in the construction of large surface combatants, submarines, or major auxiliaries. A number of other shipyards construct small combatants, amphibious warfare craft, mine warfare craft, and similar other craft. Altogether, over 300,000 people are employed in Soviet shipyards. A large percentage of them are engaged in industrial activities that are not directly related to shipbuilding, but take place in the yards.

It is difficult to obtain much solid evidence on the performance of Soviet yards producing naval vessels. It is known that Soviet yards tend to be more self-sustaining than Western yards and that each yard specializes in making a particular type of naval equipment (propellers, anchors, etc.). Many yards have steel mills nearby, and several have large foundries collocated with them.

Since 1950, naval ships have been produced in some 30 Soviet yards having over 75 slipways over 475 feet in length and more than 90 docks or transverse building positions of this size. These yards have the following capabilities:

- *Submarine production*: nuclear capability resides in five yards; total capacity is enough to build 20 to 25 submarines per year on a single shift.
- *Large surface combatant production*: nine yards have this capability, five of which only build this category (many ships are under 1,000 tons displacement).
- *Small combatant production*: over a dozen yards have this capacity.

Since 1970, the Soviet Union has directed substantial effort to improving and modernizing its shipbuilding facilities, with the most attention going to submarine overhaul and repair. Four new yards have been built, and 24 have been enlarged and modernized, mostly to expand and maintain the Soviet Navy.

In addition to acquiring ships built in the Soviet Union, the Soviet Navy orders ships from abroad, principally from Poland (amphibious warfare, oceangoing research, survey, buoy tender, repair tender, hospital, and generating ships—500 ships scheduled under the 1986 to 1990 five-year plan), Finland (cable layers and oceangoing tugs—28 ships delivered in 1983, plus 14 conversion/repair), and Sweden and Japan (floating drydocks).

The Soviet merchant marine has acquired a cargo fleet of about 1,740 ships, much of it from domestic yards. Until 1990 at least, no further growth in the number of ships will take place. Rather, the Soviet Ministry of Merchant Marine will replace obsolete ships with modern, highly specialized ships. Many have built-in features that enable them to function as naval auxiliaries and strategic sealift ships, and many will be ice-strengthened.

The Soviet military production base is kept relatively active and is close to or on a wartime footing. Industrial plants have the capability to expand production rapidly, often without installing technologically sophisticated subsystems.[28]

Conclusion

It is clear that a shipbuilding and repair base has a key role to play in mobilization scenarios envisioned in support of current national security objectives. What has not been clear is a quantitative appreciation of the requirements, enabling assessments of the sufficiency, irreplaceability, and vitality of the base. The Department of the Navy and the Maritime Administration now believe that they have the necessary insights to make such assessments. Officials and leaders in other areas are less sanguine, partly because of inaccessibility of classified planning documents and partly because of the specters of closed yards that haunt the waterfronts.

Lane Kirkland, president of the AFL-CIO, attacked the maritime policies of the Reagan administration as follows:

> Every successful industrial nation but our own has put in place a coherent national industrial policy designed to advance, promote, preserve and protect particular industries or groups of industries—new and old, sunset and sunrise—in its own national interest. What America has, by comparison, is a collection of mini-policies that never add up to a maximum national effort.
>
> We have policies that encourage the flight of American capital overseas, hiding from U.S. taxes, U.S. wage rates, and U.S. work, health and safety standards. We export capital to those places in this world where workers are docile, hungry and willing to work for pennies per hour—and there is no end to that supply. We have a trade policy that operates only on the inbound shipping lanes—and that has produced a record trade deficit this year of $120 billion—and a loss of nearly 3 million jobs.
>
> Make no mistake about it. There is an international trade war underway, a war to capture the American market at home and abroad. It is a war in which we have no allies, only adversaries. We are losing that war because this administration has not only surrendered, it has unilaterally disarmed America and is collaborating with our enemies.[29]

Congressman Charles E. Bennett (D-FL) sponsored legislation that has resulted in the authorization and establishment of a seven-member Commission on Merchant Marine and Defense. This commission, to be chaired by the secretary of the navy, is directed, among other tasks, to study "the adequacy of the shipbuilding mobilization base of the United States to meet the needs of naval and merchant ship construction in time of war or national emergency."

The president of the Shipbuilders Council of America, M. Lee Rice, bemoaned the failure of national leadership to address the basic problems confronting the industry. He concluded a recent address on the subject by saying:

> I have recited a litany of failures of national military and political leadership. At this point in time one thing is very clear. The maritime industry can do very little to influence the policies which will determine our fate. We are not alone in this lament. A national industrial policy based upon national security needs does not exist and is not planned. Our industry is, at best, a divided house. Likewise, much of the basic heavy industrial base has been segmented and stratified. Will a national calamity be required to cause focus to occur on the entire industrial base problem? A strong industrial base is at the foundation of our strategy of deterrence. Without industrial strength and the ability to engage a powerful enemy in a conventional war,

are we prepared to either lose a significant conventional military encounter or initiate a mutual nuclear act of suicide?[30]

Administration views were articulated on this subject by the Assistant Secretary of the Navy for Shipbuilding and Logistics, the Honorable Everett Pyatt:

> In the past, a significant portion of the U.S. shipbuilding and repair industry was supported by U.S. shipowners in the forms of Jones Act construction and construction for the foreign trade which is supported by the Construction Differential Subsidy (CDS). Now, it appears that not all such support is necessary to maintain an adequate shipyard mobilization base.
>
> CDS has not worked and does not appear necessary to sustain the shipbuilding base. Reliance on lower cost foreign-built and reflagged ships allows shipowners to be more competitive in the current world economic environment. This should enable them to maintain fleets which will support strategic sealift requirements.
>
> Labor has made concessions to enable the industry to become more competitive; now it is time to work on the rest of the problem. The Navy shipbuilding program has shown that shipyards can rise to the competitive challenge effectively. This same spirit must infuse management with a new willingness to find creative ways to increase business without increasing the burden on the federal treasury. The industry must meet the challenge of maintaining an adequate and viable mobilization base which offers job opportunities, pride in craft and product, and regains a competitive position in world shipbuilding and repair.
>
> We believe the current industry *can* accommodate the mobilization workloads which derive from government planning estimates. The American merchant marine and the supporting industrial base are truly in transition today. We must decide, now, whether this moment will be seized as an opportunity to meet America's needs for the future or slip from our grasp in a futile return to protectionsim.[31]

The debate will continue. Politicians will make tradeoffs among cost, defense goals, and economics; industrial leaders will fight for survival and a fair chance at profits; labor leaders will defend the quality of their workers' lives; trade representatives will decry foreign nationalism and protectionsim; and Congress will seek a consensus heavily influenced by constituency, interest rates, and the national debt. So far, no persuasive arguments have been advanced for a return to industrial protectionism in the name of national security. A comprehensive maritime policy is slowly emerging, but it is a difficult birth and one for which many participants will have to share parentage. From a national security viewpoint, at least, the nation's shipyards require no advanced life support to remain as healthy as the other maritime industries.

13 Shipyards and Ports

THE MARITIME MOBILIZATION posture of the United States rests on a triad: U.S.-flag ships, U.S. shipyards, and U.S. ports. This chapter considers the "port" leg of the triad, perhaps the least understood one, but nonetheless important. Primarily, the chapter looks at the relationship between shipyards and ports.

Ports and National Security

This book and the author's earlier *U.S. Merchant Marine: In Search of an Enduring Maritime Policy* have placed considerable emphasis on the relationship between the nation's maritime posture and national security. With respect to ships and shipyards, the relationship is easily perceived. However, the port is more abstract, primarily because of its many components—the number of berths, the loading and unloading facilities (e.g., the number of container and heavy lift cranes), the depth of the main and berth channels, ship support facilities including shipyards, navigation systems, shoreside labor and labor relations, state port authorities if the state has a large port investment, port security arrangements, available storage areas, and interfacing land transportation.

At the end of 1983, the Maritime Administration listed 183 deep-draft, U.S. commercial ports, including those of the Great Lakes and in Hawaii, Alaska, Puerto Rico, and the Virgin Islands.[1] A deep-draft port was defined as one having a minimum depth alongside of 25 feet for coastal ports and 18 feet for Great Lakes ports. These 183 ports had 2,871 deep-draft berths—1,396 general cargo, 699 dry and bulk cargo, and 776 liquid bulk facilities.[2]

The Maritime Administration report noted the defense role of seaports:

> National defense contingencies provide for augmentation or projection of U.S. forces overseas. The large volume of resources needed to make initial force deployment, to resupply those forces, and to maintain the

economic means to wage war, can only be accommodated by waterborne transport. At least 95 percent of all essential cargoes must pass through our ports . . . . The port facilities that would support our Armed Forces in time of war or other international military emergency are those developed *by local, non-Federal entities for commercial purposes in peacetime* [italics supplied].[3]

In a 1978 study, the Military Traffic Management Command evaluated 18 major U.S. ports regarding their capacity to support the early deployment of major U.S. Army tactical units.[4] Since that time a number of studies and conferences have dealt with, wholly or in part, the role of ports in a national security context.[5]

In a 1983 Report to Congress, the U.S. General Accounting Office listed 28 U.S. ports that would play a major role in a mobilization. Table 13.1 lists these ports and their emergency functions.

In its 1984 inventory of U.S. shipbuilding and repair yards, the Maritime Administration listed 83 major facilities.[6] Only a dozen were located a significant distance from the "mobilization seaports" shown in Table 13.1.[7] Those ports that have major roles in a mobilization are essentially *the same ports that host the nation's major shipyards.*

Relationship between Shipyards and Ports

As noted above "the port facilities that would support our armed forces in time of war . . . are those developed by local, non-Federal entities for commercial purposes in peacetime." Private shipyards, particularly repair yards, are included among those facilities. Together with other port components, they are an important consideration to the shipping firm when ranking the overall attractiveness of a particular port. (Additional components were listed at the beginning of the chapter.) In the total scheme of things, each positive port attribute makes its others more commercially viable; hence, a shipyard that can offer a wide range of quality repair services adds to port attractiveness, which in turn helps to increase port tonnage. Greater tonnages provide increased employment opportunities for local stevedores and vendors. It is equally true that good waterfront labor relations can influence a shipping company's choice of one port over another. This in turn increases vessel traffic, which increases the number of potential ship repair customers. This mutual support concept holds for all port components.

As a general rule, the features that make a port competitive are provided from nonfederal funds.[8] The major exception has been the dredging and deepening of main channels by the Army Corps of Engineers. Since 1981, however, the Reagan administration has made various proposals to share this cost with port users. As might be expected, port authorities and user groups have fought the concept in Congress.

Table 13.1. Mobilization seaports.

Port	Deployment	Resupply	Prepositioned ammunition permit[a]
Port Arthur, TX[b]			
*Baltimore, MD	X	X	X
*Beaumont, TX	X	X	X
*Boston, MA	X	X	X
*Charleston, SC	X	X	X
Corpus Christi, TX		X	
*Galveston, TX	X	X	X
Gulfport, MS	X	X	
*Houston, TX	X	X	
Port Hueneme, CA	X		
*Jacksonville, FL	X	X	X
Los Angeles, CA	X	X	
Long Beach, CA	X		
*Mobile, AL	X	X	
Morehead City, NC		X	
*New Orleans, LA	X	X	X
*New York, NY incl.			
Port of New Jersey	X	X	X
*Norfolk, VA incl.			
Hampton Roads		X	X
*Oakland, CA incl.			
*San Francisco	X	X	
*Philadelphia, PA		X	X
Portland, OR		X	
San Diego, CA	X	X	
*Savannah, GA	X	X	X
*Seattle, WA		X	
Stockton, CA		X	
*Tacoma, WA	X	X	X
Tampa, FL[b]			
*Wilmington, NC	X	X	X

SOURCE: U.S., General Accounting Office, *Observations Concerning Plans and Programs to Assure the Continuity of Vital Wartime Movements through United States Ports* (Washington, D.C.: U.S. General Accounting Office, 1983), Appendix I.

*Indicates ports included in the 1978 Military Traffic Management Command study on port contingency capabilities.

[a]A Coast Guard prepositioned ammunition permit allows for unit basic loads of ammunition during deployment but does not permit ammunition shipments during supply/resupply operations.

[b]In addition to deployment, resupply, and ammunition shipment functions, all 28 ports have facilities allocated to certain federal agencies that have the responsibility for moving critical commodities.

Although no proposal has received congressional approval, most observers believe some cost-sharing arrangement is inevitable. In this regard, the proposal given the best chance of becoming law includes the following provisions:

- For dredging to a depth of 20 feet, local sponsors would be responsible for 10 percent of the initial cost plus another 10 percent over the next 10 years.
- For projects between 20 and 45 feet deep, local sponsors would pay 25 percent of initial cost and 10 percent at a later time.
- For dredging greater than 45 feet, local sponsores would pay 50 percent of initial cost plus a deferred additional 10 percent.
- An .04 percent ad valorem tax would be placed on all cargo moving through U.S. ports. Proceeds of the fund would be placed in a dedicated trust fund. The administration forecast is that the federal government could recapture one-third of its outlay for operation and maintenance from fund revenues.[9]

Why, however, is there port authority (user) concern over having to pay a share of main channel dredging costs as opposed to funding other port facilities? Two reasons are paramount. First, there is the very high cost of dredging projects. In 1978, for example, the cost of increasing the depth of Baltimore's inner port and approach channel by 8 feet was estimated at $230 million.[10] The mid-1980s figure, of course, would be considerably higher. State and/or local sponsors insist that funds of this magnitude are beyond their means.[11] Moreover, it is estimated that once main channels are deepened, substantial private investment would be required at terminals to accommodate deeper-draft vessels. One study concludes that "up to 80 percent of the capital cost of the deepened channel would fall on the private sector to rehabilitate and structurally strengthen private docks."[12]

Second, ships are getting larger. The trend began with tankers in the 1960s and was extended to the dry bulk and major container trades in the 1980s. However, with larger ships, hence deeper-loaded drafts, U.S. ports suffer a significant economic disadvantage. In this respect, of the some 2,900 berths at American ports, only 11 have berthing depths of 55 or more feet, and these are all on the Pacific Coast (Puget Sound). On the other hand, many, but certainly not all, foreign ports can accommodate large, deep-draft vessels. Japan's port depths, for example, range from 52 to 80 feet. Le Havre, France has 65 feet; Rotterdam 68 feet; and Taranto, Italy 52 feet. Other countries with deep-draft ports in the 55 to 75 foot range are South Africa, Brazil, and Australia.[13] In a four-country comparison (Japan, Australia, France, and the United States), 14 percent of Japan's ports have depths between 55 and 60 feet, as have 7 percent of

Australia's, 6 percent of France's, and only 1 percent in the United States.[14]

One economic disadvantage is that large bulk carriers can only be partially loaded at U.S. ports. A 160,000-dwt-capacity coal carrier, for example, can only load 120,000 tons at Hampton Roads. With respect to grain, 75 percent of the movement from the U.S. Gulf Coast to Europe moves in the more moderate-size ships of 60,000 to 80,000 dwt.[15]

Thus, as the world's bulk carriers, and ships in general, become larger in many trades (as they are expected to do), U.S. ports with deeper channel depths will possess a considerable advantage over their more shallow-depth competitors. So also will shipyards located in deep-draft ports benefit; for the more traffic (tonnage) there is moving through a port, the better are the repair opportunities for a shipyard located at that port.

Port Competition and Ship Repair

As a general rule, competition between U.S. ports, though not especially visible, does exist.[16] Table 13.2 lists some ways, other than with deeper channels, that U.S. ports seek to attract shipping lines and shippers. Table 13.3 lists improvements on line or planned at some major European ports.

It has been maintained that having ship repair facilities in a port is a positive factor with respect to port attractiveness. But is this a case of something that is true in theory only, given the higher costs of repair work in U.S. yards? Not necessarily. The United States is at one end of the world's largest set of trading routes. Even granting higher costs, for many repair jobs it could be cost-effective to have the work done in U.S. yards rather than divert the vessel from her trade to search out low-cost repair facilities. Foreign-flag cruise ships operating from the U.S. east coast are an example.

A recent British report made essentially the same point in a hypothetical case study.[17] The authoritative *Marine Engineering/Log* summarized the case in this way:

> . . . a vessel with an insured value of $5 million . . . sustained severe bottom damage in an area with no suitable drydocking facilities. Tenders for repair ranged from $4.8 million from East Coast North America through $2.1 million from Northern Europe to $1.8 million from the Far East. Adding in towage, insurance, return voyage and superintendence fees, however, the total costs from the Far East emerged as $3.4 million and from northern Europe as $2.8 million. This suggests that even in an "open market" type of repair bid, trading route and area will remain, along with costs, a major determinant in considering tenders.[18]

Table 13.2. Recent investments to increase ports' competitive positions.

Port	Recently completed or underway investments
Boston, MA	New container terminal with two cranes serving 1,000-foot berth; contract to build a new passenger ship terminal.
Port of New York/New Jersey	VTS radar monitoring and radio advice traffic system; new terminal operation at pier 94 North River; major expansion work at Howland Hook Marine Terminal.
Philadelphia, PA, Wilmington, DE	New 150-acre terminal opened in Gloucester, NJ.
Baltimore, MD	New 1,000-foot container berth at Dundalk Marine Terminal.
Hampton Roads, VA	New auto processing facility, three new container cranes on order; dredging container berth at Norfolk to 45 feet; interstate highway linkup to Newport News Terminal.
Wilmington, NC	Added third berth and new container crane; fourth crane and berth on order.
Charleston, SC	Fourth container crane added at North Terminal; 40 acres added to Wando Terminal; North Terminal to be entirely container handling facility in 1986.
Savannah, GA	Regular piggyback service from port to Atlanta; fifth container berth and three new container cranes scheduled for 1986.
Jacksonville, FL	Multipurpose crane added to Talleyrand Docks; third container crane and multipurpose crane at Blount Island Terminal and addition of three 925-foot container berths.
Miami, FL	Two new gantry cranes and 1,000-foot berth; another 1,000-foot berth and two additional gantry cranes; deepening main channel to 42 feet.
Port Everglades, FL	New 900-foot, 44-foot-water-depth multipurpose berth.
Gulfport, MS	Direct intermodal service restored between port and midwest cities; second container crane to be installed.

Table 13.2. (cont.)

Port	Recently completed or underway investments
Mobile, AL	$250 million spent on new facilities.
New Orleans, LA	Two berths opened at Jordan Roads terminal; new midstream anchorage for bulk loading; new cruise liner terminal.
Houston, TX	New shiploader system at port's Bulk Materials Handling Plant; dredging at Bayport to deepen ship channel entrance to 42 feet.
Corpus Christi, TX	Modernization of bulk materials dock.
Los Angeles, CA	New 115-acre container terminal in San Pedro; installation of Automated Cargo Clearance Entry Processing Technique (ACCEPT) of U.S. Customs Service; new auto handling terminal and lumber depot.
San Francisco, CA	New, on-dock intermodal container transfer facility.
Portland, OR	New soda ash bulk loading facility; rehabilitation of Terminal 2.
Seattle, WA	Expansion of Terminal 18 including four new container cranes; construction of new intermodal rail yard; two new cranes at Terminal 5 and rehabilitation of Terminal 91.
Tacoma, WA	New 76-acre container terminal.
Port of Healy, AK	New coal terminal under construction.

Source: "Ports Woo Shipping Lines with Better Facilities and Access," *Marine Engineering/Log*, March 1985, pp. 26–27.

A second consideration that will make a shipyard an increasingly important port asset is the forecast of increasing ocean trade moving through U.S. ports. One estimate is that metric tons moved will increase to 5.22 billion in 1990 from a 1982 figure of 3.72 billion, and to 6.53 billion in 1995 and 7.84 billion in the year 2000.[19] More cargo means more ships, and it follows that with more tonnage it is quite important for a port to have a ship repair capability. Looking at ships instead of cargo, in January 1984, the world's merchant fleet totaled 25,579 vessels of 666,404,000 dwt. This represented a gain of 3,979 vessels of 220,034 dwt since 1973.[20]

Table 13.3. Selected European port investments.

Port	Investment
Felixstowe, England	Increased minimum depth of main approach from 8.9 to 11 meters (29 to 36 feet). Two new container cranes ordered.
Kings Lynn, England	New container berth with 25-ton jib crane.
Falmouth, England	New 80-acre container port planned.
Le Havre, France	Accommodation for bulk vessels up to 250,000 dwt. Two new gantry cranes on order. New storage facilities planned.
Antwerp, Belgium	New 68-ton container crane in operation. New port radar system installed. New lock planned to allow 150,000-dwt vessels access to bulk facilities on Scheldt River.
Rotterdam, Netherlands	Deepening channel for bulk cargo ships to increase drafts from 72 to 73 and 74 feet.
Genoa, Italy	Plans to double container handling capacity by 1987 with addition of seven new container cranes.
Bremen–Bremerhaven, West Germany	Major container terminal expansion, including storage area and new container cranes completed.

SOURCE: "European Ports Launch a Variety of Programs to Attract Shippers," *Journal of Commerce*, 25 September 1984, p. 13A.

At this writing (1986), the international maritime community is still struggling with a worldwide shipping recession, with most tanker and bulk trades overtonnaged. However, if increased U.S. trade projections are reasonably close to the mark, then tonnage entering American ports should increase substantially, with increased opportunities for U.S. ship repair facilities.

Conclusion

U.S. shipyards, particularly those limited to repair work, are heavily dependent on naval budgets for their existence. In fact, many have made substantial investments in anticipation of this business. However, as has been stated time and again, the Navy cannot support the nation's maritime industries. Admiral Thomas J. Hughes, Deputy Chief of Naval Operations (Logistics), recently asserted, "The [maritime] problem is bigger than Navy or even Defense [and] in no way can the Navy solve the overall dilemma of the U.S. maritime industry."[21]

Granted this naval assessment, can anything be done? This chapter proposes that one of the first steps to action is understanding that our maritime posture is made up of mutually dependent entities—ships and seamen, shipyards and shipyard workers, and ports, including all their constituent components. Simply put, our maritime posture is a maritime *system*, and a system is only as strong as its weakest link. From this departure point, the following steps may be taken:

- The federal government must ensure that whatever cost-sharing arrangements are worked out respecting the dredging of our ports, the arrangement does not work to the disadvantage of smaller and medium-size ports. Table 13.1 listed 28 ports with a primary mobilization role. They cannot all be "load centers."[22]
- The federal government must accept unequivocally that the present level of shipyard work (now mostly naval work) will not sustain an adequate shipyard mobilization base over the long term. Chapter 11 addressed the issue of federal support options.
- State and local governments that now aggressively seek shippers and shipping firms as port customers must plan to finance port investment in ways heretofore not considered. One possibility is to offer economic incentives to private investors willing to invest in port facilities such as shipyards, marine terminals, and warehouses. Another is the joint venture, an approach that was extolled at a recent meeting of the American Association of Port Authorities. The opening session was told that port investment will be so vast that "the public purse isn't big enough to handle it." Port managers were advised to develop "a capital acquisition strategy" that would emphasize joint ventures with the private sector.[23] If foreign U.S. trade grows as projected, the return to the taxpayer and the private investor will be substantial in terms of jobs, a larger tax base, and profits.

The most important thing, however, is for the federal government to recognize that in a mobilization the great majority of port assets on which a successful mobilization depends are those assets that are maintained by nonfederal dollars—primarily piers, terminals, warehouses, port security systems, and shipyards—and that keeping them in place depends upon the continued economic viability of the port.

14 Essential Elements of a Shipbuilding Policy

THE SHIPBUILDING and ship repair industry of the United States stands at a crossroads in the mid-1980s. While the nation possesses a not insubstantial shipbuilding and repair capability, its major support is derived almost entirely from the construction of combatant new buildings for the Navy and auxiliaries to be operated by the Military Sealift Command (T-ships), and the naval overhaul and repair program.[1] With the imminent completion of the T-ship programs and the stretching out of the naval overhaul and repair programs, combined with the total absence of a commercial shipbuilding program (not one commercial shipbuilding contract for an oceangoing vessel was placed in 1983), the shipyard capability of the nation will continue to atrophy at an alarming rate. The number of U.S. shipyards capable of building an oceangoing vessel of over 1,000 gross tons (GT) was reduced from 27 in 1982 to 23 in 1985. This dramatic reduction in active yards has had a concomitant effect on the number of active shipyard employees, production and staff alike, and a predictable impact on design and engineering support and the industrial supplier base. Many of these shipyard assets cannot be readily replaced.

Few of the 23 active shipyards are operating at or near optimum capacity; reportedly, some 73 percent of the Navy's 1985 ship construction budget was spent in but three major shipyards.

Although the reduction in shipyard capability is obvious and dramatic, a number of studies conducted by the Navy and the Maritime Adminstration conclude that inventories of these ever-contracting assets are adequate to satisfy the requirements of a major mobilization. Unfortunately, only excerpts of these government studies have been shared with the industry; the full studies and the assumptions upon which they are based have never been officially released, so evaluation of the validity of their conclusions is difficult. Nevertheless, the announced conclusions encourage the suspicion that they are based more on political than military judgments; for in order to avoid sounding the alarm on the inadequacy of the shipyard mobilization base, self-serving studies would project a growth in yard capability and supporting manpower, at the onset of hostilities, at a rate far beyond reasonable expectation.

Analysis of the shipyard mobilization base is particularly troublesome because the adequacy of the base depends on the questionable assumption that any future conflict would require the nation to respond with the resources it had in being. Current general cargo, U.S.-flag vessel assets are of dubious value, since they constitute, in the main, container vessels ill-suited for wartime requirements. Reliance on effective U.S.-controlled ships for wartime sealift is equally unsupportable, for this fleet is essentially composed of large tankers and bulkers of little value for military support.[2] Moreover, these vessels are manned by alien crews whose dependability to respond at a time of mobilization is in grave question. In addition, from a practical point of view, the trading patterns of these vessels are such that they rarely are in U.S. and allied ports.

Thus, resolution of the problem posed by the rapidly shrinking shipyard base is difficult to achieve, since the problem is not universally agreed to exist, much less have efforts been made to quantify it. Nevertheless, the Shipbuilders Council of America, as the generally accepted spokesman for the industry, has consistently argued that it is in the national interest to maintain a U.S. private sector shipbuilding industry capable of building and repairing naval and merchant ships in time of emergency. The joint responsibility of the Departments of Defense and Transportation to implement such a policy has emphasized the dilemma facing the nation—with both agencies unprepared to confront, accept and respond to the issue, usually with the explanation that adequate funding is not available in either of their respective budgets to carry out the policy. Nevertheless, the Shipbuilders Council has called upon the DoD and DoT, in consultation with the U.S. private sector shipbuilding industry, jointly to develop and maintain a national shipyard mobilization plan that would define both the need in time of emergency and the minimum peacetime shipbuilding base required for the construction and repair of oceangoing self-propelled vessels. These agencies would be charged with the identification of those shipyards capable of either building or repairing oceangoing self-propelled vessels, monitoring their resources with a view to their current and long-term potential capability. It has consistently been the industry position that all oceangoing self-propelled vessels owned or employed by any agency of the U.S. government should be built and repaired in U.S. private sector shipyards, and that all U.S.-flag domestic trade vessels and offshore structures owned by private citizens should be built and repaired in U.S. private sector shipyards. To the extent that satisfying these requirements does not provide enough work to maintain the shipyard mobilization base, then the DoD and DoT should jointly cause those numbers of ships to be built and repaired in U.S. private sector shipyards adequate to maintain such a base.

While the U.S. shipbuilding and repair industry has not stood still, it is fair to state that it cannot compete effectively with foreign shipyards because of gross disparities in labor and material costs and productivity. While hundreds of millions of dollars have been invested in modern facilities (in many respects based on foreign technology) and millions of dollars have been spent on computer-assisted manufacturing and design and other technological innovations, the level of overall technological achievement in the United States has not matched the level achieved by Far Eastern yards. There, new shipyards located on greenfield sites have been build over the last decade with little concern for costs. Moreover, the lack of repetitive orders has denied to U.S. yards the efficiency that serial production would provide. In the face of this competitive challenge, American shipyard workers have proved to be increasingly flexible in assisting yard management in striving for cost parity through improved work practices. Labor negotiations in the mid-1980s have generated "take-back" contracts, reducing the base level of wages and benefits; and two-tier agreements, which maintain the level of wages on current employees while reducing by some two to three dollars per hour the rate to be paid to new hires, are increasingly in vogue. But despite the best efforts of labor and management alike to reduce the cost disparity, U.S. yards can do little to respond to the challenge of foreign yards, with their reduced, below-cost, selling values and financing incentives—provided, in many cases, with the assistance of foreign governments desirous of maintaining full employment. Consequently, certain of the programs hereafter enumerated are of increasing importance if the American shipbuilding and repair industry is to survive.

Jones Act

A provision of the Merchant Marine Act of 1920 provided that no merchandise can be transported by water and/or land or water, on penalty of forfeiture of the merchandise, between points in the United States, either directly or via a foreign port, in any vessel other than a vessel built in the United States, documented in accordance with U.S. laws, and owned by U.S. citizens. This legislative codification of cabotage laws has provided over the years a substantial source of employment for American shipyards. A 1985 survey by the Shipbuilders Council of America emphasized the importance of this program, determining that for the ten-year period 1975–84 the aggregate contract value of Jones Act cargo vessels was $4.1 billion, involving 63 new building construction and 23 major conversions. One American yard had over $1 billion worth of work over the decade, and another had some 16 new buildings. However, for the years 1983–85, only five vessels, aggregating less than $300 million, were contracted for—reflecting the depression visited upon the domestic U.S. merchant marine. The outlook for further Jones Act construction is clouded by the Department of Transportation's determination in 1985 that certain vessels previously constructed with a construction differential subsidy would be permitted to refund such subsidy as a condition of entering the domestic trades of the United States. While this governmental action has generated strong opposition from those operators currently in the Jones Act trade and U.S. shipbuilders, the issue has not been resolved.

Nevertheless, support of maintenance of the Jones Act has consistently been declared an administration position; and although critics will continue to seek specific exceptions to its applicability, a certain amount of construction for Jones Act trades will continue to provide limited construction in U.S. shipyards, especially in view of the provisions of the Port and Waterways Safety Act, mandating increased safety measures, that came into full effect on 1 January 1986.

Policy Options

The alternatives available to the nation to support the shipbuilding mobilization base take three forms: subsidies, cargo preference, and direct government procurement.

Subsidy

The keystone of support for American shipbuilding, since passage of the Merchant Marine Act of 1936, had been the construction differential subsidy program, whereby the differential between the cost to the shipowner of construction in U.S. and foreign shipyards, up to a maximum of 50 percent of such vessel cost, was directly funded by the federal government. Under this program, some $3.8 billion in the aggregate of annual appropriations generated the construction and conversion of hundreds of vessels, principally for the liner segment of the foreign commerce of the United States. With the election of President Reagan, this program was terminated in 1981, with immediate and dramatic effect on U.S. shipbuilding orders. Table 14.1 shows orders placed in U.S. yards during 1973–83.

Continuing financing and tax support programs include:

- *Investment tax credits*: These are available for shipowners for funds invested in vessels, in the same manner that investors in new capital equipment are entitled to such credits in other businesses.
- *Capital construction funds*: This program permits deferral of federal taxes on funds deposited in a capital construction fund established by

Table 14.1. Merchant ship orders awarded to U.S. shipyards, 1973–83 (ships 1,000 gross tons and over).

Calendar year	Total number of ships	Gross tonnage
1973	41	1,978,000
1974	15	1,113,300
1975	11	507,900
1976	16	339,400
1977	13	265,500
1978	30	394,000
1979	21	487,200
1980	7	116,200
1981	8	148,000
1982	3	19,900
1983	0	0

SOURCE: United States, Department of the Navy, *Annual Report on the Status of the Shipbuilding and Repair Industry of the United States* (1982). The 1983 information is from the Shipbuilders Council of America.

a shipowner and on funds withdrawn if such funds are employed for the construction or reconstruction of vessels in U.S. shipyards or for the acquisition of U.S.-built ships. Some $2.4 billion was deposited in such funds during the period 1971–81, and some $2 billion was withdrawn from the funds during that period.

• *Ship mortgage guarantees (Title XI)*: Pursuant to Title XI of the Merchant Marine Act of 1936, the government was authorized to guarantee up to 87.5 percent of the purchase price of vessels built in U.S. shipyards. Guarantee limits under this program have been successively raised over the years to a ceiling of $12 billion, but the program is currently receiving close scrutiny due to heavy demands made upon the fund (attributable to the recent high incidence of defaults). The Maritime Administration now can reasonably be expected to administer the program most conservatively because of the dramatic depletion of the guarantee reserves.

Although these programs have been suggested to enhance the attainment of national objectives, they are subject to periodic congressional scrutiny.

Cargo Preference

Cargo preference initiatives designed to grant U.S.-flag shipping exclusive rights to carry a percentage of certain cargoes have been in limited effect for some time. These cargo reservation programs devolve about military support, carriage of U.S.-government-impelled agricultural products, maintenance of strategic petroleum reserves, and other government-supported initiatives. These programs collectively have not generated enough cargo to support either the types of vessels contemplated by the 1936 Act or the nation's shipyard mobilization base. Therefore, over the past decade, a number of efforts have been made to enact legislation that would effectively reserve varying percentages of U.S. bulk cargoes for U.S.-flag ships. While the cost penalty of carriage of such cargoes would not be a charge against the government, the consumer would be compelled to pay for the additional costs for the cargoes carried under these programs. Legislative efforts to achieve these objectives have repeatedly failed, owing to the strong and unyielding opposition of major bulk traders (i.e., the petroleum, mining, and agricultural industries), who have succeeded in defeating these initiatives on the basis that enactment of such legislation would impose a further countercompetitive burden on U.S. foreign trade. While efforts have been made to transfer some or all of the cost burden of cargo preference to the government, in the form of tax credits for shippers who must pay higher freight rates because of preference requirements, general support for this alternative has not been obtained. Another criticism of the legislation is that it can by no means guarantee that vessels that might be constructed to engage in cargo preference trades would be of military utility.

Direct Procurement

A more forthright and uncomplicated solution to the problem is available through direct government procurement and/or operation and/or lease of vessels that would precisely respond in numbers and kinds to satisfy military requirements. This method was employed in accordance with Title VII of the Merchant Marine Act of 1936 to generate the substantial tonnages required by World War II, and, most recently, in the Mariner Program, devised in 1951, which resulted in the construction of 35 vessels in some seven yards over a two-year period.

Despite initial industry resistance, the vessels constructed under the Mariner Program were profitably employed for decades by commercial operators in the trade routes of the United States. Reflecting their versatility, they performed in a highly satisfactory manner as military auxiliaries, with five of the vessels being transferred outright to the Navy for conversion to amphibious warfare ships and test ships for the Polaris Missile Program.

With the current problems confronting the industry paralleling those of the early 1950s, a Mariner II program would be most welcome and timely. The vessel produced would be versatile; for instance, a flexible vehicle carrier capable of carrying wheeled vehicles sized from compact cars to large outsize construction units of up to 100 tons. The vessel would have the capability of carrying containers and palletized cargo, with slewing stern ramps and ramped side doors providing maximum flexibility for loading and unloading. A representative five-ship program for the construction of such vessels might require annual funding of some $400 million to $500 million, but it would provide excellent value in a commercially attractive vessel with military utility. Such a vessel would be significantly more efficient than its predecessors, carrying more than twice the cargo, requiring less than half the crew, and consuming less than half the fuel; and it would provide the base to support two essential shipyards.

The mechanics for vessel acquisition could be through the Maritime Administration, which would procure the vessels by competitive bidding among U.S. shipyards, contracting cost-effectively for their design and construction. On completion, the vessels would be offered for sale or charter, either singly or in groups, to any qualified U.S. owner at prices and rates calculated and/or negotiated competitively in the world market. A potentially attractive commercial market exists in the carriage of automobiles from exporting nations to the United States. With the lifting of quotas on the importation of such automobiles into the U.S. market, the government could negotiate a requirement, as a condition of free access to the lucrative U.S. auto market, that a percentage of these vehicles be transported in U.S.-flag vessels. Not only would such a program have a positive impact on the shipbuilding industry, but benefits would extend beyond the yards to the industrial base. Moreover, the project would generate a welcome addition to the sealift capabilities that are vital to national security; for in the event of mobilization, five such vessels would be capable of moving at least 15,000 men with supporting equipment, and they could easily be converted to serve as full or partial troop ships or hospital ships. Annual review of such a program would be desirable to ensure the maintenance of the essential shipyard mobilization base and military sealift requirements.

Maritime Development Bank Charter Act of 1985

In order to "stimulate innovation, increase productivity and improve the competitiveness of the maritime industry in the U.S.," legislation has been introduced to establish a privately capitalized government-sponsored organization, to be known as the Maritime Redevelopment Bank of the United States, structured with mixed private and governmental owners. The bank would be initially capitalized from funds provided from the Capital Construction Fund, the Federal Ship Financing Fund, the Ship Trade-in Program, the sale of obsolete vessels from the National Defense Reserve Fleet, and monies received by repayment of loans extended by the bank. The primary purpose of the bank's creation would be to finance construction, reconstruction, and reconversion of commercial vessels. Another initiative of the legislation would be to establish a privately financed, government-sponsored corporation known as the National Shipbuilding and Development Corporation. This enterprise would conduct research regarding the development of manufacturing technologies applicable to the products of domestic shipyard and component manufacturers. Under its roof would be joined many of the fragmented research and development efforts conducted by the maritime industry and the government. While the intent of the legislation is laudable indeed, it has not been received with enthusiasm by either maritime labor or management because the legislation would fail to address the gross disparity between domestic and foreign costs of construction and financing, and it would do little to generate the cargo without which ships would not be built in any event.

Military Sealift Enhancement

To increase the size of the U.S.-flag sealift fleet, the Department of Defense has instituted a number of programs designed to enhance the sealift capability necessary to support the extension of military forces abroad. The Military Sealift Command in concert with the Maritime Administration is engaged in an ambitious program to replace the war-built tonnage in the National Defense Reserve Fleet with more modern and efficient vessels. Not only are these vessels obtained by trade-in by U.S.-flag operators, but the worldwide shipping depression has served to make a number of highly fuel-efficient and versatile foreign-flag vessels available as well. Moreover, an aggressive program is in place designed to modify some 40 container ships in the U.S.-flag commercial fleet to enable them to carry large and heavy military cargo. The use of specially designed pallets (flat racks) and open-topped oversized containers (sea sheds) enables container vessels to increase their ability to satisfy military requirements. Sealift enhancement features are designed to improve the ability of these vessels to communicate, refuel, and off-load in hostile environments. Moreover, the Navy has announced a program designed to encourage the incorporation of "military sealift enhancement features" into newly built tonnage which would provide improved military usefulness for these commercial vessels.

It is anticipated that these programs will be broadened to narrow the gap currently existing in the military support capability of the U.S. merchant fleet.

Conclusion

In the face of the worldwide malaise in shipping, in an environment that finds foreign government support aggravating an already pronounced cost disparity, there can be little economic justification for the construction of oceangoing vessels in American shipyards. Nevertheless—despite a lack of unity within the U.S. government on the issue—Secretary of Defense Caspar Weinberger clearly stated the problem when he wrote:

> The Navy's current and planned shipbuilding and repair programs are, by themselves, insufficient to support the Nation's present shipyards at an efficient level of production. Moreover, a further decline in the number of shipyards would reduce the competitive base for these essential Navy programs. Clearly what is needed is a revitalization of the commercial segment of the maritime industry.[3]

All elements of the American maritime community agree that revitalization of the commercial segment of the maritime industry depends on development of a long-overdue comprehensive cargo policy for the United States. But development of such a policy requires coming to grips with a number of very complex economic and political issues, making prompt attainment of such a policy realistically beyond short-term accomplishment. While the numerous initiatives directed to grappling with this problem should be encouraged, a more realistic short-term response to the problem would appear to lie with direct governmentally initiated construction and conversion programs. While providing no panacea to the underlying ills of the shipbuilding industry, direct procurement would buy time while the answers to the more fundamental issues were being sought.

Satisfying Department of Defense requirements or Jones Act construction will not provide a sufficient volume of new building orders to maintain the shipbuilding mobilization base in the United States. Without direct government support or enactment of a cargo preference program that would generate cargoes for commercial vessels, the American shipbuilding industry can anticipate continued downsizing. However, nothing in the declared position of the Reagan administration indicates that there is any basis for optimism that these trends will be reversed in the near term.

15 Maintaining a U.S. Shipyard Industry

> If a man does away with his traditional way of living and throws away his good customs, he had better first make certain he has something of value to replace them.
>
> —Basuto proverb*

Defining the Shipyard Mission

At first glance, a discussion of "Defining the Shipyard Mission" seems redundant. The mission (purpose) of shipyards as part of the country's national security posture has been cited and expanded upon on numerous occasions in different chapters of this book. However, asserting in general terms that U.S. shipyards have a mobilization mission is one thing; precisely defining that mission over a wide range of scenarios, assigning specific tasks to shipyard resources that may or may not be in place at some future time, is quite another. The difficulty of precisely defining and tasking the mission of U.S. shipyards in a national emergency is the basic reason why reasonable and informed persons disagree on the required size and composition of a shipyard mobilization base and the question of how best to manage and maintain it.

Some of these disagreements have been pinpointed and discussed in this book, and a brief review of the more important areas of agreement and disagreement is a worthwhile exercise before steps are recommended to ensure that a U.S. shipyard industry remains in place down the road.

Disagreements

Unlike ships, which are movable assets, shipyards have fixed locations. Thus, while a British or West German RO-RO may meet a mobilization requirement in a NATO conflict as well as an American-flag vessel, a shipyard in Bremerhaven is a tenuous and limited substitute for a ship-

*Quoted in *Something of Value* by Robert Ruark (Garden City, N.J.: Doubleday, 1955).

yard in New Orleans. The fact that a shipyard has a place utility, that is, its value depends largely upon its geographic location, mandates that the United States possess a shipyard mobilization base of some specified size and composition. But from this point, disagreements become the rule rather than the exception, including disagreements about the size of the base (number of shipyards), capabilities of the yards within the base (number of building ways and degree of technological sophistication), and location (east coast, west coast, Gulf). Moreover, disagreements about the mission of shipyards change over time. A U.S. General Accounting Office (GAO) analysis of a 1975 Department of Defense–Maritime Administration study, "Adequacy of the U.S. Shipbuilding Industry as a Mobilization Base," is a case in point.[1] Interestingly, a fair amount of the report dealt with the question of rebuilding shipping capacities *after* a conflict has ended, particularly how much and how fast. In the mid-1980s, postwar maritime recovery is almost a nonissue. In any event, the then–assistant secretary of commerce for maritime affairs concluded that the 1975 base was adequate, in effect repudiating an

Ingalls' shipyard in full production. A total of 23 naval ships are shown in various stages of production. (Courtesy Shipbuilders Council of America and Ingalls Shipbuilding Corporation)

earlier Maritime Administration assessment that the base was but one-third the necessary size.

More recently, the Shipyard Mobilization Base (SYMBA) study identified a 1982 base of 110 yards. However, before SYMBA was published, 16 of the shipyards in the base closed because of lack of work. This loss in base numbers necessitated a follow-on study, the National Defense Shipyard (NADES) study, using *different* assumptions. The 1985 NADES base was made up of 66 shipyards including the nine publicly owned naval and Coast Guard shipyards. The adequacy of this figure was endorsed by Everett Pyatt, Assistant Secretary of the Navy (Shipbuilding and Logistics), in March of 1985 when he stated that "through 1990, the national security interests do not require substantial government intervention in or support for the [present] shipyard mobilization base."[2] But even before the NADES study was officially released, General Dynamics announced it planned to close its Quincy, Massachusetts shipyard with a loss to the industry of approximately 4,000 employees; and in late 1985 it was announced that the Boston Shipyard would close in 1986.

Captain Ralph V. Buck, USN, currently serving as deputy for systems in the Office of the Assistant Secretary of the Navy (Shipbuilding and Logistics) and the author of Chapter 12 of this book, probably comes as close to the mark as is possible when he notes that "there is no uniformly accepted definition of what the term [mobilization base] means."[3]

Agreements

While there is disagreement over what the size and composition of the shipyard mobilization base should be, many facts are self-evident, and there is general agreement on others.

Foremost, perhaps, is that the United States is a high-cost producer of commercial ships and ship repairs. Many types of ships can be built in foreign yards for 40 to 50 percent of the U.S. cost (in 1986), while ship repairs are, on average, 30 percent higher. And while it is true that much of this higher cost is attributable to higher American wages, it is also true that U.S. maritime (and most other) American wages have been higher than their foreign counterparts since the founding of the republic. High U.S. wages and living standards are not a new phenomenon, and it adds little to an understanding of our shipyards and their current problems to imply that relatively high shipyard wages somehow came about in the post–World War II period and are solely attributable to carelessly managed government support programs and/or incompetent shipyard management. Rather, the issue that must be focused upon in the remaining years of this century is that of how to make shipyard labor more productive—in economic terms, how to increase the value of shipyard labor's marginal product.

Moreover, over 80 percent of shipyard revenues come from Department of Defense budgets (1986 figures), primarily from naval (including Military Sealift Command programs) building and repair funds. The remainder comes from some foreign ship repair revenues and building/repairing U.S.-flag ships enrolled in the protected domestic ocean trades. However, naval building and repair budgets are expected to decrease over the next 10 years. Thus, while the Navy will continue in percent terms to be the major source of shipyard revenues, the dollar amounts will be smaller. The Basuto proverb quoted above then becomes quite meaningful—what of value *will* replace this source of funds?

Finally, it is generally agreed that in a completely competitive world and a world without war or the threat of war, the United States would not be a producer of commercial ships and would, at best, have only a moderate repair capability. However, the world shipbuilding and repair marketplace is light-years away from any competitive norm. Government intervention through subsidies, direct and indirect, and various preference and exclusionary laws, is the rule rather than the exception. And however fervently we might wish otherwise, we live in a high-risk world where the threat of conflict is always present. The question then is not whether we need a shipyard mobilization base, but how we can maintain one over the long term, at the same time realizing that it is better to err on the high side rather than the low.

Essentially Nonbudgetary Considerations

Before examining the more complex problem of how the federal government might (most efficiently) sustain a shipyard mobilization base by use of public monies and its inherent sovereign powers, some considerations that do not directly impact on the federal budget must be thought through and dealt with.

1. The number and capability of shipyards that constitute an adequate mobilization base must be specified. In this respect, it is not acceptable, and is essentially dishonest, to change the assumptions about what is required of a shipyard mobilization base in order to rationalize changes taking place within the industry. For example, if there are 100 shipyards in the base in 19XX and mobilization plans are formulated around this number, then reasonable persons can only be suspicious if three years later it is asserted that 70 yards are, in fact, adequate.

Naval construction work is now concentrated in relatively few yards. The same is becoming true with respect to complex repair and overhaul contracts. Only two private shipyards, Newport News and Electric Boat, are certified to work with nuclear reactors. In large measure this concentration has occurred because some yards have been willing to invest in the technology necessary to do complex work. If such investment leads to a concentration of naval contracts in a relatively few yards, then govern-ment should maintain a nominal hands-off policy but at the same time recognize that there are *geographic* constraints on such concentrations.

2. The shipyard mobilization base must have some minimum geo-graphic dispersion. In other words, a high concentration of shipyards on a particular coast would entail unacceptable risks in an emergency. Since, as has been argued from the beginning of this book, shipyards are national defense assets, it is a proper role of government to ensure that each of our coasts, east, west, and Gulf, has some minimum capability irrespective of other considerations.

In 1985 the role that west coast yards would play in a national emer-gency became an issue when the Navy decided against any requirement that would mandate a share of new construction on the west coast. The issue was later exacerbated when the decision was made to overhaul Pacific fleet aircraft carriers on the east coast. J. T. Gilbride, president of the Todd Shipyard Corporation, argues the case for private west coast shipyards in Appendix C.

3. A definitive answer to the recurring question of how naval overhaul and repair work will be apportioned between naval and private sector shipyards is long overdue. An even more fundamental question is whether naval shipyards should be sold or contracted out to private sector management. The issue is not unique to the United States. In July 1985 the British government made the decision to contract out the manage-ment of the Royal Dockyards at Devonport and Rosyth. A part of the official relevant communication reads:

> Under this arrangement, separate substantial private sector companies, selected by competition to meet the Navy's requirements, will run each dockyard at Devonport and Rosyth initially for a fixed term, probably 5–7 years, being subject to competition for renewal if deemed appropriate; the circumstances under which a further competition would be necessary have not yet been defined. The dockyard assets of land, buildings and machinery will remain in government ownership and will be used by the contractor to carry out a substantial portion of the refit task. The balance will be open to competition between the dockyard and the rest of the commercial ship repair industry. The dockyards will be free to take on non-naval work provided the Navy's needs are met. The management and workforce of the two dockyards will cease to be civil servants and will transfer to new dockyard companies taken over by the successful contractors. Should the contractor change, these new dockyard companies will remain in being to ensure continuity of employment and expertise, but their ownership will transfer to the incoming contractor.[4]

4. In 1985 the Department of Defense decided against allowing private shipyards to build diesel electric submarines for the navies of

friendly powers. The argument cited was the possibility of compromising U.S. submarine technology. The question still to be answered is, in what respect does nonnuclear submarine technology differ so markedly from the technology of first line military aircraft? In the latter case, the United States aggressively pursues foreign sales. The eight-page report arguing against submarine sales was an in-house Department of Defense study. At a minimum, the assumptions and conclusions of the report should be evaluated by the U.S. General Accounting Office. Not only should GAO look at the submarine technology issue; it should also recommend clear and unambiguous guidelines with respect to a full range of possible naval ship and ship system foreign sales.

5. The fact that a trade-off exists between the types of ships shipyards build for the Navy or merchant marine and the cost of maintaining a shipyard mobilization base in place must be, at least implicitly, recognized. The issue is not new. It essentially turns on the question of whether merchant ships, fitted out with national defense features, can adequately perform many naval underway replenishment tasks. It has never been disputed that merchant ships are cheaper to build than naval vessels; the issue is whether they can perform the task. If, for example, two merchant ships can be had for the price of one naval auxiliary, then two possibilities arise. The obvious is that two orders instead of one can be placed in shipyards that are not capable of building technologically complex combatants, but are nonetheless an important part of the mobilization base. On the other hand, if only one ship is ordered, the savings would approximately equal the construction subsidy needed to build a conventional merchant ship in an American yard.

The question of using merchant ships fitted out with national defense features has been debated ever since an off-the-shelf merchant tanker, modified with defense features costing $30,000, was successfully used to underway-replenish fleet combatants in 1972. Following the test, in April 1973, a joint Navy–Maritime Administration Design Team was established to recommend national defense features for merchant ships that would make them militarily useful in wartime. However, there was little enthusiasm for its mission in the Navy, and the team was eventually dissolved.

A 1973 cost comparison of a merchant T6-S-93a hull modified for naval underway replenishment use and a naval AO-75 tanker, showed the merchant ship cost to be $36.5 million in a series of five builds versus an AO-75 cost of $51 million in a series of 10 builds. The naval tanker had a capacity of 120,00 barrels, a speed of 20 knots, an endurance of 6,000 miles, and a shaft horsepower of 24,000. The merchant tanker had a capacity of 266,500 barrels, a speed of 19.5 knots, an endurance of 7,000 miles, and a shaft horsepower of 36,000.[5]

In 1977 the question was again raised of why standard design merchant tankers and fleet tugs could not be adapted for naval use. The issue was extensively debated in the House of Representatives, but with predictable results.[6] The Navy remained adamantly opposed to the concept.

The last time the question arose—of what does the Navy build and at what cost, and how does it impact on the shipyard mobilization base—was in 1983, in the form of a proposal to build four smaller, oil-fired, aircraft carriers for the price of one *Nimitz*-class nuclear carrier.[7] The suggestion was put forward by J. J. Henry, a respected naval architect with a long record of design achievements.[8] The Henry proposal had the twin aims of increasing the Navy's capability to project power and providing additional work for hard-pressed U.S. shipyards. The possibility of export sales was also noted. Nothing came of the proposal.

6. It is essential to recognize the role legislation (or lack of it) plays in the fortunes of American shipyards. In Chapter 3, it was noted that the British Acts of Navigation and the way that a ship was taxed inhibited innovative vessel designs. The result was that British-built ships remained expensive and noncompetitive in world trade for almost half a century. Currently, several areas beg U.S. legislative initiatives.

First, Congress or one of its internal support agencies (Congressional Budget Office or Office of Technology Assessment) must examine the feasibility of renewing a U.S. commitment to nuclear-powered merchant ships. In the mid-1980s, nuclear power in its various forms does not enjoy wide public support; but it is the role of Congress to lead, not to follow public opinion. In this respect, it is interesting to note that the Soviet Union plans a fleet of nuclear-powered barge carriers. The first of the class, the 26,400-ton *Sevmorput*, was scheduled to enter Pacific service in 1986.[9]

Another area where a regulatory thicket must be cleared is the extent to which foreign components can be utilized in American-built vessels. The position of the Maritime Administration in 1985 was that if the hull and housing were built in a U.S. yard, other vessel components, including the main power plant, could be of foreign manufacture. To a certain extent this was a discretionary Maritime Administration decision.[10] Not only should Congress give the option a firm legislative imprint, but it should also make exercising the option by American shipyards as easy as possible.

In 1983, Andrew Gibson, then president of Delta Steamship Lines and a former maritime administrator, noted the addition to vessel cost of complying with American construction and safety standards, that is, meeting the requirements for U.S. registry.[11] While this is properly more of a concern to the shipowner, it also impacts to a certain degree on American shipyard competitiveness. For example, meeting a specific

American registry requirement in a U.S. shipyard might add $1 million to a vessel's cost; meeting the same requirement might add only $300,000 if the vessel were built in a foreign yard. While the cost of the vessel has increased in both cases, if a construction subsidy program is in place, the additional cost of the U.S. registry requirement increases the cost to the taxpayer of supporting a shipyard mobilization base by means of a construction subsidy program. The perceived high cost of the CDS program inaugurated in 1936 was the major rationalization for canceling it in 1981. If an effort is to be made to decrease the gap between U.S. and foreign building costs, then a review of U.S. registry standards and the added vessel cost that they impose is worthy of the attention of Congress.

Finally, Congress should determine whether any impediments exist to foreign investment in American shipyards, particularly repair yards. It was pointed out in Chapter 13 that by being at one end of the world's largest set of trading routes, the United States will always have a potential market for its repair facilities. If it means building new facilities from the ground up, as in the case of Japanese-owned, U.S.-located automobile plants, Congress should recognize such foreign investment as highly desirable and in the national security interest. Moreover, positive encouragement of such investments would not be out of order.

7. Chapter 5 strongly suggested that a comprehensive review of Section 27 of the Merchant Marine Act of 1920 (Jones Act) is past due. Current odds are long that very much of the present domestic trade tanker fleet will be renewed, particularly those vessels engaged in Gulf–Atlantic coast petroleum shipments. However, some modifications to the Jones Act could improve not only our shipbuilding posture but our shipping capabilities as well. One is to allow U.S.-owned, foreign-flag ships into the nation's domestic contiguous trades in exchange for investing in U.S.-flag, foreign-trade tanker and bulk tonnage. This possibility will be discussed in a later section of the chapter.

8. Since 1981, bills have been introduced in Congress to require users to pay a share of the cost of port improvements, costs once exclusively borne by the federal government. While the intent of the legislation cannot be faulted, it is important to recognize that ports, like shipyards, have a place utility. In terms of national security, the extent to which one port can be substituted for another is limited. In other words, a geographic dispersion of economically viable ports is an important defense consideration. Thus, whatever cost-sharing arrangement becomes law, it must not have the effect of concentrating foreign trade tonnage at a few large ports while a larger number of smaller ports lose their national defense value because of a lack of investment in port facilities (e.g., shipyards).

Reducing U.S. Shipbuilding Costs Has Limits

Historically, U.S. wages including maritime wages have tracked higher than their foreign counterparts. In the country's early history, as noted in Chapters 2 and 3, American shipbuilders and operators were able to overcome the wage disadvantage through building and operating innovations—design innovations coupled with cheap raw materials in the first case and smaller crews in the latter.

Following World War II the differential between American and foreign building costs increased faster than cost differentials between most other American and foreign products. Quite correctly, much of this increase was due to the sedative effect of operating and construction differential subsidies. The point to understand, however, is that some, *but not all*, of the large maritime wage increases and additions to building costs attributable to management inefficiencies, were due to government support programs. If this proposition is accepted, it can be agreed that while U.S. shipbuilding/repair costs must be substantially reduced as a condition for continued government support of the industry, there is no chance that American building costs will ever approximate those in most foreign yards. There are several reasons for this.

1. A relatively high and accepted American standard of living sets a floor on shipbuilding wages. It might be noted in this respect that the officially recognized poverty level for a family of four in the United States is an annual income of anything less than $10,128 (1985). This would represent an extremely high family income in many major shipbuilding countries.

2. There are relatively few international patents on shipbuilding technology. Many of the publicized shipbuilding concepts used in foreign yards originated in the United States. In this regard, much is made of the techniques of prefabrication and building in series without remembering that these techniques were the hallmark of American ship production in World War II. With respect to technologies such as computer aided design (CAD) and computer aided manufacturing (CAM), use of robotics, preassembly, and modular construction, the best the United States can do is keep pace. However, just by keeping pace American shipbuilding costs *can be* reduced.

3. Shipyard workers in the United States are highly unionized. Collective bargaining as an adversary proceeding is the rule rather than the exception. This has been so almost since the beginning of the union movement. It is considerably different from the more paternalistic approach used in many Far Eastern shipbuilding countries. Nonetheless, there are opportunities to reduce labor costs. Among those cited in Chapter 8 were revamping union work rules to improve productivity,

obtaining labor's support for the introduction of automated production techniques, moderating wage increases, and implementing two-tier wage scales for new hires.

4. It must be understood that commercial shipbuilding/repair earnings are a large part of the gross national products of many foreign shipbuilding nations, while the contribution of commercial shipwork to the U.S. GNP is negligible. This fact alone ensures that these foreign governments will continue to subsidize, directly and indirectly, and to the extent necessary, their shipbuilding industries. Chengi Kuo, Professor of Ship and Marine Technology at the University of Strathclyde in Scotland, believes that Japan, for example, is prepared to use its huge surplus trade balances to subsidize its shipbuilding industry indefinitely. He argues that the Japanese will match ship price cuts anywhere in the world, including South Korea, to maintain their market share. As Professor Kuo sees it, the first problem vis-à-vis Japan as a shipbuilding competitor, is to correct its trade imbalance with the rest of the world.[12]

Making Up the Difference

In the previous sections it was suggested that even if American shipyards were to (a) employ the most advanced shipyard technology, (b) follow the most advanced management techinques, and (c) utilize foreign-built components to the fullest, and if shipyard labor were (a) to streamline work rules and (b) tailor wage demands to reflect the economic condition of the industry, a significant price differential would still remain between U.S.- and foreign-built commercial ships.

But if, as argued throughout this book, a shipyard mobilization base is essential to the national security of the United States, a government support program for the industry must be put into place.

In fashioning a support program, the beginning of wisdom is to recognize that maintaining a shipyard mobilization base is going to cost the taxpayer. For, as economists are prone to point out, "There is no such thing as a free lunch." There are, however, guidelines to which any program should adhere. One is that since maintaining a shipyard capability is properly a national defense expenditure, its cost should be spread among the beneficiaries (the general public) as evenly as possible. Another is that it should not be disruptive in terms of foreign relations, particularly with respect to the nation's allies. A third is that it should be supportive of the country's maritime posture. Fourth, it should impose the least possible cost on the taxpayer, given the stated objectives of the program. Finally, the program should address the long as well as the near term, that is, look to the time when naval work will play a lesser role in supporting an adequate mobilization base.

Chapter 11 notes and reviews a number of ways in which the federal government could support shipyards. Appendix A lists the major studies published over the past four years, several of which analyze possible support options.

The program favored here was discussed in Chapter 5. Essentially, it has two parts. The first part is a reinstitution of a construction differential subsidy program directed toward building and maintaining a moderate-size U.S.-flag, U.S.-built, foreign trade bulk and tanker fleet, a fleet that is all but nonexistent in the mid 1980s.[13] Two incentives would drive such an investment. First, construction subsidies would equalize foreign and U.S. vessel costs with respect to the shipowner's investment. Second, the Jones Act would be amended to allow U.S.-owned, foreign-built, foreign-flag shipping into the nation's domestic contiguous (but not noncontiguous) trades, *provided* the operator agreed to build in the United States and operate under the American flag, a bulk or tank vessel in an American foreign trade. The vessel would be built under the CDS program, and the exchange would be on a one-for-one basis.* Long-term commitments to replace such vessels would be a part of the package. National defense features, as recommended by the Navy, would be a Department of Defense expenditure. However, should foreign-flag, foreign-built tonnage prove noncompetitive with U.S. land systems, then acquiring a U.S.-flag, U.S.-built, foreign trade bulk and tanker fleet would be entirely dependent upon implementing the second part of the program.**

The second part of the program would be to encourage investment in U.S.-built, U.S.-flag, foreign trade bulk/tanker shipping by negotiating bilateral cargo-sharing agreements with the country's bulk and petroleum trading partners.

---

*One major detail that cannot be overlooked in any swap of a U.S.-flag, domestic, contiguous trade fleet for a U.S.-flag, foreign-trade tanker and bulk fleet is how to compensate the owners of relatively new domestic trade tonnage built in higher-priced U.S. yards as per Jones Act requirements, since this tonnage could in no way compete with lower-priced foreign-built vessels. Some possibilities to level the playing field include accelerated depreciation schedules or outright sale of such vessels to the government for inclusion in the National Defense Reserve Fleet or the Military Sealift Command active fleet. In any case, the number of relatively new ships in the domestic, contiguous trades is not large. The main consideration is to ensure that equity is done.

**In a 1984 address before the American Petroleum Institute Tanker Conference (3–6 June 1984 at Boca Raton, Florida) Frank J. Iarossi, president of Exxon Shipping Company, noted the decline of the domestic tanker business. He stated that "In 1971, domestic crude production along the Gulf Coast began to decline, and with it the demand for U.S. tankers to move Gulf coast crude to East coast refineries. Today this trade, once over 25 percent of our tanker movements, has essentially disappeared. The second component of the Gulf to East coast tanker business began a rapid decline in the late 70s as the overall demand for petroleum products decreased while product pipelines continued to expand . . . . The tanker demand prompted by the need to move petroleum cargoes from the Gulf to East coast is only one-third of what it was 20 years ago."

While bilateral agreements have been criticized on the ground that the higher costs of a U.S.-flag operator are passed on to the foreign and domestic consumer, whether bilaterals, in fact, would increase shipping rates above some "competitive norm" is debatable, given that some U.S.-flag liner companies successfully compete in foreign trade without an operating subsidy and presumably without passing higher American operating costs on to the consumer. Moreover, with ever smaller crew sizes almost routinely accepted by seagoing unions, crew wages as a percent of vessel operating costs are decreasing, lending weight to the argument that American-flag firms can compete once a ship is in hand.

But even granting that consumer prices might be higher, the national security consideration is still overriding. In this respect, one of the great economists of the twentieth century, the late G. Warren Nutter of the University of Virginia, noted that in some instances intervention by government in trading arrangements is not only acceptable but necessary. He wrote in this regard:

> The classic case for free trade derives from a time in which the totalitarian state had not entered the scene and commerce was therefore overwhelmingly in private hands, regardless of the forms of government under which trading partners lived. Almost all economists, myself included, find it painful to admit that there are legitimate political arguments for controlling foreign trade, primarily because time-worn arguments based on spurious economic reasoning quickly masquerade as the newly justified political ones. But we cannot escape the fact that the spread of state trading, particularly as practiced by totalitarian states, makes it necessary for us to qualify the normal case for free trade.
>
> More fundamentally, the state has as much right to employ trade policy as an instrument of national power as it has to employ anything else. Trade policy deserves no special immunity as long as it is a legitimate and effective means for achieving a legitimate end.[14]

Aside from the philosophical debate over government intervention, bilateral agreements have two other advantages. As noted in an earlier chapter, they are the least disruptive in terms of foreign relations. But, more important, they spread any additional cost of maintaining a maritime posture as equitably as possible over the beneficiaries. The Center for Naval Analyses study discussed in Chapter 11 estimated that the annual cost to support a bulk fleet of some 300 vessels carrying 20 percent of the nation's bulk cargoes would be between $1 billion and $2 billion without operating and construction differential subsidies.[15] If the data are adjusted linearly for a fleet of 150 bulk/tank vessels carrying 10 percent of the country's bulk imports and exports, then a range of $500 million to $1 billion is a reasonable cost estimate for a bilateral trade program. Spread over the U.S. population as a whole, its cost is about $4 for every man, woman, and child, considerably less than that imposed by the present sugar quotas. (Appendix I calculates the present cost to U.S. consumers of sugar quotas.) Note, however, that the CNA estimates assumed no CDS payments. With CDS payments limited to 35 percent, the total program cost, including possibly higher consumer prices and CDS payments, should be around $750 million annually. And while the exercise is not performed here, this figure should be further reduced by reduced shipping rates in the domestic contiguous trades and the tax return to government occasioned by more fully employed maritime resources.

Conclusion and a Recommendation

The government-owned merchant marine (Military Sealift Command and RRF ships in the National Defense Reserve Fleet) is increasing, while the number of privately owned ships is declining. Public shipyards perform the lion's share of naval overhaul and repair work, while only two private shipyards are certified to work on nuclear reactors, in contrast to six public shipyards that have this capability. Whether intentionally or not, the United States is moving inexorably toward a nationalized maritime industry.

At the end of World War I the country was faced with a similar situation. The federal government was, by far, the nation's largest shipowner and shipbuilder. Senator William H. King of Utah engaged in the debate on what to do with these essentially private sector assets, in words as relevant today as in 1920:

> . . . the Government cannot operate more economically and efficiently ships and railroads than it can operate its own business. There is not a businessman in the United States of any acumen who could not take possession of the governmental agencies and instrumentalities functioning in Washington and elsewhere and conduct the Government business in a more efficient manner than it is being conducted by the Government of the United States at a cost of 33 percent of that now paid by the United States.[16]

In 1981 the Maritime Administration was transferred from the Department of Commerce to the Department of Transportation. Whether this move could be considered a proximate cause of the rapid decline of U.S. shipping and shipbuilding over the past six years is open to debate. What can be stated is that the move in no way improved the fortunes of the maritime industries. Maritime decisions have been formulated at the White House and transmitted to the Maritime Administration for execution with the admonition to make the decisions as palatable as possible in terms of public opinion. Nor has industry input fared any better. The Reagan administration–initiated Maritime Advisory Committee, set up in 1981 to consult and advise on maritime policy, was disbanded in 1985.[17]

The conclusion of a 1985 draft report published by the Center for Strategic and International Studies is hardly encouraging. It states:

> Given current administration policy, by 1989, domestic shipping and ship-building industries could decline by as much as a third or more from today's levels. The U.S. flag fleet is likely to decrease from the current 401 active oceangoing vessels (as of 2/1/85) to less than 350. . . .
>
> The Active Shipbuilding Industrial Base, consisting of 24 major and about 85 smaller private yards, could decline to 17–20 major yards and perhaps to 50 smaller ones.[18]

If the above conclusion is anywhere near the mark, more than sufficient reason exists to create an independent Maritime Administration, and one insulated to the greatest extent possible from political considerations and purely political appointees. Should Congress in its wisdom will such a change, the responsibilities of such a commission should be limited to overseeing the economic well-being of our merchant marine, shipyards, and ocean ports. These are the three vital private sector components of our maritime defense posture. Other Maritime Administration responsibilities could remain in the Department of Transportation or be abolished. Ideally, the new commission would be lean, mean, and single-purposed—such purpose being to ensure that our maritime assets are fully capable of meeting mobilization requirements.

Epilogue

WHEN THE ORIGINAL draft of the manuscript for this book was completed and submitted to the publisher in December 1985, it was recognized that a number of relevant legislative proposals would subsequently be debated in the second session of the Ninety-Ninth Congress, in addition to discussions held within the executive branch and Congress on several earlier maritime initiatives. Where possible, data and information that became available after December 1985 were directly incorporated into the text during proof stages. In some cases, however, new material did not lend itself to this technique, either because the material was too voluminous, or there was no appropriate section of the text to which it could be added. In general, material in this epilogue became available in December 1985 or during the first two months of 1986.

The Shipyard Mobilization Base

In 1982, there were 110 private shipyards and 9 public yards (8 naval and 1 Coast Guard) in what the Shipyard Mobilization Base (SYMBA) Study (Chapter 12) identified as the potential U.S. shipyard mobilization base. Twenty-seven of these shipyards comprised the active shipbuilding industrial base (ASIB) in 1982. The ASIB yards, as defined by the Maritime Administration, are the benchmark of U.S. shipbuilding capability.

At the beginning of 1985 the potential shipyard mobilization base had decreased to 93 private and 9 public yards (Appendix H). Twenty-three yards were included in the ASIB. Nine months later (October 1985) the potential base was down to 88 private yards and 9 public yards. This downward trend in numbers continued when, in late 1985 and early 1986, three major yards and one smaller yard announced they were closing. One of the major yards, the General Dynamics facility in Quincy, Massachusetts, was in the ASIB. Two others, Todd Shipyard in New Orleans and the Boston (Massachusetts) Shipyard, while not in the ASIB, had the capability of building/drydocking a ship of at least 400 feet in length. The smaller yard was Jeffboat, Inc. of Jefferson, Indiana. At the time of the

SYMBA study it was one of the largest builders of barges and towboats in the United States.

The question for the 1980s and beyond is the same question addressed by the SYMBA study in 1982: how many shipyards, with what capabilities, are enough?

The National Defense Shipyard (NADES) Study (see comments under SYMBA study, Appendix A), which was a follow-on to the earlier SYMBA analysis, hypothesized the worst-case scenario with respect to the number of shipyards that would be available in a 1988–90 time frame. It estimated this number to be 57 major private yards and 9 public shipyards. The study concluded that this number was sufficient for a shipyard mobilization base. In 1986, fifty-six of the private shipyards identified in the NADES study, in addition to the eight naval yards, are the key yards in a national security context.[1]

The Mariner Revolving Fund

As the first session of the Ninety-Ninth Congress moved toward a December 1985 adjournment, it earmarked $852 million of unspent naval shipbuilding funds as seed money for a revolving fund that would be used to construct, and lease to U.S.-flag operators, militarily useful merchant vessels.[2] Although the $852 million is locked in place for the moment, additional legislation will be required before it can be spent (see Table 4.3). The Reagan administration has been ambivalent in its position on the legislation.

Since the envisioned militarily useful ships will be built in higher-priced American shipyards, most maritime observers view the legislation as a partial substitute for the former construction differential subsidy (CDS) program, which was canceled by the Reagan administration in 1981.

The proposed Mariner Fund has both partisans and critics. Proponents of the initiative argue:

- The program will provide work for hard-pressed U.S. shipyards.
- The national security will benefit to the extent that new, militarily useful merchant ships will be added to a dwindling U.S.-flag merchant marine.
- The fund would be replenished by charter monies received from U.S. operators. The most optimistic scenario is that over the long term, the fund would be self-supporting and not a drain on the taxpayer.

Critics contend:

- The long-term viability of the fund is highly unlikely given that world shipping in the mid-1980s is overtonnaged by as much as 30 percent.

To make charter terms attractive in this environment, charter rates would have to be cut well below the break-even point, which in turn would mean serious shortfalls with respect to monies flowing into the fund.

- The need for *more* U.S.-flag tonnage can only be rationalized if there is a government program in place that guarantees additional cargo to U.S. operators.
- There is no analysis of where implementation of the revolving-fund concept might lead 10 or 15 years down the road. In this respect, in 1986 government-owned merchant-type tonnage (including naval auxiliaries) exceeded that of the private sector. The Mariner Fund approach would exacerbate this trend, in that new construction under the program would be *Navy-owned*. Equally important is the question of whether, and to what extent, the initiative is a substitute for already existing programs such as the Military Sealift Command's T-Ship programs, and the Navy-funded Ready Reserve Force of the National Defense Reserve Fleet. To the extent that it is a substitute program, the question that must be answered is, is it a cost-effective substitute?[3]
- The program, as presently envisioned, is limited to new, general cargo construction. This limitation ignores one of the most pressing merchant marine issues of the 1980s insofar as national security is a concern. At the beginning of 1986 there were only 32 bulk and tanker vessels, including tug-barges, tanker-barges, and liquid natural gas carriers (LNGs), in the U.S. foreign trade fleet. The United States, in effect, was hostage to foreign-flag ships (nations) with respect to its strategic mineral and petroleum imports.[4]
- The revolving-fund concept contemplates a standard-design, general cargo vessel, built in series. While such a vessel would be constructed with as much use-flexibility as possible, by definition it would still be first a militarily useful vessel, and second, a ship that would have to satisfy unknown trade requirements 20 or more years down the road.[5]

If the entire $852 million is spent on vessels such as the West German multipurpose cargo ship described in note 5, at best only about 16 could be built in American yards. This calculation assumes that it would cost at least twice the West German price of $26 million per ship to build a similar vessel in the United States. On the other hand, if a series of moderate-size bulk carriers were built at a 50 percent construction subsidy rate ($20 million per ship) as noted in Chapters 9 and 11, some 40 vessels could be constructed for $852 million.

Cargo Preference, the Build-Foreign Option, and Title XI

The bitter and acrimonious debates in 1985 over interpretation of existing cargo preference laws with respect to U.S. agriculture shipments carried over into 1986. On one side was the Department of Agriculture. It wanted to limit preference-eligible cargo to donation-type (giveaway) programs (i.e., where the cargo was donated to the recipient nation). It opposed cargo preference for commercial shipments that were only "assisted" by U.S.-backed financial arrangements. Maritime interests adamantly opposed this interpretation of existing law. Their position was upheld by a federal court in February 1985. In December 1985 a compromise was reached with passage of Public Law 99-198. Maritime interests backed away from their insistence that 50 percent of all government-impelled, commercial-type cargoes be moved in U.S.-flag ships, while agricultural interests agreed that 75 instead of 50 percent of donation-type cargoes (e.g., the Food for Peace Program) be carried in American ships.

In 1986 the Reagan administration, which generally opposes cargo preference as a too costly way of ensuring freight for American-flag ships, continued to search for a least-cost way around the requirements of Public Law 99-198 without unduly antagonizing maritime industry supporters in Congress.

In January 1986 two other cargo preference initiatives were dropped into the congressional hopper. One would require the Postal Service to use American-flag ships exclusively in moving U.S. mail. The only exception would be lack of service by U.S. carriers at fair and reasonable rates. Another bill, introduced by Walter Jones, chairman of the House Merchant Marine and Fisheries Committee, would require that half of Japanese car imports be carried in U.S. vessels.

The relevance of cargo preference legislation and the economic well-being of American shipyards has been noted throughout this book. In essence, if there is no guarantee of cargo, there obviously is no incentive for new construction. The 1986 debates in Congress on maritime policy thus far have, if anything, strengthened a major conclusion of this study. If a modest-size, privately owned bulk and tanker segment of the nation's foreign trade merchant marine and a reasonably secure shipyard mobilization base are desirable, then a limited construction differential subsidy (CDS) program (for bulk carriers and tankers) must be reestablished *in conjunction with bilateral shipping agreements* between the United States and its bulk cargo trading partners (Chapter 11).

In 1981 operationally subsidized U.S.-flag operators were given the option of building vessels in foreign shipyards without penalty. This option was allowed under Section 615 of the Merchant Marine Act of 1936 when no construction differential subsidy monies were available (Chapter 1, note 6). The option expired on 30 September 1983. Since that time the Reagan administration has made strenuous efforts to have the "build foreign" alternative reinstated. In 1986 the option is on the table as a bargaining chip. Maritime industry supporters in Congress have indicated a willingness to support the administration on "building foreign" in return for administration support on one or more cargo preference bills.

Title XI of the Merchant Marine Act of 1936 guarantees payment by the federal government to a lender should a vessel mortgagee be in default on a loan (Chapter 11). Historically, Title XI has been cited as self-supporting, in that assessed fees paid by mortgagees covered the costs of administering the program. In 1985, and the first part of 1986, Title XI was badly shaken by a series of defaults that depleted the fund, and in turn required the Maritime Administration to borrow money from the U.S. Treasury.

As in the case of other shipyard support programs, Title XI has both its partisans and detractors. The Reagan administration is opposed to continuing the program. No funds were requested for Title XI in the FY 1987 budget. On the other hand, many maritime industry supporters in Congress are not convinced that a series of defaults is incontrovertible evidence that Title XI is fatally flawed. They point to its previous history as a soundly administered program. In general, supporters of a loan guarantee concept fault the Maritime Administration for approving, in their opinion, a series of questionable loan guarantee applications.

Balanced Budget and Emergency Deficit Control Act of 1985 (Public Law 99-177)

As Congress reconvened in January 1986, the most pressing monetary and financial issue before it was how to implement the budget cuts mandated by Public Law 99-177, the so-called Gramm-Rudman-Hollings bill.[6] In contemplation of Gramm-Rudman-Hollings, President Reagan's FY 1987 budget was both good and bad news for shipyards. The good news (for shipyards engaged in naval work) was that the defense buildup was to be continued. In addition to sustaining conversion and overhaul work at close to present levels, funds were requested for 21 new ships. The bad news was that (1) no funds were requested for CDS, (2) no new funds were requested for operating differential subsidy (ODS) contracts, and (3) no new loan guarantee authorizations (Title XI) were requested beyond 1986.

However, major disagreement on which programs to cut and by how much, was the rule rather than the exception in Congress. Leadership in the House of Representatives was adamant that defense spending be significantly scaled down.

Many maritime observers believe that passage of Gramm-Rudman-Hollings makes a slowdown in naval construction inevitable. Government authorities, typified by Captain Ralph Buck, USN (author of Chapter 12), continue to forcefully defend a naval construction program that includes at least twenty new starts each year. They caution that further reductions in the active shipbuilding base could severely curtail wartime shipbuilding options, but stress that a diversified ship repair base is even more essential.

Until the impact of Gramm-Rudman-Hollings becomes clearer, it is unlikely that any major shipyard support legislation will be passed by Congress. On the other hand, should naval construction and repair funding be significantly cut early on resulting in the closing of more shipyards, then all earlier proposals, as well as some new ones, in support of shipyards and shipping will again be on the table.

Commission on Merchant Marine and Defense and Congressional Maritime Caucus

Section 1536 of the Department of Defense Authorization Act of 1985 states:

> (a) There is hereby established a commission to be known as the Commission on Merchant Marine and Defense (hereinafter in this section referred to as the "Commission").
>
> (b) The Commission shall study problems relating to transportation of cargo and personnel for national defense purposes in time of war or national emergency, the capability of the United States merchant marine to meet the need for such transportation, and the adequacy of the shipbuilding mobilization base of the United States to meet the needs of naval and merchant ship construction in time of war or national emergency. Based on the results of the study, the Commission shall make such specific recommendations, including recommendations for legislative action, action by the executive branch, and action by the private sector, as the Commission considers appropriate to foster and maintain a United States merchant marine capable of meeting national security requirements. The recommendations of the Commission shall be provided in the reports of the Commission due on September 30, 1985, and September 30, 1986, under subsection (g).
>
> (c)(1) The Commission shall be composed of seven members, as follows:
>
> (A) The Secretary of the Navy (or his delegate), who shall be the chairman of the Commission.
>
> (B) The Administrator of the Maritime Administration (or his delegate).
>
> (C) Five members appointed by the President, by and with the advice

and consent of the Senate, from among individuals of recognized stature and distinction who by reason of their background, experience, and knowledge in the fields of merchant ship operations, shipbuilding and its supporting industrial base, maritime labor, and defense matters are particularly suited to serve on the Commission.

Legislation authorizing the commission was passed by Congress and signed into law by President Reagan in late 1984. As of 1 March 1986 nominations for commission membership had not been announced, although commission office space had been set aside at the Center for Naval Analyses in Alexandria, Virginia.[7]

While (c) (1) (C) of Section 1536 was generally broad with respect to what constitutes acceptable "background, experience, and knowledge," for a commission member, various maritime interest groups quickly staked out claims to representation. Among them were shipyards, vessel operators, and organized labor. Every indication is that the Reagan administration will acquiesce to these pressures, and that appointments will follow the Supreme Court pattern of setting aside a certain number of places for particular interest groups. It must be noted, however, that *every* maritime industry segment, including the below-cited Congressional Maritime Caucus, has been publicly critical of the Reagan administration for the 15-month delay in naming the commission.

In the summer of 1985, Walter B. Jones, chairman of the House Merchant Marine and Fisheries Committee, took the lead in forming the Congressional Maritime Caucus, made up of 75 House members who supported a strong U.S. maritime posture.

The first business of the caucus was to establish the Maritime Advisory Board, composed of a cross-section of maritime interests. Included were representatives of the administration, carriers, shpiyards, port interests, and organized labor. The purpose of the advisory group was to frame, and submit to the caucus, a firm maritime policy proposal by March 1986. A number of advisory board meetings were held, and suggestions were made by each of the industry sectors represented.[8]

In a 7 February 1986 letter, Chairman Jones requested the secretaries of defense and transportation, or their representatives, to brief the advisory board with respect to several key maritime issues. Topics included a Department of Defense assessment of "current national security requirements for the maritime industry, including numbers and types of vessels, seagoing personnel, and shipyard capacity, and projections as to the likely needs in the coming decade."

The request to the secretary of transportation was essentially similar to that of DoD. Requested was an accurate assessment of "the numbers and types of vessels, shipbuilding capacity and personnel that the nation needs [which] should include both national security and commercial requirements."[9]

The concept of maritime advisory committees or commissions is hardly new. In 1981 the Reagan administration established such a committee. (See Chapter 15, note 16.) The committee was little used and listened to less, and was finally disbanded in 1985.

Insofar as framing an enduring maritime policy, the odds are no better than even money that the Merchant Marine and Defense Commission can succeed. Its interest-group approach almost ensures that political compromises will drive policy recommendations. To the extent, however, that the commission is composed of recognized and respected merchant marine and naval authorities, such as retired admirals James Holloway, Issac Kidd, and George H. Miller, naval architects such as J. J. Henry, and labor statesmen of the stature of the late Paul Hall, so will the odds improve that an economically sound report can emerge from its deliberations.

Of the two committees (commissions), the Maritime Advisory Board of the Congressional Maritime Caucus probably stands the better chance of framing a long-range maritime policy. While it must also contend with special-interest views, it is not required to meet a specified deadline with respect to its recommendations as the Merchant Marine and Defense Commission must. Its charge can carry over into the presidential election year of 1988, the earliest likely date that anyone in the executive branch of government is willing to take maritime issues seriously.

Notes

1. The National Defense Shipyard Study (NADES) included the Quincy, Massachusetts shipbuilding facility of General Dynamics. This yard is scheduled to close in 1986. The small Coast Guard shipyard located at Curtis Bay, Maryland is not considered to be a key yard in mobilization planning.

2. Section 8103(b) of the Conference Report on H.J. Resolution 465 of the Continuing Resolution for FY 1986 provided that "$852,100,000 shall be available only for the Mariner Fund and may not be obligated or expended for any purpose until enactment of legislation establishing a Mariner Fund program for construction and lease of militarily useful vessels. . . ." The legislation was signed into law by President Reagan.

3. Actually, the Mariner Fund initiative is a made-to-order fallback position for the Navy. If naval construction funds are cut as a result of Gramm-Rudman, the Navy can then logically support the construction of militarily useful merchant vessels as a nondefense expenditure, not a naval expenditure. And if ships are built under the program and it is later found that there are no charter takers because of lack of cargo, the vessels will still be Navy-owned. One likely use would be their employment as Navy-crewed, naval auxiliaries, ships now built with Navy-appropriated construction funds.

4. While a significant share of America's strategic imports are carried in U.S.-owned, foreign-flag ships, few, if any knowledgeable authorities outside the federal government attach any national security value to this shipping. (See Chapter 11.)

5. An editorial in the January 1986 issue of *Marine Engineering/Log* suggested the ideal militarily useful ship for the Mariner Fund plan would be a state-of-the-art, multipurpose container ship recently built in West Germany. This 27,000 dwt ship has a 1,600 twenty foot equivalent unit (TEU) container capacity, can be operated by a crew of 16, and is fuel-efficient at 17 knots. The vessel's cargo hold can accept containers, large bulk, and outsize-type cargo. Built in West Germany, the ship cost $26 million. Whether this vessel would satisfy U.S. military logistics requirements is an open question. The strength of the proposal is that, by definition, the ship would be a commercially useful ship first, and militarily useful second.

6. In essence, Gramm-Rudman-Hollings mandated that the federal budget be reduced to zero by FY 1991. The reduction would take place in stages. If in any year the target deficit is not attained, then the legislation requires across the board reductions in federal spending or an increase in taxes.

7. Merchant Marine and Defense Commission offices are located at the Center for Naval Analyses, 4401 Ford Avenue, Room 1233, P.O. Box 16268, Alexandria, Virginia 22302.

8. Legislative successes in which the Congressional Maritime Caucus played a part included keeping, in the face of administration opposition, the capital construction fund (CCF). CCF is a government-administered account into which ship operator earnings can be deposited on a tax-deferred basis for the ultimate purpose of building or acquiring U.S.-flag, U.S.-built vessels. A second success for which the caucus could claim a share of the credit was keeping cargo preference for agricultural shipments on the books in some form. This legislation is discussed in the body of this epilogue.

9. Letters date 7 February 1986 to Elizabeth H. Dole, Secretary of Transportation, and Caspar Weinberger, Secretary of Defense, from Walter B. Jones, Chairman, Congressional Maritime Caucus.

Appendices

A   Summary of Major Shipping/Shipyard Studies and Analyses, 1983–85

Shipping, Shipyards and Sealift:
Issues of National Security and Federal Support

(This is a discussion draft report and subject to change.)

By: National Advisory Committee on Oceans and Atmosphere.
Year of Issue—1985. Approximately 125 pages.
   The report is made up of three chapters and a number of appendices, which are listed below.

   Chapter I. Industry Review: Status and Problems in Shipping and Shipbuilding.
   Chapter II. Defense Concerns: Sealift and Shipyard Mobilization Base.
   Chapter III. Discussion of Proposed Solutions.
   Appendices 1–7.

Summary. The report is a follow-on to an earlier 1983 NACOA study, "Marine Transportation in the United States." The report concludes that government policies, as enumerated in the Merchant Marine Act of 1936 and subsequent maritime promotional legislation, have been ineffective with respect to maintaining a shipping and shipyard mobilization base.
   Principal conclusions respecting shipyards are:

(a) Despite some yard closings, there is sufficient capacity in those yards expected to survive to meet wartime needs.
(b) Effort should concentrate on building up viable federal and commercial fleets in peacetime, rather than preserving sufficient shipyard capacity for wartime shipbuilding.
(c) Build U.S. requirements have failed and imposed the cost of preserving a shipbuilding base on the ship operator rather than the general taxpayer.

Principal recommendations are:

(a) The administration and Congress should not fund any program for building commercial merchant ships that requires major federal expenditures.

(b) National shipbuilding and shipping policies should be delinked, including allowing operating differential subsidies for foreign-built, U.S.-flag ships; allowing Capital Construction Fund tax-deferred funds to be used for foreign-built vessels; allowing Title XI federal loan guarantees for foreign-built ships; allowing foreign-built vessels to carry government-impelled cargo; amending the Jones Act to allow some foreign-built ships into the U.S. domestic trades on an approximately one-for-one basis.

Comment. This report repudiates an earlier 1983 study that recommended a number of positive government support actions for U.S. shipyards. By and large it endorses the present laissez-faire Reagan administration policies with respect to foreign trade shipping and shipbuilding.

Toward More Productive Naval Shipbuilding

By: Marine Board, Commission on Engineering and Technical Systems, National Research Council:
Year of Issue—1984. 197 pages.
The report is composed of seven chapters and a number of appendices. Chapter titles are listed below.

Chapter I. Summary, Conclusions and Recommendations.
Chapter II. Shipbuilding in the United States.
Chapter III. Investment, Profitability, Naval Ship Acquisition, and Productivity.
Chapter IV. Modernizing Shipbuilding Technology: Integrating Engineering and Production to Support Zone-Oriented Ship Design and Construction.
Chapter V. Modernizing Shipbuilding Technology: Production Management Systems.
Chapter VI. Suppliers and Navy Shipbuilding.
Chapter VII. Cross-Cutting Issues and Needed Developments.
Appendices 1–5.

Summary. "This report . . . . reflects a point of view that productivity improvements are more readily initiated by the customer [the Navy] than the manufacturer [the shipbuilder and shipbuilding supplier] . . . . As a result, the Navy, to a greater extent than shipbuilders and suppliers, is the subject of critiques, conclusions and recommendations in the report."

Principal recommendations are:

(a) The Navy should employ contracts that maximize opportunity for larger production runs, and that also contain provisions for contractors to assume greater risk in exchange for greater reward for productive performance.

(b) The Navy should continue to provide financial support to the National Shipbuilding Research Program.

(c) To foster the use of zone-oriented ship construction, the Navy should develop means to apply the technology in preliminary and contract designs, educate its personnel on the advances being embraced by shipbuilders so that naval practices and procedures can be adapted in support of them, and work together with its shipbuilders to provide a receptive environment for use of productivity-improving technology.

(d) A generic specification is needed for computerized shipbuilding industry management systems.

(e) The Navy should establish a task force on computerization in concert with its shipbuilding, ship design, and supplier industry.

(f) The Navy should establish productivity improvement goals and incentives for its shipbuilding programs.

(g) The Navy should establish a focus for productivity improvement within its organization.

Comment. The report does not address the adequacy of the present shipyard mobilization base, nor does it make any recommendations for maintaining it. Primarily, it concentrates on improving productivity in U.S. shipyards. The role of the supplier as a part of the Navy–shipbuilder system is examined, a role that is being increasingly recognized as a critical one. Several case studies of capital improvements made by shipyards are included in the Appendix. The report is well researched and comprehensive but basically written for those familiar with the industry and having a technical background.

An Assessment of Maritime Trade and Technology

By: Office of Technology Assessment (U.S. Congress)
Year of Issue—1983. 231 pages.

This study is made up of seven chapters and three content appendices, which are listed below.

Chapter I. Summary.
Chapter II. World Trade and Shipping.
Chapter III. U.S. Shipping Industry.

Chapter IV. The U.S. Shipbuilding Industry: Status and Trends in Technology and Productivity.
Chapter V. Status and Trends in Ship Design and Operating Technology.
Chapter VI. U.S. Maritime Policies.
Chapter VII. International Trade and Cargo Policies.
Appendices 1–3.

The principal conclusion is that "the United States has no overall, coordinated and effective maritime policy that responds to the major trends and realities confronting the U.S. maritime industry in the increasingly competitive and complex arena of world seaborne trade. Existing maritime policies are a patchwork of measures adopted at various times to address specific needs. The principal recommendation is "that major new or revised policies are needed if the U.S. maritime industries are to remain healthy in the decades to come."

Comment. This frequently cited report, the most comprehensive of recent maritime studies, is the primary source document for many later studies. (This book is indebted to it for much of its research.) While the draft National Advisory Committee on Oceans and Atmosphere report generally supports the Reagan administration view of the maritime industry—there really is no policy—the OTA study is much more sympathetic to the maritime policy initiatives proposed in Congress. However, it is still a balanced effort. Its greatest strength is the in-depth research on current maritime issues.

U.S. Shipping and Shipbuilding: Trends and Policy Choices

By: Congressional Budget Office (U.S. Congress)
Year of Issue—1984. 119 pages.
The report is composed of five chapters and several appendices, which are listed below.

Chapter I. Introduction.
Chapter II. Historical Review of U.S. Shipping and Shipbuilding Policies.
Chapter III. Current U.S. Shipping and Shipbuilding.
Chapter IV. Shipping, Shipbuilding, and National Security.
Chapter V. Maintaining the Maritime Industries for National Security: Alternative Strategies.
Appendices 1–5.

Summary. The report reviews early U.S. shipping and shipbuilding policies as background to an analysis of current maritime industry problems. A major part of the report, approximately one-half, deals with national security considerations. The principal conclusion is that governments can support their merchant marines (and shipyards) in three ways:

(a) Direct or indirect subsidies to operators and builders.
(b) Cargo reservation.
(c) Government operation of shipping.

All options involve significant costs—about $1 billion per option annually in addition to current outlays for maritime support programs. No option is recommended, although advantages and disadvantages of each are noted.

Analysis of the International Competitiveness of the U.S. Commercial Shipbuilding and Repair Industries

By: U.S. International Trade Commission.
Year of Issue—1985. 221 pages.

This report was requested by the House of Representatives Committee on Ways and Means in October 1984. The study is divided into six subject areas, which are listed below. Documentation is extensive and supported by 70 tables and figures. Much of the data is original, having been obtained from questionnaires returned by industry.

Chapter I. U.S. Industry Profile.
Chapter II. U.S. Government Involvement.
Chapter III. World Industry and World Market.
Chapter IV. Competitive Position of the U.S. Commercial Shipbuilding and Ship Repairing Industries in the World Market.
Chapter V. Ocean Freight Shipping.
Chapter VI. Recent Initiatives on Behalf of the U.S. Shipbuilding and Ship Repairing Industries.

Major findings of the report are:

(a) The United States has the largest shipbuilding and repair industrial base in the Western world.
(b) In recent years, production and repair of commercial ships have shifted from developed countries in Europe to developed and developing countries in Asia.
(c) U.S.-built commercial ships take twice as long to build and cost two times as much money as many comparable foreign-built vessels.
(d) U.S. construction and repair of commercial ships has decreased greatly from the levels reached in 1979 and 1980. In 1984 only 9 percent of the U.S. shipbuilding and repair industries net sales were derived from commercial shipbuilding and repairing.

(e) Employment in the U.S. shipbuilding and repair industries increased during 1979–84, but employment in the commercial ship sector declined significantly.
(f) Despite the decline in economic activity, U.S. shipyards have retained a relatively high level of capital expenditures.
(g) The U.S. shipbuilding industry exports little or none of its production, as opposed to many foreign competitors.
(h) The supplier base of the U.S. maritime industries has also declined as a result of the lack of commercial shipbuilding activity in the United States.
(i) Foreign shipbuilders and ship repairers enjoy a competitive advantage in the cost of raw and semifinished materials, the availability and cost of capital, and the cost of labor.
(j) U.S. and foreign shipbuilders and repairers were judged to be equally competitive in the areas of availability of raw and semifinished materials, availability and skill level of labor, product quality, and level of technology.

Shipyard Mobilization Base (SYMBA) Study

(Executive Summary, unclassified)

By: U.S. Navy and U.S. Maritime Administration.
Year of Issue—1984. 9 pages.

Summary. This study was intended "to serve as an input to maritime policy formulation and as a 'datum' for recurring analysis of this subject." The report assesses the ability of the present (and future) shipyard mobilization base to meet a wartime scenario. Conclusions are highly dependent on simulation modeling.

Conclusions:

(a) The minimum number of facilities required for an adequate base is 51 building positions, 41 graving docks, and 56 floating drydocks.
(b) Naval work is projected to employ about 125,000 shipyard workers, about 40,000 short of the 1988 D-day number required. Naval work alone will not sustain an adequate mobilization base.
(c) Naval work is concentrated in a relatively few shipyards. However, most of the yards modeled in the SYMBA study are primarily commercial building/repair yards.

Note: While the SYMBA study was being researched, a number of additional shipyards were closed, shrinking the 110 yards in the SYMBA base. Given this development, an extension of the SYMBA study was begun in 1983—the National Defense Shipyard (NADES) Study. The NADES base is comprised of 66 shipyards, including the eight navy yards and one Coast Guard yard. The NADES report has not been approved for release.

Defense and Economic Aspects of HR 1242
(Competitive Shipping and Shipbuilding Act of 1983)

By: Center for Naval Analyses.
Year of Issue—1983. 174 pages.
This report is composed of five sections and several extensive appendices. There are 40 tables and illustrations. The five major sections are listed below.

Section 1: Introduction and Summary.
Section 2: U.S. Flag Merchant Marine as Naval Auxiliary.
Section 3: The Estimated Effects of HR 1242 on the U.S. Merchant Fleet.
Section 4: Military Utility of the Contract (Bulk) Shipping Fleet.
Section 5: Conclusions.
Appendices 1–4.

Summary. The report was requested by the Assistant Secretary of the Navy (Shipbuilding and Logistics). It evaluates the effect of HR 1242, an act intended to increase the bulk fleet (dry and liquid cargo) by reserving a 20 percent share of U.S. bulk trades to U.S.-flag/built ships. The CNA analysis concentrates on the potential national defense benefits of HR 1242 insofar as it would expand the sealift available to the United States in time of emergency.
Findings include:

(a) An estimated net gain of approximately 300 ships is expected 16 years after enactment of the legislation.
(b) Once the 20 percent preference requirement was in place, a larger shipyard mobilization base would be sustainable. Importers and exporters would pay an additional $1–2 billion annually in higher shipping costs.
(c) Higher U.S. shipping costs would increase the delivered price of American bulk products and hence reduce foreign demand for these products.
(d) There is no incentive for shipbuilders or operators to incorporate national defense features into bulk ships.

The major national defense recommendation is to provide a mechanism whereby national defense features can be incorporated into the additional tonnage generated by HR 1242. The CNA study did not make a judgment as to whether national defense benefits outweighed the costs imposed by the legislation.

B American Clipper Ships, 1845–60

Ship[a]	Designer	Builder	Gross tons	Speed, knots
Sovereign of the Sea	Donald McKay	Donald McKay[b]	2,421	22
James Baines	" "	" "	2,525	21
Champion of the Sea	" "	" "	2,447	20
Stag Hound	" "	" "	1,534	20
Lightning	" "	" "	2,083	19
Donald McKay	" "	" "	2,594	18
Flying Cloud	" "	" "	1,800	18
Red Jacket	Samuel Pook	Deacon-Thomas	1,700	16
Defiance	" "	not known	1,690	20
Game Cock	" "	Samuel Hall[c]	1,392	18
Surprise	" "	" "	1,261	18
Rainbow	J. W. Griffiths	Smith-Dimon	752	16
Sea Witch	" "	" "	890	17
Challenge	William H. Webb	William H. Webb[d]	2,006	18
Ocean Monarch	" "	" "	2,145	18

SOURCE: Carl C. Cutler, *Greyhounds of the Sea*; O. T. Howe and F. C. Matthews, *American Clipper Ships 1833–1858*; George F. Campbell, *China Tea Clippers*; and Carl E. McDowell and Helen M. Gibbs, *Ocean Transportation*.

[a]Between 1845 and 1860 a number of clipper ships were built in Great Britain. On average, they were generally smaller than their American counterparts. Some of the better known were the *Sea Witch* (337 gross tons), the *Stornoway* (527 gross tons), the *Challenger* (699 gross tons), the *Lord of the Isles* (770 gross tons), and the *Robin Hood* (852 gross tons).

[b]Other clippers built by McKay were the *Star of Empire* (2,050 gross tons), the *Chariot of Fame* (2,050 gross tons), and the *Empress of the Seas* (2,200 gross tons).

[c]Other clippers built by Hall were the *Akbar* (650 gross tons), the *Coquette* (420 gross tons), and the *Gilpin* (1,089 gross tons).

[d]Other clippers built by Webb were the *Montauk* (690 gross tons), the *Panama* (670 gross tons), the *Helena* (598 gross tons), the *Cohota* (690 gross tons), the *Isaac Wright* (1,300 gross tons), the *Ivanhoe* (1,300 gross tons), the *Yorktown* (1,300 gross tons), and the *London* (1,300 gross tons).

C West Coast Shipyards: An Endangered U.S. Resource

IN A WORLD of rapid and continuous change, we have come to accept many situations and events that, just a few years ago, we would have thought "could never happen": the first man on the moon, Japan's technological ascendancy over many major U.S. industries, $33-per-barrel oil, the breakup of the world's best telephone system, and a trillion-dollar national debt, to name just a few. Most of us would not have conceived of such developments very long before they occurred, and I do not believe our foresight is greatly improved now.

I shall discuss an eventuality that probably has not been given much thought because it is in that "it could never happen" category. What would happen if, by the year 2000, there were no longer any privately owned, full-service shipyards, that is, shipyards capable of doing both naval and commercial work, operating on the west coast? What economic, social, and military impact would such a development have on the nation and on the Pacific region?

The immediate response, understandably, might be that such a development is highly unlikely and could easily be avoided by common-sense government and public opinion. As a person who has been intimately involved with shipbuilding for over 40 years, I must reply that, no, this possibility is not unlikely, but, yes, it can be avoided with political and public support.

Let me review some of the reasons why I do not think this possibility can be easily dismissed.

It is well known that the U.S. shipbuilding industry is currently undergoing a drastic shakeout caused by a variety of factors:

First, commercial ship construction and repair work in 1985 was at an all-time low. Shipyards solely dependent on this sector are desperately short of work, and many have closed. Todd Shipyards Corporation has

This appendix was contributed by J. T. Gilbride, Chairman, Todd Shipyards Corporation.

not been exempt; we shut down our Brooklyn and Houston divisions in 1983.

Second, current government policy through the Maritime Administration (MarAd) has eliminated construction differential subsidies and actually will use operating differential subsidies to promote the construction of ships for the U.S. merchant fleet in foreign shipyards. Jones Act protection is in jeopardy and, in my opinion, is very likely to disappear.

Third, the few healthy yards remaining are engaged in naval construction and repair, but, as Vice Admiral Joseph Metcalf, Deputy Chief of Naval Operations (Surface Warfare), recently said: "The Navy simply cannot generate the work required either in repair, new construction or conversion to maintain the existing industrial base in any condition of profitability. We are almost the only game in town but we are by no means a large enough game to support so many players."[1]

Which facilities are likely to succumb? The industrial base to which Admiral Metcalf referred is currently comprised of 23 shipyards, not all of which have work today and only five of which are located on the west coast: one in San Diego, one in Los Angeles, and three in Seattle. Obviously, any further shakeout on the west coast would be a severe blow to the national security interest and to the Pacific region.

Last summer, the local ship supervisor of shipbuilding for the Navy, who was also in charge of naval repair contracts in the northwest, was quoted by the press as saying that unless shipyards out there got their wage costs more in line with eastern competitors, they could not expect to get any more work.[2] This apparently reflected the Navy's "low-bid" procurement policy, which has ignored the need to maintain shipbuilding resources on all coasts and has resulted in the overwhelming majority of new construction contracts being awarded to east and Gulf coast operations. For instance, only 4 percent of fiscal 1984 new naval construction expenditures were apportioned to the west coast, while the east and Gulf coasts received 74 percent and 21 percent, respectively. Todd's two major competitors for frigate/destroyer/cruiser type ships, one of which is on the east coast, the other on the Gulf, will share an estimated $11 billion of ongoing work during the next five years, including 27 Aegis cruisers (CG 47) and several Aegis destroyers (DDG 51). The opportunities available to all five west coast mobilization base shipyards are a small fraction of that amount during the same period.

This lack of work has impacted employment unfavorably in the Seattle and Los Angeles areas. In the past three years, 6,000 jobs have been lost in the northwest (3,000 at Todd's Seattle Division), and employment at Todd's Los Angeles Division had dropped from 4,700 to 2,400 workers as of June 1985.

What is the cost differential between east and west coast private shipyards that has led to such a harsh procurement policy toward Pacific coast shipyards? An October 1984 MarAd report estimated west coast shipbuilding costs to be 4.6 percent higher than in the east and 9.2 percent higher than in the Gulf.[3] Is this such a considerable difference that our nation can risk losing its west coast private shipyard capability to build and support the Pacific Fleet, plus the U.S. merchant fleet and ships owned by nations of the Pacific Basin, our number one trading area? And, what will the real defense costs be after the initial savings by low-bid, or "low balling" procurement have been realized?

For the Navy, follow-on cost increases would be unavoidable for normal peacetime operations and would be greatly increased under emergency conditions. Why? Let me describe a few "could never happen" scenarios based on a series of interrelated events that are pure fiction today but have enough plausibility to be seriously considered for contingency planning.

Scenario Number One

The Panama Canal is blocked by terrorist action. As a result, submarines, cruisers, and other ships built in the east and assigned to Pacific fleet duty, which normally travel an average of over 5,000 miles to west coast ports, must now travel around the tip of South America, adding over 8,000 miles to the voyage. Clearly, this compromises fleet readiness and rapid deployment, increases operating costs, exposes the ships to unnecessary risk, and involves the crews and ships in weeks of nonproductive activity.

Scenario Number Two

Government-owned shipyards replace the private sector on the west coast. Since naval yards had not been building naval vessels, they are not able to overhaul and repair them as cost-effectively as the experienced private builder. Furthermore, in my judgment, having dealt with relative costs of private and government ships since before World War II, the cost of doing work in government nontaxpaying yards in terms of dollars, time, and bottom-line results is 30 percent higher than that of private yards. The cost variance would be further increased by west coast navy yard's wage rates, which are 18.7 percent higher than their east coast counterparts, as stated in the 1984 MarAd report.[4] Over the 30-year life expectancy of the ships, therefore, the added cost of life-cycle support services required to keep a ship in state of readiness would far exceed any savings realized from initial low-bid purchase.

Scenario Number Three

The national shipbuilding industrial base is reduced to eight east and Gulf coast yards because west coast yards, forced to bid for new business at a

4.6 percent to 9.2 percent loss by naval procurement policy, are eventually closed down. New construction and repair competitions fail to reduce prices because fewer competitors exist—the inevitable economic result of creating near-monopolistic conditions—and government yards are overloaded. "Surge" capacity is nonexistent, labor strikes for less overtime, and crew morale sinks because of overhaul delays and prolonged separations from families at home ports. The problem is particularly acute for the nine Pacific Fleet aircraft carriers and their Aegis-equipped cruiser and destroyer escorts, some of which must return to the east for major overhaul. The fleet is put at greater risk when a South American country, denied further credit by the United States, gives the Soviet Union rights to establish a naval base in return for economic aid.

Scenario Number Four

Foreign-flag fleets join the Soviet Union in boycotting U.S. ports. Shipping activity slows to a trickle as a majority of African nations join the Soviet Union in boycotting the United States to protest its South African and Israeli policies. Credit-poor South American nations consider support of the boycott, as do Pacific Basin countries objecting to U.S. intervention in a Philippine insurrection. The president orders activation of the 116-ship Ready Reserve Force (30–60-day delays anticipated from shipyard overloading), initiates an emergency training program for able seamen, recalls the 300-ship U.S.-flag merchant fleet, and appeals to allies and neutral-block nations (including Japan) for use of sealift resources.

Implausible as these fictional scenarios may seem, present government maritime policy and procurement actions are heading the nation toward an era of maritime insufficiency that could bring them about. By allowing the active U.S.-flag merchant fleet to decline (to 403 ships as of 1 October 1985, down 57 units from 1983), by concentrating the overwhelming majority of the nation's fleet construction and repair resources in the eastern half of the country, and by allowing west coast resources to wither, government policy surely will lead the United States into economic, military, and political decline by abdicating the nation's position of supremacy at sea and leaving the world's sealanes open to nations with the ability to command or interdict them. Lack of sealift capacity spells weakness to our opponents just as surely as does lack of domestic sources of basic commodities and strategic materials. Admiral Ike Kidd said it concisely: "If the (merchant ship) owning nations chose to deny sealift to us, the result could be economic blackmail to which we could not respond in peacetime, much less in war."[5]

This concern was dramatized in the following fictional scenario by Harlan Ullman in the May 1985 issue of the Naval Institute *Proceedings*, a picture that, if present downward trends continue for the U.S. merchant marine and west coast shipbuilding industry, could be tomorrow's reality.[6]

Scenario Number Five

It is winter 1990. The war in the Persian Gulf between Iran and Iraq, after ten years of bloodshed, has finally spilled over. As a result of a series of bone-chilling winters and other economic factors, Western dependence on Persian Gulf oil grew significantly in the latter part of the 1980s. A Western naval task force, largely composed of U.S. forces, was ordered into the Gulf to protect both the shipping routes and the oil-producing facilities on the Arabian Peninsula. Conflict resulted, and large numbers of Western forces were brought to bear. Unfortunately, because of the spread of advanced weapons to the belligerent states and terrorist groups acting in their behalf, Western naval losses, including warships and merchantmen, have been heavy. But worse, after several months of a grinding campaign of attrition, the United States has found itself increasingly hamstrung by lack of a merchant fleet. It has only limited ability to provide the wherewithal for Western forces engaged in the region and the cargo capacity to compensate for the economic embargo imposed by nonaligned states against all belligerents. Further, erosion of the U.S. shipbuilding base has made repair work on damaged ships a very lengthy process.

Surely, this scenario suggests that now is the time to return to reality, and a good start would be to observe the law of the land. In 1956, Congress recognized the importance of maintaining a geographically dispersed shipbuilding mobilization base to enable ships to be built when and where they are needed, on all three coasts. The enacted statute states that "the Department of the Navy shall have constructed on the Pacific Coast of the United States such vessels as the President determines necessary to maintain shipyard facilities there adequate to meet the requirements of national defense."[7]

Second, in regard to shipbuilding and repair, the government should not be involved in any activity that the private sector can do better and at less cost—and that applies on all our coasts.

Third, we must face up to the real cost of not maintaining total seapower resources. The difficulties we face in making such an analysis have been the lack of an overall maritime strategy, the mistaken belief that U.S. maritime industries must survive under "free market" conditions, and the misconception that the Navy can fulfill its peacetime and military missions effectively with its own sealift resources and a greatly diminished shipbuilding industrial base. Again I quote Ike Kidd: "Investment right now in better balanced East and West Coast shipbuilding, merchant and naval, would provide an unmistakable message to Moscow that we have no intention of defaulting anywhere."[8]

Without a clear national policy to maintain adequate seapower resources, it is difficult to define accurately how much of each resource (naval, merchant, and industrial) is needed, and how we can pay for it.

This subject needs urgent consideration at the highest policy levels, according to the Center for Strategic and International Studies' recent report "Forecasts for U.S. Maritime Industries in 1989: Balancing National Security and Economic Considerations."[9] This report concludes: "U.S. commercial maritime capabilities will probably decline by a third or more by this decade's end. That condition may or may not be in the national interest. That decline must not, however, occur by default. Broader public debate and discussion are essential. The issue is too vital to be resolved through inaction."

This issue, we believe, transcends partisan and parochial interests and is truly a national issue. Furthermore, it is an issue on which we have clear historical perspective. Two world wars demonstrated beyond all argument the essentialness of maintaining three-coast shipbuilding capacity. As reported in Frederick Lane's *Ships for Victory*, a comprehensive history of World War II shipbuilding: "In 1940 and 1941, the Maritime Commission and the leaders of the shipbuilding industry attempted to apply lessons learned from 1917–1919. Recalling the over concentration in the Northeast, they wisely placed many new shipyards on the Gulf and Pacific Coasts." Of four administrative offices established, "the most important regional office was that in Oakland, California," which from 1939 to 1945 delivered 10.2 million displacement tons of ships, all from west coast commercial yards, compared with 7.7 and 3.9 million displacement tons, respectively, on the east and Gulf coasts.[10]

Should the citizens of the Pacific coast, and indeed the nation, be concerned about these "could never happen here" events? They certainly should. The public must understand that the lessons of history and certain economic and security concerns are being ignored on the naval side with low bid only, not ultimate cost, and on the commercial side with the exercise of so-called free market competitive forces. The latter would be fine if fair international free market conditions existed, which they do not, as I observed over a three-year period as a member of a presidential commission on world shipping and shipbuilding, which found evidence of overt and covert government aid worldwide for shipping and shipbuilding.

It is appropriate and urgent that Americans, as a nation, commit themselves to preserving their important maritime heritage, which is in real danger of becoming just a memory. All U.S. citizens, not just those in the 11 western states, must realize that they have a stake in maintaining a healthy private west coast shipbuilding industry and must act to convince government decision makers to redirect national policy toward preserving balanced maritime resources.

As things now stand, the Pacific coast is the area most severely impacted by government misdirection. It is nevertheless a strategically located maritime/industrial area of immense importance and value to the nation's security and economic well-being—rich in skilled labor, deepwater ports, and supporting industrial infrastructure. It would be ironic if the country's leadership allowed these resources to disappear at a time when the nation's greatest adversary for political and commercial influence in the Pacific Basin has spent, and continues to spend, billions of rubles attempting to replicate U.S. resources on the same waters.

Secretary of Defense Caspar Weinberger recently stated: "The United States has made a fundamental decision that we are a Pacific nation, that we will remain a Pacific power and a force for peace and stability in the region. Our nation's future does indeed lie in the Pacific."[11] This declaration lacks the credibility, in my judgment, that only a swift and common-sense change in government maritime policy can provide. In view of present circumstances, only decisive action can prevent the nation's adversaries from confidently ignoring the secretary's caveat: "Let no one misread the past, or misjudge our resolve."[12]

Notes

1. Shipbuilders Council of America, *Shipyard Weekly*, 13 December 1984, p. 1.

2. Letter from Supervisor of Shipbuilding, Conversion and Repair, U.S. Navy Seattle, Washington, dated 25 July 1984, to Todd Shipyards Seattle Division, re: The Future of Navy Work in the Pacific Northwest.

3. U.S., Department of Transportation, Maritime Administration, *Relative Cost of Shipbuilding*, p. 2.

4. Ibid., p. 12.

5. Issac C. Kidd (USN Ret.), "Shipbuilding and U.S. Sea Power Credibility," *The Washington Times*, 5 February 1985, p. 6.

6. Harlan K. Ullman and Paula J. Pettavino, "The Dreary Future of U.S. Maritime Industries," *U.S. Naval Institute Proceedings*, p. 136.

7. *Construction on the Pacific Coast, Statute 10.7302* (August 10, 1956, c. 1041, 70A Stat. 451).

8. Issac C. Kidd (USN Ret.), p. 6.

9. Harlan C. Ullman and Paula J. Pettavino, *Forecasts for U.S. Maritime Industries in 1989: Balancing National Security and Economic Considerations*, p. 36.

10. Frederick C. Lane, *Ships for Victory* (Baltimore, Md.: The Johns Hopkins Press, 1951), p. 43.

11. Harry V. Martin, "Our Nation's Future Does Indeed Lie in the Pacific," *Defense Systems Review*, May 1985, p. 18.

12. Ibid.

D   Naval Shipyards: History and Present Mission

Portsmouth

The Portsmouth Naval Shipyard is located in Kittery, Maine, although it takes its name from neighboring Portsmouth, New Hampshire.

"Sails to Atoms" is an apt motto for this shipyard, which was the first government-owned shipbuilding and repair yard, authorized in 1799 and established in 1800. One of the yard's first commanders was Commodore Isaac Hull, who was in command of the USS *Constitution* when she defeated HMS *Guerriere* during the War of 1812.

During the Civil War over 2,000 workmen were employed in both shipbuilding and ship repair. The keels of the nine-gun steam sloops of war *Ossipie* and *Kearsarge* were laid in 1861. The latter was the best known of the early ships built at Portsmouth. She was a steam screw sailing sloop of war, who on 21 June 1864 defeated the Confederate raider CSS *Alabama* off the coast of Cherbourg, France.

In 1905 the world's attention focused on the Portsmouth Naval Shipyard when, on 5 September 1905, the Treaty of Portsmouth was signed ending the Russo-Japanese War. President Theodore Roosevelt had invited the envoys of Russia and Japan to negotiate the terms of a peace treaty at Portsmouth.

Because of the interest in submarine warfare generated by World War I, the Navy Department made the decision to plan and build a submarine at a navy yard. Heretofore, the Electric Boat Company at Groton, Connecticut, and the Fore River Shipbuilding Company at Quincy, Massachusetts, held a monopoly on submarine construction. Portsmouth was selected to build the first submarine constructed at a naval shipyard. The

Captain Wilbur J. Mahony, USN (Ret.), author of Chapter 7, "Naval Shipyards," researched and wrote this appendix on the history and mission of the present naval shipyard complex.

Each naval shipyard has its own seal. The seal of the Norfolk Naval Shipyard notes the yard's existence under four different national flags.

keel of the L-8 was laid in 1914. The yard was designated a submarine yard by the secretary of the navy in 1923.

During World War I, the yard reached a peak employment of 5,722, including approximately 1,000 women. The yard laid the keels of six submarines between March 1917 and October 1918.

In World War II, the yard reached a peak of 20,466 employees. A total of 98 vessels were constructed during the period September 1939 to August 1945, including 85 submarines.

Following World War II, Portsmouth was in the forefront of advanced submarine design and construction. Here, 20 World War II fleet-type submarines were converted to the more capable, snorkel-equipped, Guppy-type boat. (The term Guppy is derived from the major aim of the program, to provide Greater Underwater Propulsion Power.)

Later years saw the construction of the *Albacore* (a streamlined diesel-powered experimental submarine), *Barbel*, *Swordfish*, *Seadragon*, *Thresher*, *Abraham Lincoln*, *John Adams*, *Nathanael Greene*, *Grayling*, *Dolphin*, and *Sandlance*. The *Sandlance* was the 134th and last submarine built at Portsmouth, being commissioned on 25 September 1971.

Along with seven other sister shipyards, Portsmouth is now completely committed to overhaul, conversion, and repair. But unlike most other yards, Portsmouth is still a submarine shipyard. The facilities and capability to build submarines lie latent, and could be activated should additional building capacity be needed.

Philadelphia

The Philadelphia Naval Shipyard is located at the confluence of the Schuylkill and Delaware rivers in the southern part of the city of Philadelphia. The Delaware River forms its main waterfront.

During colonial days, Philadelphia was one of the largest shipbuilding ports on the east coast. Many of the early American privateers were built there. A Philadelphia naval architect, Joshua Humphries, was the first "Chief Constructor" in the U.S. Navy and was assigned the task of fitting out the first fleet of the Continental Navy. The *United States*, the first ship ever built for the U.S. Navy, was constructed in Philadelphia.

The Philadelphia yard, along with Washington, Portsmouth, Boston, and Norfolk, was authorized in 1799 and established in 1801. Initially, it was only 11 acres in size. However, with the additional work generated by the Civil War, it was recognized that the original site was too small. In 1862, Congress authorized the acceptance of the present League Island location which was donated by the city of Philadelphia for $1. The shipyard is now joined to the South Philadelphia mainland and is considered to be a part of the port of Philadelphia. A 40-foot-deep channel provides access to the sea some 90 miles away down the Delaware River.

Shipyard employment has varied widely over the years. In recent years, employment reached a peak of 12,300, at a time when conventionally powered surface ships were being constructed at the yard. In 1974, employment dropped to 7,000 when all new naval construction was assigned to the private yards.

However, Philadelphia still has the capability for surface ship new construction in the event this capability is needed. The yard has what is considered to be the best propeller casting and manufacturing capabilities in the world. All of the Navy's large casting capability on the east coast is consolidated at Philadelphia. The casting and propeller manufacturing mission is concentrated in one production group, which is unique among naval shipyards.

When the New York Naval Shipyard was ordered closed in 1964, Philadelphia was assigned as the alternate site to Norfolk for repair and overhaul of aircraft carriers. In recent years the USS *Saratoga* has undergone overhauls at Philadelphia, once a regular overhaul and again as a part of the carrier Service Life Extension Program (SLEP).

Conversion of the USS *Forrestal* (CV 59) under the SLEP program began on 21 January 1983. Conversion of the USS *Independence* (CV 62) started in April 1985. During the Vietnam War, the Philadelphia yard activated the battleship USS *New Jersey*. After a second reactivation at Long Beach, the *New Jersey* is once again on the active ship list.

Norfolk

The seal of the Norfolk Naval Shipyard indicates long involvement in maritime activity, "Service to the Fleet—Under Four Flags." Operations were started in 1767 under the British Flag. During the American Revolution the site was taken over by the Navy of Virginia.

A British brigadier general may have sealed the fate of Cornwallis at Yorktown when he ordered his troops to torch the site of the Norfolk Naval Shipyard, then the Gosport Yard, during the War for Independence. Sent ashore by Commodore Sir George Collier to occupy the Gosport Yard, Brigadier General Edward Matthew and his 1,800 troops went even further; they burned the yard and 47 ships of 9 May 1779.

The action prevented the British from using and benefiting from the assets of what was then the largest and best equipped shipyard in colonial America. Lord Cornwallis was forced to surrender at Yorktown to George Washington when the British fleet could not break through a combined French–American blockade and provide the beleaguered British troops with ammunition, food, and supplies. The 47 ships destroyed with the shipyard could have been a decisive force in the blockade battle.

Norfolk was established as a government navy yard under the U.S. flag in 1801. It was extensively damaged by the British in the war of 1812.

During the Civil War, the shipyard played one very significant role in the history of naval warfare. At the start of the Civil War, the frigate USS *Merrimac* was berthed in the yard. She was burned to the waterline and sunk by Union forces. However, the scuttled ship was raised and refitted as the CSS *Virginia*, an "armored floating battery" that initially wreaked havoc on wooden Union warships in Hampton Roads. The Union response was the USS *Monitor*, also an ironclad. While the classic battle of 9 March 1862 between the two ships was inconclusive, it did effectively usher in the age of the ironclad warship and turret gun.

During the 1920s the shipyard converted the collier USS *Jupiter* into the world's first aircraft carrier, the USS *Langley*.

Production during World War II exceeded the combined efforts of all past wars as shipyard employees serviced 6,850 vessels and built new ships and craft, including three aircraft carriers, the *Lake Champlain*, *Tarawa*, and *Shangri-La*.

The Norfolk Naval Shipyard is located in the city of Portsmouth, Virginia directly across the Elizabeth River from the city of Norfolk. Norfolk is one of the great natural harbors in the world, and the shipyard is ideally located to service the large numbers of the U.S. Atlantic Fleet ships using the Norfolk area as an operating base. One hundred twenty-three ships were home-ported in the Norfolk area in 1983, making the base the largest home port for U.S. naval ships. The Norfolk Naval Shipyard was awarded the Naval Material Command's productivity award in 1981, 1982, and 1984, in recognition of its effective effort to be a leader in productivity and productivity improvements. This shipyard is the only federal activity to have been awarded the U.S. Senate Productivity Award and the only one to have received a Presidential Unit Citation.

Charleston

Charleston is a relatively new shipyard, having been established in 1901, a century later than those discussed previously. Strategically, it is the only facility of its kind from Hampton Roads to the Gulf of Mexico and, therefore, it is vital to South Atlantic and Carribbean naval operations. The Charleston Naval Shipyard is on the Cooper River, just north of the city of Charleston. Access to the Atlantic Ocean is by way of the Cooper River with a channel depth of 35 feet and a bridge clearance of 150 feet. The depth and bridge constraints permit entry to the shipyard by most active combatants except aircraft carriers. Charleston is assigned depot level maintenance support responsibility for submarines and surface combatants. Because Charleston is a nuclear submarine refueling shipyard, the workload in the shipyard has been more than 50 percent submarine work in recent years.

At various times until the end of World War II, Charleston engaged in new construction. During World War I, employment peaked at 5,600, approximately 1,000 of whom worked in the naval clothing factory, which occupied the building now used by the shipyard quality assurance department. By 1932 the yard employed 515 civilian workers and 26 naval officers. In 1933 the shipyard resumed new construction, and by 1939, civilian employment at the yard had increased to 2,395. During World War II the shipyard workforce peaked at 25,943. New construction continued, but the largest and most intense effort during the World War II years was battle damage repairs. After World War II, the Charleston yard no longer built ships, and its building ways were subsequently dismantled.

In 1948, the secretary of the navy announced that the Charleston Naval Shipyard would be a submarine yard. With the start of the Korean conflict in 1950, shipyard employment steadily increased. From a post–World War II nadir of 4,614 in December 1949, yard employment reached its post–World War II high of 9,220 in 1952. In 1956, Charleston was designated as one of six shipyards authorized to work on nuclear submarines.

In 1985, the shipyard had 8,600 civilian employees and 60 military managers assigned. The Charleston Naval Shipyard was awarded the

Chief of Naval Material Productivity Excellence Award for 1983, which culminated several years of diligent effort to improve shipyard performance.

Puget Sound

The Puget Sound Naval Shipyard possesses the widest range of capability in the naval shipyard complex. This range includes nuclear and conventionally powered aircraft carriers, surface combatants, submarines, missile ships, and large auxiliaries.

The Puget Sound Naval Shipyard is located in the city of Bremerton, Washington. The distance to Seattle across Puget Sound is 16 miles to the east, and the shipyard waterfront is approximately 1 mile long. Employing approximately 10,000 people, the shipyard is the major industrial activity of the Bremerton area.

Naval interest in Puget Sound dates at least as far back as 1841, when Lieutenant Charles Wilkes, renowned for Antarctic exploration, described Puget Sound as "The best harbor north of San Francisco." The current shipyard site was established as a naval station in 1891 and was designated a naval shipyard in 1945.

Puget Sound Naval Shipyard is the west coast naval shipyard with the capacity for surface ship new construction. The facilities to construct ships include a structural shop that has been considered one of the finest in the industry. With a floor area of 400,000 square feet, it is equipped to cut, form, and weld high-strength alloy steels with automatic machinery. The ability to process large volumes of steel plates and shapes is very important to efficient ship construction.

Puget Sound Naval Shipyard has the responsibility of producing the Navy's requirements for large castings and large volumes of castings for west coast naval shipyards. The foundries in the other shipyards have been reduced in size and manning so that only small emergency requirements are met from these local facilities.

Because of its strategic location in the northwest, the shipyard is an important facility in support of naval operation in the northern Pacific and Alaska waters. Puget Sound personnel have been deployed throughout the world in support of a variety of ship repairs.

Mare Island

The choice of the shipyard's name, and later the horse's head on its emblem, is credited to Mexican General Mariano Guadalupe Vallejo, who left his imprint in many ways on the local area surrounding the shipyard. The city of Vallejo, California, across the Napa River causeway on the mainland, bears his name.

Seal of the Mare Island Naval Shipyard. The horse head is a symbol of the name of the island, "Isla de la Yegua" (Island of the Mare), where the yard is located.

While stories vary as to the details of how General Vallejo's highly prized white mare was lost, she reportedly was found on the island, which was then named by Vallejo "Isla de la Yegua," or "Island of the Mare."

In 1853, the island was purchased for $83,491 for the purpose of establishing a navy yard; and Commander David Glasgow Farragut was assigned to duty as its first commandant. Mare Island was the first naval establishment on the west coast.

The first ship built by Mare Island was the *Saginaw*, a four-gun, wooden hull, steam-driven, side-paddle-wheel gunboat. The USS *Saginaw* was commissioned on 5 January 1860 and set sail a few days thereafter to the Western Pacific to show the flag in the Far East.

While eastern navy yards were split in support of either the Federals or the Confederates during the Civil War, Mare Island remained firmly in the Union camp.

During the Spanish-American War, Mare Island participated in the overhaul, repair, or stores and ammunition loading of many ships that fought the Spanish, in either Cuba or Manila Bay. Again, in the prewar buildup and during the course of World War I, Mare Island activity increased. The workforce was at about 3,000 the day war was delcared, growing to 4,500 by the end of 1917 and to 10,000 during the next two years. The keel of the *California*, the first superdreadnought to be built on the Pacific Coast, was laid on 25 October 1916.

In World War II, shipbuilding at Mare Island adopted the practice of "farm-out." In this respect, the yard claimed the longest assembly line and the highest building ways in the country. All the destroyer escorts and landing craft launched at Mare Island were constructed a mile above sea level, in Denver, Colorado, and they all crossed the Rocky Mountains on their way to the sea.

The intended commitment of Mare Island Naval Shipyard resources to construction and repair of nuclear-powered ships was announced at the 1954 Centennial Celebration. The first nuclear-powered ship constructed on the west coast was the *Sargo*, an attack submarine. Beginning with the *Theodore Roosevelt* and ending with the *Mariano G. Vallejo*, Mare Island was among the shipyards building Polaris submarines. The last ship constructed by Mare Island was the *Drum*, another nuclear attack submarine, launched in May 1970.

The Mare Island Building ways, which have a four-ship capacity, are now put to other uses, but they could be reactivated in a naval expansion program.

Long Beach

The Long Beach Naval Shipyard occupies what is known as Terminal Island, an area that has a history as an Indian burial ground and, prior to World War II, a fashionable bathing beach. In 1940, Congress appropriated funds to establish the Navy Dry Docks on Terminal Island. The site was purchased from the city of Long Beach for $1, and construction began. The first ship was dry-docked in 1942. The yard was formally established in 1943 and reached a peak employment of 16,000 employees in August 1945.

Since the drawdown in employment from World War II, the shipyard workforce has remained between 6,000 and 9,000. The shipyard is favored with deep water throughout its waterfront, with depths varying from 35 to 60 feet.

Probably the most distinctive part of the Long Beach Naval Shipyard's skyline is "Herman"—the largest, self-propelled floating crane in the world. Built in 1941 by the Germans at Bremerhaven, the crane served the Germans in the Baltic Sea, German North Sea ports, and Denmark. It is now designated YD-171. It and a sister crane were captured by the British in Kiel in May of 1945, and it was dismantled and transshipped to Long Beach. The crane's erection at Long Beach was completed in January 1948, and after extensive tests it was placed in operation.

The most notable work accomplished by Long Beach in recent years was the activation and modernization of the World War II battleship *New Jersey*.

Long Beach has the strategic location, facility installation, and repair and overhaul experience to continue to be an important asset to the operating fleet in Southern California.

Pearl Harbor

Pearl Harbor is the only naval shipyard located outside the continental United States. It is situated on Oahu in the Hawaiian Islands, 2,500 miles west and south of Los Angeles. King Kalakaua granted the United States exclusive rights to establish a naval base at Pearl Harbor in 1887, and the navy yard at Pearl Harbor was officially established in 1908. Its dry docks, the only ones in Hawaii available to handle large ships, are put to frequent use in emergency repairs.

The facilities and manpower levels at the Pearl Harbor Naval Shipyard are designed to support the combination of overhaul of home-ported ships and emergency repair work guaranteed by the shipyard's strategic location. The yard is tasked to accomplish extensive repairs to both nuclear and conventionally powered aircraft carriers. Manpower levels have frequently been supplemented from mainland shipyards to meet the three-shift, seven-day-a-week schedule required to get a fleet carrier back on line.

The level of employment in recent years has varied between 5,000 and 7,000, depending on the anticipated workload, much of which is unplanned. The all-time peak employment was in June 1943, when the shipyard workforce numbered 24,910. After World War II, the employment level dropped rapidly to 3,800, but during the Korean War, the personnel strength increased, rising to a peak of 7,600.

Pearl Harbor is one of the six naval shipyards authorized to work on nuclear-powered ships. The overhaul and refueling of nuclear submarines home-ported at Pearl Harbor is an important element of the workload, providing a continuing base of capability from which emergent repairs to nuclear ships deployed to the Western Pacific can be staged when required.

One of Pearl Harbor's greatest assets is its strategic location, which places fleet support 2,500 miles closer to major Far Eastern operating areas, compared to west coast ports.

E   Summary of Main Provisions of Shipbuilding and Ship Repairing Labor Agreements— International Brotherhood of Boilermakers, Iron Shipbuilders, Blacksmiths, Forgers, and Helpers

THE INTERNATIONAL BROTHERHOOD has 23 major shipbuilding and repair agreements with 59 employers. Contract provisions differ among employers; hence, the provisions cited below do not apply to every contract. They do, however, apply to one or more agreements in force, and in most cases to a majority of agreements.

Hourly Wage Rates

	Low rate	*Medium*	*High*
Loftsman	$9.56	$10.38	$13.74
Layerout	9.43	11.17	13.74
Mechanic	9.20	10.18	13.49
Helper	5.94	7.94	13.19
Laborer	5.96	7.93	13.19

Wage Premium

1. Premium paid if employee reports to work without having been notified not to report.

Source: *An Analysis of Shipbuilding and Marine Industry Labor Agreements* (prepared for the 1983 Conference of the Shipbuilding and Marine Industry), Washington, D.C., 16 March 1983.

2. Premium paid if employee called back to work after his normal shift.
3. Premium paid for second- and third-shift work.

Overtime

1. Time and one-half after 8 hours of work.
2. Double time after 10 hours of work.
3. Time and one-half for Saturday work.
4. Double time for Sunday work.
5. Double time on holidays in addition to holiday pay.

Fringe Benefits

1. Number of holidays ranges from 10 to 13.
2. Vacations range from 4 to 6 weeks annually.
3. Funeral leave with pay, 2 to 3 days.
4. Jury duty pay.

Insurance

1. Life insurance. Employer pays all or part of cost.
2. Accident and sickness benefits, maximum of 26 weeks. Employer pays all or part of cost.

Hospital and Surgical Insurance

1. Semiprivate room accommodations ranging to 365 days.
2. Fee payment for surgical benefits.
3. Major medical payments with $50 or $100 deductible.
4. Dental provision.
5. Prescription drug provision.

Pensions

1. Median benefit is $14.00 per month for each year of service; range is $8.00 to $16.00. Median employer contribution to pension plan is 30¢ per hour; range is 10¢ to $1.45.

Cost of Living Clauses

1. Agreements tied to cost of living index. Some have "cap" or maximum; some do not.

F

Minimizing Shipyard Costs by Varying Amounts of Labor and Capital Used in the Production Process

A SPECIFIC OUTPUT level (tons of shipping or number of ships) can be produced by using a range of possible input combinations. Since inputs will have different prices, the firm must decide on the optimum input combination in terms of minimizing its costs.

Assume that a firm utilizes two inputs, capital (C) and labor (L), and that these inputs are purchased in competitive markets; that is, the firm can obtain as much as it wants of a particular input at a set price. Its total cost (TC) for a specific amount of C and L would be:

$$TC = xC + yL$$

where x is the unit price of input C and y is the unit price of input L.

However, the amount used of a particular input is subject to diminishing marginal returns. This simply means that given a fixed amount of capital equipment for a completely outfitted shipyard, as more workers are hired, the marginal output of each additional worker increases as the labor requirement is better matched to existing capital equipment. For example, the addition of a second worker to a crew might result in an additional 10 tons of output, and a third worker might add 15 tons. At some point, however, one more additional worker will not add, but will actually cause the total output to decrease. (An easily understood example would be deciding how many teenage boys to hire to mow, rake, hoe, trim shrubs, and fertilize a yard and garden. If the yard owner believed more is better, he would quickly learn otherwise.)

Thus, while some minimum amount of labor is needed to achieve *any* production, there is an upper limit on the total amount of the input to be employed.

A similar example could be made with respect to capital. Given a fixed-size work crew with no capital (tools), then each increment of capital added would add a greater output than the preceding unit of capital, but only up to a point. When more capital units are added to a fixed crew size than the crew can use, utilization of existing space will become inefficient, while a part of the crew now must be responsible for security and maintenance. Total output will decrease.

The next step in our example is to specify a price for a unit of capital and labor. If, for example, a unit of labor cost $10/day and daily cost of a unit of capital is calculated at $100/day, then the cost of producing some specific output can be calculated. If 500 tons is the desired output, and it can be achieved with 5 units of labor (L) and 8 units of capital (C),

$$\text{Total Cost} = \$10 \times 5 + \$100 \times 8 = \$850.00$$

However, it can be reasoned from the above that different amounts of capital and labor can be used to produce 500 tons. In fact, any combination of inputs that satisfies the equation $\$850 = \$10L + \$100C$ is theoretically possible. Solving the equation for C:

$$C = \frac{\$850}{\$100} - \frac{\$10}{\$100} L$$

$$C = 8.5 - .10L$$

When $L = 1$, $C = 8.4$; $L = 2$, $C = 8.3$; . . . $L = 5$, $C = 8$.

The managerial goal is to achieve an output of 500 tons at the least possible cost, that is, search out the optimum combination of labor and capital, given the cost of each input. Theoretically, in the above example, it is possible to use 1 unit of labor and 8.4 units of capital; and indeed, in industries that are automated, such a combination is feasible.

Shipyard work, however, is labor-intensive, which is another way of saying that even the theoretical minimum amount of labor in a capital-intense shipyard operation will be quite large. In fact, the range of possible labor inputs is relatively limited in shipyard work when compared with other manufacturing industries. This does not suggest that U.S. shipyards cannot substitute capital for labor in many operations and achieve lower total costs; but there is an upper limit to the amount of capital that can be substituted for labor.

The conclusion is that as much emphasis should be put on reducing labor unit costs as on reducing units of labor, in attempting to reduce total shipyard costs.

G Nations Having Ship Repair Capabilities

EIGHTY-SEVEN nations/territories have repair facilities—from Nassau in the Bahamas, with a 50-ton travel hoist, to the seven yards of the giant Hitachi Shipbuilding and Engineering Company in Japan, the latter having the ability to handle 500,000-dwt ships at its Ariake Works. A list of these countries follows:

Abu Dhabi	Finland
Algeria	France
Angola	German Democratic Republic
Argentina	German Federal Republic
Australia	Ghana
Austria	Gibraltar (Great Britain)
Azores (Portugal)	Greece
Bahamas	Greenland
Bahrain	Guatemala
Bangladesh	Guinea
Belgium	Guyana
Bermuda	Hong Kong (Great Britain)
Brazil	Hungary
Bulgaria	Iceland
Canada	India
Chile	Indonesia
China, People's Republic	Iran
Colombia	Ireland
Cyprus	Israel
Denmark	Italy
Dominican Republic	Japan
Dubai	Kenya
Egypt	Korea, South
Fiji Islands	Kuwait

Apendix G (cont'd)

Malaysia	Sierra Leone
Malta	Singapore
Martinique	South Africa
Mauritius	Spain
Mexico	Sri Lanka
Morocco	Sudan
Netherlands	Sweden
Netherland Antilles	Switzerland
New Zealand	Syria
Nicaragua	Taiwan
Nigeria	Thailand
Norway	Trinidad
Pakistan	Tunisia
Panama	Turkey
Peru	U.S.S.R.
Philippines	United Kingdom
Poland	United States
Portugal	Uruguay
Saudi Arabia	Yemen
Senegal	Yugoslavia

SOURCE: Marine Engineering/Log, *Marine Directory 1983–84*, pp. B34–92.

H

Shipyards in the Mobilization Base

THIS LIST OF YARDS is derived from the Navy/Maritime Administration Shipyard Mobilization Base (SYMBA) Study, which used an October 1982 data base. Figure H.1 shows the regional distribution of the original 119 yards in the SYMBA base. Some facilities have changed ownership and name since then. At the end of 1984, eighteen yards on the SYMBA list had closed (including Munro, shown on the October 1984 list, Table H.1), and one new yard had appeared (North Florida Shipyards, Jacksonville, with 308 production workers on 1 October 1984). American Shipbuilding, Toledo, Ohio, was reported about to reopen in 1985 under the ownership of the Toledo–Lucas County Port Authority. All yards on the list have the capability of working on a ship at least 400 feet in length. Twenty-three yards are on the MarAd Active Shipbuilding Base list (noted by #). Sixty-three yards are capable of constructing or drydocking a ship at least 400 feet in length (noted by *).

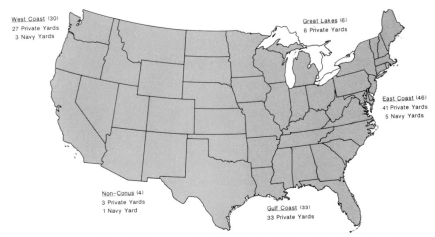

West Coast (30)
27 Private Yards
3 Navy Yards

Great Lakes (6)
6 Private Yards

East Coast (46)
41 Private Yards
5 Navy Yards

Non-Conus (4)
3 Private Yards
1 Navy Yard

Gulf Coast (33)
33 Private Yards

Figure H.1. Location of shipyards identified in the Shipyard Mobilization Base (SYMBA) Study. (Non-Conus = not in continental United States.)

Table H.1. Shipyard mobilization base.

Shipyard		Production Workforce		Minimum water depth (feet)
		October 1982	October 1984	
EAST COAST				
Allied Repair Service Norfolk, VA		150	50	16
Atlantic Dry Dock Corp. Fort George Is., FL	*	86	256	12
Bath Iron Works Bath, ME	*#	7,432	5,500	20
Bath Iron Works Bath, ME	*	80	575	Unk.
Bethlehem Steel Sparrows Point, MD	*#	480	1,500	27
Boston Marine Ind. Pk. Boston, MA	*	100	20	32
Boston Shipyard Corp. Boston, MA	*	100	308	28
Braswell Shipyards Mt. Pleasant, SC	*	142	300	12
Caddell DD & Repair Staten Island, NY	*	160	150	20
Coastal DD & Repair Brooklyn, NY	*	635	846	23
Colonna's Shipyard Norfolk, VA		205	135	22
Detyen's Shipyards Charleston, SC	*	332	240	14
General Dynamics/EB Groton, CT	*#	20,993	20,000	29
General Dynamics Quincy, MA	*#	1,491	3,960	30
General Ship Corp. Boston, MA	*	352	326	21
Hoboken Shipyards (BSI) Hoboken, NJ	*	0	300	32
Jackson Engineering Staten Island, NY	*	98	100	32
Jacksonville Shipyard Jacksonville, FL (incl. Bellinger)	*	2,000	1,175	30

Table H.1. (cont.)

Shipyard		Production Workforce		Minimum water depth (feet)
		October 1982	October 1984	
Jonathan Corp. Norfolk, VA		139	295	28
Metal Trades, Inc. Hollywood, SC		175	111	20
Metro Machine Corp. Norfolk, VA	*	238	330	25
Moon Engineering Co. Norfolk, VA		84	110	17
Munroe Drydock, Inc. Chelsea, MA		85	30	24
Newport News Shipbuild. Newport News, VA (incl. commercial sites)	*#	19,121	20,485	45
Newport Offshore, Ltd. Newport, RI		119	125	16
Norfolk Shipbuilding and Drydock Norfolk, VA	*#	3,019	2,350	29
Pennsylvania Shipbuild. Chester, PA	*#	1,093	880	26
Perth Amboy Drydock Perth Amboy, NJ	*	76	65	28
Promet Marine Corp. E. Providence, RI		25	22	36
Reynolds Shipyard Corp. Staten Island, NY		40	30	30
Robert Derecktor Middletown, RI	*	700	780	35
Rodermond Industries Jersey City, NJ	*	100	75	18
South Portland Shipyard South Portland, ME		38	15	40 (channel)
Tracor Marine, Inc. Port Everglades, FL		280	170	32
Charleston Naval Shipyard Charleston, SC	*	4,602	5,087	37

Table H.1. (cont.)

		Production Workforce		Minimum water depth (feet)
Shipyard		October 1982	October 1984	
Norfolk Naval Shipyard Portsmouth, VA	*	8,084	7,825	40
Philadelphia Naval Shipyard Philadelphia, PA	*	6,825	7,418	40
Portsmouth Naval Shipyard Kittery, ME	*	4,754	4,501	35
U.S.C.G. Shipyard Curtis Bay, MD		500	517	25
Total				
34 private yards		60,168	61,614	
5 public yards		24,765	25,348	
39 east coast yards		84,933	86,962	
GULF COAST				
ADDSCO Mobile, AL	*#	158	370	28
American Marine Corp. New Orleans, LA		400	200	20
Avondale Shipyards Avondale, LA (incl. Westwego)	*#	4,392	3,300	20
Bender Shipbuilding and Repair Mobile, AL	*	640	535	13
Bethlehem Steel Beaumont, TX	*#	695	1,485	30
Bludworth Bond Shipyard Houston, TX		180	125	22
Boland Marine New Orleans, LA		320	75	24
Buck Kreihs Co. New Orleans, LA		180	108	30
Coastal Iron Works Corpus Christi, TX		100	90	12
Delta Shipyard Houma, LA		190	131	15

Table H.1. (cont.)

Shipyard		Production Workforce		Minimum water depth (feet)
		October 1982	October 1984	
Dixie Machine Welding New Orleans, LA		300	180	25
Equitable Shipyards Inc. New Orleans, LA	#	150	80	24
Gulf-Tampa Drydock Tampa, FL		170	290	30
Halter Marine Chicasaw, AL	*#	530	60	30
Hendry Corp. Tampa, FL		80	180	18
Litton/Ingalls Pascagoula, MS (east and west banks)	*#	9,040	5,300	38
Marathon Le Tourneau Brownsville, TX	*	849	1,092	18
Marine Maintenance Houston, TX		105	250	20
McDermott Shipyard Morgan City, LA		320	682	13
Misener Industries Tampa, FL		250	210	18
Newpark Shipbuilding Houston, TX		50	198	25
Runyan Machine Pascagoula, MS		50	50	13
SBA Shipyards Jennings, LA	*	100	30	18
Tampa Shipyards Tampa, FL	*#	633	750	20
Texas Gulfport Shipbuilding Port Arthur, TX	*	250	175	20
Todd Shipyards Galveston, TX	*#	770	460	34
Todd Shipyards New Orleans, LA	*	340	185	35
Total 27 private yards		21,242	16,591	

Table H.1. (cont.)

Shipyard		Production Workforce		Minimum water depth (feet)
		October 1982	October 1984	
GREAT LAKES				
Bay Shipbuilding Sturgeon Bay, WI	*#	690	52	21
Fraser Shipyards Superior, WI	*	17	28	27
Marinette Marine Corp. Marinette, WI	#	475	467	18
Petersen Builders Sturgeon Bay, WI	#	475	964	16
Total				
4 private yards		1,657	1,511	
WEST COAST				
Continental Marine San Francisco, CA		231	213	Unk.
FMC Corp. Portland, OR	*	325	40	30
Kaiser Steel Napa, CA		612	246	15
Lake Union Drydock Seattle, WA		85	70	30
Larson's Boat Shop Terminal Island, CA		80	80	15
Lockheed Shipbuilding Seattle, WA	*#	2,611	2,096	30
Marine Power and Equip. Seattle, WA	*	400	300	21
National Steel and Shipbuilding San Diego, CA	*#	4,575	3,200	28
Pacific Drydock Oakland, CA		131	30	20
Port of Portland Portland, OR		1,730	1,590	30
Port Richmond Richmond, CA	*	70	175	30

Table H.1. (cont.)

Shipyard		Production Workforce		Minimum water depth (feet)
		October 1982	October 1984	
RMI National City, CA		91	110	21
Rowe Machine Works Seattle, WA		20	15	30
Service Engineering Co. San Francisco, CA		428	120	30
Southwest Marine San Diego, CA	*	598	254	30
Southwest Marine San Pedro, CA	*	200	264	25
Southwest Marine San Francisco, CA	*	137	262	Unk.
Tacoma Boatbuilding Tacoma, WA	*#	2,075	1,334	30
Todd Pacific Shipyards San Pedro, CA	*#	3,739	2,877	35
Todd Shipyards San Francisco, CA	*	419	340	30
Todd Shipyards Seattle, WA	*#	3,328	1,280	45
Triple A Machine San Francisco, CA	*	910	230	32
Triple A South San Diego, CA		132	400	20
West Winds San Francisco, CA		97	75	35
U.S. Naval Station San Diego, CA	*	0	0	30
Long Beach Naval Shipyard Long Beach, CA	*	4,659	4,492	35
Mare Island Naval Shipyard Vallejo, CA	*	6,803	5,739	35
Puget Sound Naval Shipyard Bremerton, WA	*	7,245	7,969	45

Table H.1. (cont.)

Shipyard	Production Workforce		Minimum water depth (feet)
	October 1982	October 1984	
Total			
25 private yards	23,024	15,601	
3 public yards	18,707	18,200	
28 west coast yards	41,731	33,801	
OUTSIDE CONUS			
Dillingham Shipyard Honolulu, HI	200	60	34
Pacific Marine Honolulu, HI	100	80	20
Puerto Rico Drydock * San Juan, PR	150	70	30
Pearl Harbor Naval Shipyard * Pearl Harbor, HI	4,161	4,099	40
Total			
3 private yards •	450	210	
1 public yard	4,161	4,099	
4 out-CONUS yards	4,611	4,309	
GRAND TOTAL			
93 private yards	106,541	95,527	
9 public yards	47,633	47,647	
102 yards	154,174	143,174	

■ Economic Cost of U.S. Sugar Quotas, 1983

HISTORICALLY, the United States has imposed high import quotas on foreign sugar. The cost of these quotas falls on the consumer; the benefit is incurred by approximately 16,000 U.S. sugar producers.

The aggregate annual additional cost to the consumer was estimated to be $1.17 billion, or a per capita cost of $5.00 in 1983. Calculations are as shown below.

Domestic sugar production (thousands of short tons) in 1983	5,680
Imported sugar (thousands of short tons) in 1983	3,168
Total	8,848[1]

The 1983 resident U.S. population was estimated at 234 million, having a per capita sugar consumption of 71 pounds, of which 64 percent was supplied domestically.[2]

The world price of sugar in July 1983 was approximately 12.45¢/pound. The U.S. domestic price was 22.75¢/pound.[3]

22.75¢ minus 12.45¢ = 10.3¢ (per pound additional cost for 5.68 million short tons of sugar)
5.68 million short tons = 11.36 billion pounds of sugar
11.36 billion pounds × 10.3¢ = $1.17 billion ($5.00 per capita)

SOURCES: U.S., Bureau of Census, *Statistical Abstract of the United States 1985* (Washington, D.C.: U.S. Government Printing Office, 1984), pp. 121 and 665. *Wall Street Journal*, 31 May 1983, p. 50, and *Wall Street Journal*, 27 August 1985, p. 50.

[1] The production and consumption figures are very close. Consumption was estimated to be 8.9 million short tons.

[2] Consumption is the residual after nonfood use and ending stocks are subtracted. This explains the discrepancy of 8.9 million short tons divided by 234 million, which equals 76 pounds per capita.

[3] The January 1986 future world price was estimated at 4.77¢/pound; the January 1986 future domestic price at 21.05¢/pound. Assuming the same amount of sugar consumed in 1986 as in 1983 and a 1986 population of 245 million, then the cost to the U.S. economy would be $1.84 billion or $7.51 for every man, woman and child in the country.

[4] A recent study published by the American Enterprise Institute estimated the net cost of the sugar program in 1983 as $1.3 billion. See Andrew Schmitz, *The U.S. Sugar Program under Price Uncertainty*.

Notes

Chapter 1

1. Recent private studies include, H. Ullman, Center for Strategic and International Studies, *Crisis or Opportunity? U.S. Maritime Industries and National Security* (1984) and H. Ullman and P. Pattavino, Center for Strategic and International Studies, *Forecasts for U.S. Maritime Industries in 1989: Balancing National Security and Economic Considerations* (1984).

2. U.S., Navy and U.S. Maritime Administration, *Shipyard Mobilization Base (SYMBA) Study* (Executive Summary), February 1984, p. L-4. This study is discussed in Appendix A.

3. Ibid., p. L-6.

4. Harold U. Faulkner, *American Economic History* (8th ed.), p. 228.

5. U.S., Maritime Administration, *Annual Report FY 1975* (Washington, D.C,: U.S. Government Printing Office, 1976), p. 1.

6. Under the Merchant Marine Act of 1936, U.S. ship operators engaged in foreign trade who received a government operating differential subsidy (ODS), were required to build in U.S. yards. U.S., non-ODS foreign trade operators could build in foreign yards, or American, as they chose. However, under Section 615 of the Merchant Marine Act of 1936, as amended, when no construction differential subsidy (CDS) funds were available, operators could apply for a waiver to build in foreign yards. Section 615 authority for U.S. subsidized operators to build foreign in lieu of CDS funding expired 30 September 1983. The Reagan administration has asked Congress to reinstate the option.

7. For example, only Newport News Shipyard and Electric Boat (General Dynamics) can build a Trident *Ohio*-class nuclear ballistic missile submarine; only Newport News can build a *Nimitz*-class attack carrier.

8. "Calhoon: Ship Industry at a Turning Point," *The Journal of Commerce*, 26 December 1984, p. 1.

9. "Maritime Policy and National Security," *Shipyard Weekly*, 27 December 1984, p. 3.

10. The National Defense Reserve Fleet (NDRF) was created by the Ship Sales Act of 1946. This fleet is composed of inactive, government-owned merchant-type ships. In 1977 a program to upgrade a part of this fleet was funded. In

January 1986 there are 72 ships in the NDRF that can be reactivated and on berth in a 5–10-day time frame.

11. The 119 yards referred to in the SYMBA study account for 90 percent of the worker base and all of the major facilities (ways, drydocks) in the base.

12. Although there is debate within the Department of Defense as to whether the Soviet Union would accept the expected high aircraft losses in attacking NATO shipyards, particularly in Great Britain and southern Europe, the fact remains that the Soviets do possess such a capability.

13. John Lehman, "Interview," *Seapower*, April 1983, pp. 59–60.

14. U.S., Navy and U.S. Maritime Administration, *Shipyard Mobilization Base (SYMBA) Study*, p. L-10.

Chapter 2

1. In 1947 Thor Heyerdahl and five others sailed from Peru to the Pacific Polynesian islands. Their "ship" was actually a raft made of 40-foot balsa logs. Construction materials and techniques were of the prehistoric period. The *Kon-Tiki* had two masts with a square sail between; the living accommodation was an open bamboo cabin. The purpose of the voyage was to demonstrate the possibility that Polynesia could have been settled by peoples from South America.

2. Charles E. Gibson, *The Story of the Ship*, p. 6.

3. This glimpse of the early history of shipbuilding neglects developments taking place in the Far East (China, Japan) primarily because the American shipbuilding industry evolved from the designs and concepts of Mediterranean and European builders.

4. G. S. Baker, *The Merchant Ship: Design Past and Present*, p. 20.

5. Maurice Griffiths, *Man the Shipbuilder*, p. 21.

6. "U.S. Merchant Shipbuilding: 1607–1976," *Marine Engineering/Log*, August 1976, p. 67.

7. The first American ship for export was built at a shipyard established by one John Winter near Portland, Maine ("U.S. Merchant Shipbuilding: 1607–1976"). The colonists, while building for the mother country, also built for themselves, and in so doing competed with English shipowners, an activity not in keeping with mercantilist doctrine.

8. In 1675, over 600 New England vessels were engaged in cod fishing, employing approximately 4,000 men. One hundred years later, in 1775, in addition to the fishing fleets there were over 300 ships engaged in whaling (Harold U. Faulkner, *American Economic History*, p. 87).

9. John G. B. Hutchins, *The American Maritime Industries and Public Policy, 1789–1914: An Economic History*, p. 153.

10. Faulkner, *American Economic History*, p. 85. Carl E. McDowell and Helen M. Gibbs, *Ocean Transportation*, p. 21, estimate this tonnage to be 210,000 out of 600,000 gross tons of British-owned shipping in the 1770s.

11. Faulkner, *American Economic History*, p. 84.

12. Carl C. Cutler, *Greyhounds of the Sea*, p. 7. Colonial ships frequently logged speeds of over 9 knots. In 1762, for example, the schooner *John* logged a noon-to-noon run of 208 miles.

13. E. B. Potter, *The Naval Academy Illustrated History of the U.S. Navy*, p. 9.

14. Numerous examples of the effect of American vessel speed are recorded. In 1777 the privateer *Revenge* of 10 guns defeated two English ships of 14 guns each. In 1780 the American *Pickering* of 180 tons and 14 guns forced the larger British *Achilles* (three times larger, with three times as many guns) to break off the engagement. Greater speed and maneuverability gave the edge to the American ship. (See Cutler, *Greyhounds of the Sea* for this and other examples.)

15. Edgar S. Maclay, *A History of American Privateers*, p. 506.

16. Cutler, *Greyhounds of the Sea*, p. 53.

17. Ibid., p. 54.

18. Some writers credit French designs as the inspiration for the fast American ships and ultimately the clipper ship. The best evidence, however, suggests this evolution was uniquely American.

19. Cutler, *Greyhounds of the Sea*, p. 13.

20. John G. B. Hutchins (*The American Maritime Industries and Public Policy, 1789–1914*) cites the "cotton freighters" of the first part of the nineteenth century as another example of American maritime innovation. Hutchins notes that these large, broad-beam, and well-constructed ships could carry 2,000 pounds of cotton per registered ton, compared to 900 pounds for smaller, earlier ships. A unique feature of these vessels was their flat bottoms so as to transit the Mississippi River bar.

21. Hutchins, *The American Maritime Industries and Public Policy, 1789–1914*, p. 261.

22. David R. MacGregor, *Merchant Sailing Ships, 1815–1850*, p. 168.

23. Hutchins, *The American Maritime Industries and Public Policy, 1789–1914*, p. 267.

24. The record clipper passage from New York to San Francisco was 89 days, set by the *Flying Cloud* in 1851.

25. The best recorded time for an American ship in the so-called tea trade was the *Oriental* of New York (1,050 tons), Hong Kong to London in 97 days.

26. In colonial times and the early nineteenth century, the American shipowner not only depended upon a well-constructed and innovatively designed vessel, but on innovatively *employing* his ship. Where there were trade imbalances, the so-called triangle trade resulted (e.g., from the North American colonies with agricultural products to southern Europe, from there to England with Mediterranean products, and from England to the colonies with manufactures). A modern-day example would be the innovative employment of Bethlehem Steel's ore fleet in carrying coal outbound and iron ore inbound. See: Wolf Dieter Bender, "The Optimum Size of an Iron Making Firm's Fleet for Ocean Dry-Bulk Transportation" (Ph.D. dissertation, Clemson University, 1975).

27. Clinton H. Whitehurst, Jr., "The Aging Mariners," *U.S. Naval Institute Proceedings*, April 1980, p. 124.

Chapter 3

1. John G. B. Hutchins, *The American Maritime Industries and Public Policy, 1789–1914: An Economic History*, p. 303.

2. Ibid., p. 306.

3. Carl E. McDowell and Helen M. Gibbs, *Ocean Transportation*, p. 22.

4. Hutchins, *The American Maritime Industries and Public Policy, 1789–1914*, p. 297. In 1860, skilled British shipyard workers earned 4s to 7s per day. This pay rate was 50 percent less than in the United States.

5. While American ship costs were much lower than those of Great Britain, Canadian-built ships were roughly competitive with U.S. ships. In the first part of the nineteenth century the ports of Saint John and Quebec emerged as shipbuilding centers.

6. Compared to the typical clipper ship, the extreme clipper was longer, narrower of beam, and had a deeper hull depth so as, when loaded, to better carry greater sail.

7. G. S. Baker, *The Merchant Ship: Design Past and Present*, p. 36.

8. Maurice Griffiths, *Man the Shipbuilder*, p. 59. The single cylinder steam engine was patented by James Watt in 1769. Earlier French and British inventors had demonstrated the potential of steam; Watt was the first to put it to practical use.

9. Ibid., p. 67.

10. David R. MacGregor, *Merchant Sailing Ships, 1815–1850*, p. 13.

11. Hutchins, *The American Maritime Industries and Public Policy, 1789–1914*, pp. 444–46.

12. David R. MacGregor, *Merchant Sailing Ships, 1815–1850*, p. 15.

13. Samuel E. Morison and Henry S. Commanger, *The Growth of the American Republic*, pp. 615–16.

14. Harold U. Faulkner, *American Economic History*, p. 230.

15. Hutchins, *The American Maritime Industries and Public Policy, 1789–1914*, p. 266.

16. Robert A. Kilmarx, ed., *America's Maritime Legacy: A History of the U.S. Merchant Marine and Shipbuilding Industry since Colonial Times*, p. 68.

17. Hutchins, *The American Maritime Industries and Public Policy, 1789–1914*, p. 455.

18. Kilmarx, ed., *America's Maritime Legacy*, p. 81.

19. Hutchins, *The American Maritime Industries and Public Policy, 1789–1914*, p. 457.

20. J. Russell Smith, *Influence of the Great War Upon Shipping*, p. 31.

21. Kilmarx, ed., *America's Maritime Legacy*, p. 125.

22. A congressional report in 1921 stated "that considering the program as a whole, the accomplishments in the number of ships constructed, the tonnage secured, and the time within which the ships were completed and delivered, constitute the most remarkable achievement in shipbuilding that the world has ever seen." Quoted in Kilmarx, ed., *America's Maritime Legacy*, p. 141.

23. Ibid., p. 149.

24. A major problem was that a specific amount of tonnage had been contracted for by the government. When the war ended sooner than anticipated, the government was still committed to honoring its contracts, and ship deliveries continued.

25. U.S., Congress, *Congressional Record, May 25, 1920 to June 5, 1920*, p. 8466.

26. In 1935, a trophy was donated by Harold Hales, a member of the British Parliament, for the fastest North Atlantic passage. The run was between Bishops Rock, England, and the New York Ambrose lightship, a distance of 2,900 miles. The trophy is commonly referred to as the Blue Riband Trophy.

27. John G. Bunker, *Liberty Ships*, p. 17.

28. A detailed description of the World War II building program is provided in: David R. Dorn, "Ships for Victory," *U.S. Naval Institute Proceedings*, February 1985, p. 68.

29. Phillip Andrews and Leonard Engel, *Navy Yearbook*, p. 20.

30. Melvin Maddocks, *The Great Liners*, p. 29.

31. The *Alabama* was the first warship designed as a commerce raider from the keel up. She had a 300-horsepower engine plus sails rigged on three masts. When she was under sail, her propeller could be detached from the shaft and lifted out of the water. She had a condenser for making fresh water and exceptionally large (coal) bunker spaces. The *Alabama* was not designed for speed but for endurance. (Her best speed was no more than 13 knots.) Her armament was relatively light, but sufficient to engage a warship of equal weight should it become necessary. The Imperial German Navy gave much credit to the *Alabama* in its building and operating commerce raiders in World War I.

32. Hutchins, *The American Maritime Industries and Public Policy, 1789–1914*, p. 549.

33. Ibid. Hutchins notes that the competition ultimately faced by the wooden schooner was the towed barge. As tugs became more powerful, tows became larger, and rates on bulk movements fell. The schooners had no place to profitably go. Foreign trade was dominated by steel steamships. Moreover, steamships had become larger, and in some cases, specialized. Coal colliers and oil tankers are particularly good examples in this regard.

Chapter 4

1. An Act Imposing Duties on Tonnage, 1st Cong., 1st sess., 20 July 1789, Chapter 3, sec. 1. An Act Imposing Duties on the Tonnage of Ships or Vessels, 1st Cong., 2d sess., 30 July 1790, U.S.-built and -owned vessels paid a duty of 6¢/vessel ton against 30¢/ton for U.S.-built, foreign-owned ships. Fifty cents a ton was levied on foreign-built, foreign-owned vessels.

2. Robert A. Kilmarx, ed., *America's Maritime Legacy: A History of the U.S. Merchant Marine and Shipbuilding Industry since Colonial Times*, p. 125.

3. The issue of what the actual cost differential was as between U.S. and foreign yards continued after World War II. The case of American Export Line's *Constitution* and *Independence* is an example. Initially, the government subsidy was figured at approximately 50 percent of vessel construction cost. Recalculation reduced this to about 28 percent; the final government share was approximately 45 percent. For a detailed discussion of CDS calculation in the postwar period, see the *Annual Report of the Federal Maritime Board/Maritime Administration, 1951*, pp. 24–27.

4. U.S., Maritime Commission, *Economic Survey of the American Merchant Marine*, p. 64.

5. A review of the "Mariner program" can be found in Clinton H. Whitehurst, Jr., "The Aging Mariners," *U.S. Naval Institute Proceedings*, April 1980, p. 124.

6. U.S., General Accounting Office, *Cargo Preference Programs for Government Financed Ocean Shipments Could Be Improved*, p. 6.

7. U.S., Maritime Administration, *Annual Report For FY 1984* (Washington, D.C.: Maritime Administration, 1984), p. 3. See also note "c" Table 4.1.

8. "A Cost Watching Navy Snubs U.S. Shipyards," *Business Week*, 10 November 1980, pp. 39–40.

9. "Letters," *Marine Engineering/Log*, February 1985, p. 19.

10. Address before Maritime Trades Department, AFL-CIO at Bal Harbor, Florida, 15 February 1985.

11. Aside from completely ignoring the additional cost to the consumer of reserving U.S. domestic ocean *commercial* cargoes to U.S.-flag ships, differentiating government-sponsored cargoes from commercial cargoes fails on logical grounds. For example, assume that Congress appropriates $500 million for wheat to be shipped to a famine-stricken African nation. The $500 million appropriation will cover the cost of the wheat and transportation. If U.S. ships are used, assume $50 million for transportation; if foreign vessels, $25 million. In the first instance, $450 million is left to purchase wheat; in the second, $475 million. In using U.S. ships, the taxpayer is "getting" less wheat. If the amount of wheat is held constant in both cases, the average cost per ton will increase by using U.S.-flag ships. This is the indirect cost the taxpayer bears.

Chapter 5

1. U.S., Congress. Merchant Marine Act of 1920, Section 27 (41 Stat. 988, Chapter 250).

2. John G. B. Hutchins, *The American Maritime Industries and Public Policy, 1789–1914: An Economic History*, p. 543.

3. Panama Canal Act of 1912 (37 Stat. 560, 566–67).

4. Hutchins, *The American Maritime Industries and Public Policy, 1789–1914*, p. 543.

5. Clinton H. Whitehurst, Jr., *American Domestic Shipping in American Ships: Jones Act Costs, Benefits, and Options*, p. 19.

6. The Reagan administration considers the "build foreign" option an essential part of its maritime program. On 2 April 1985 the secretary of transportation sent to Congress a legislative proposal that would make permanent authority for an operator receiving an operating subsidy to acquire his vessels overseas.

7. Whitehurst, *American Domestic Shipping in American Ships: Jones Act Costs, Benefits, and Options*, p. 18.

8. Ibid., pp. 17, 20

9. Shipbuilders Council of America, *Statistical Summary*, pp. 1, 8.

10. Vessels of foreign registry may transport between U.S. ports empty cargo vans, shipping tanks, and barges carried on board ship that are used in the vessel's foreign trade, as well as transfer cargo between barges. This privilege requires reciprocal rights for U.S. vessels.

NOTES   251

11. U.S., Congress. Public Law 89, 81st Cong., 27 December 1950. Before a waiver is granted, the Maritime Administration must first attempt to arrange the needed transportation in a U.S.-flag vessel.

12. The most recent exception was proposed on 9 January 1985 by the U.S. Customs Service. It would allow a foreign-flag vessel to take on a passenger at a U.S. port, proceed to a foreign port, and make one or more calls at U.S. ports, ultimately landing the passenger at his original port of embarkation.

13. "Free the Alaska 600,000," *The Wall Street Journal*, 19 August 1981, p. 28. An Alaska Statehood Commission study in 1982 estimated the cost of using American ships in moving Alaska oil to the continental United States to exceed the foreign-ship alternative by 40 percent.

14. One recent order for domestic tanker tonnage highlights the importance of the Jones Act to U.S. shipyards. In 1984, Exxon ordered two 209,000-dwt tankers at a price of $125 million each.

15. The large American-flag cruise liners are the *Constitution* and the *Independence*, owned by America-Hawaii Cruises. The small cruise ships are the *Newport Clipper* and the *Nantucket Clipper*, owned by Coastal Cruise Lines. In 1984, six additional U.S.-flag cruise ships were in the planning stage. For a discussion of the cruise ship market and American participation in it, see: Clinton H. Whitehurst, Jr., "U.S. Flag Passenger Ships and National Security," *Marine Policy Reports*, Vol 7, No. 1, September 1984.

16. U.S., Congress, *U.S. Shipping and Shipbuilding: Trends and Public Choices*, p. 64.

17. U.S., Congress, Office of Technology Assessment, *An Assessment of Maritime Trade and Technology*, p. 168.

18. Arthur J. Haskell, "Discussion—The Jones Act: Foreign Built Vessels and the Domestic Shipping Industry," *Society of Naval Architects and Marine Engineers Transactions* 91, 1983, pp. 184–85.

19. Letter from Maritime Administrator Harold E. Shear, to Lawrence French, President, American Society of Naval Architects and Marine Engineers, 12 October 1983.

20. "Washington News," *Marine Engineering/Log*, April 1984, p. 21. On 13 July 1985 President Reagan signed legislation limiting the export of Alaska crude oil. However, a review of the present incentives to produce Alaska oil, including export restrictions, were also mandated by the act.

21. Warren G. Leback and John W. McConnell, Jr., "The Jones Act: Foreign Built Vessels and the Domestic Shipping Industry," *Society of Naval Architects and Marine Engineers Transactions* 91, 1983, pp. 169–84.

22. Clinton H. Whitehurst, Jr., *The U.S. Merchant Marine: In Search of an Enduring Maritime Policy*, Chapters 6 and 20.

Chapter 6

1. U.S., Office of Management and Budget, *Standard Industrial Classification Manual* (Washington, D.C.: Government Printing Office, 1972), p. 199. Included are the building and repairing of barges, cargo ships, combatants, dredges, drilling platforms, fireboats, fishing vessels, hydrofoils, lighters, passenger ships, transports, tugboats, and yachts.

2. Marine Engineering/Log, *Marine Directory*, 1984.

3. U.S., Department of Transportation, Maritime Administration, *Relative Cost of Shipbuilding*, p. 4.

4. *Standard and Poor's Register of Corporations, Directors, and Executives, 1984*, Vol. 3, pp. 283–84.

5. Shipbuilders Council of America, *Shipyard Weekly*, 12 July 1984, p. 3.

6. U.S., Department of Transportation, Maritime Administration, *Relative Cost of Shipbuilding*, p. 4.

7. Parent companies with shipyard subsidiaries are Congoleum Corporation, Manitowoc Company, Bethlehem Steel Corporation, General Dynamics, Litton Industries, Lockheed Corporation, Morisson-Knudsen, Tenneco, and Trinity Industries. In July 1985, the Ogden Corporation sold its Avondale Shipyards subsidiary to a new employee-owned corporation—the Avondale Corporation.

8. The active shipbuilding industrial base (ASIB) decreased from 27 yards in 1982 to 23 yards in 1985. The four yards dropping out were closed or in caretaker status.

9. "U.S. Naval Shipbuilding Program 1982," *U.S. Naval Institute Proceedings*, January 1983, pp. 120–21.

10. As a rule major overhauls are performed in large private or naval shipyards. For example, the reactivation of the battleship *Iowa* was awarded to Avondale Shipyards.

11. Since December 1982, sixteen shipyards have dropped out of the mobilization base. Four of these were build-capable yards in the ASIB.

12. Gene D. Heil, "U.S. Ship Repair," *Marine Engineering/Log*, May 1984, pp. 57, 59.

13. "Elimination of Duty on Foreign Repairs," *Marine Engineering/Log*, February 1985, p. 49.

14. M. Lee Rice, "The Tie That Binds: Navy Ship Repair and American Shipyards," *Naval Engineers Journal*, January 1985, p. 44.

15. U.S., Congress, House, Committee on Armed Services, Defense Department, Authorization and Oversight Hearings FY 1985, Part 5, 98th Cong., 2d sess., p. 721.

16. A Booz, Allen and Hamilton study, "Outlook for Naval Ship Conversion and Repair," sees the most likely naval ship repair market as about $6.8 billion in 1988.

17. U.S., Congress, Committee on Appropriations, *Report on Department of Defense Appropriations Bill 1985*, 98th Cong., 2d sess., p. 62.

18. Ibid.

19. U.S., Department of Transportation, Maritime Administration, *Relative Cost of Shipbuilding*, pp. i and 12.

20. U.S. Congress, Committee on Merchant Marine and Fisheries, *Hearings on Maritime Redevelopment Bank*, p. 1175.

21. John G. B. Hutchins, *The American Maritime Industries and Public Policy: 1789–1914*, p. 280.

22. U.S., Congress, House, Seapower Subcommittee on Armed Services, *Hearings on Current Status of Shipyards, 1974*, Part 2, 93d Cong., 2d sess., p. 855.

23. "Interview With SNAME President Larry French," *Seapower*, October 1984, p. 19.

24. Navy League of the United States, *The Almanac of Seapower 1985*, p. 94.

Chapter 7

1. *Cradle of American Shipbuilding, Portsmouth Naval Shipyard*, Library of Congress #LC78-600146, Portsmouth, N.H., 1978. In 1798, the Secretary of the Navy Benjamin Stoddard instructed Joshua Humphries, the first chief naval constructor, to make surveys for possible sites for government-owned navy yards. The portion of his survey from New London, Connecticut to Wisasset, Maine reported that Fernald's (Dennet's) Island near Portsmouth, New Hampshire was the best site for a government shipyard in that area. Land was also purchased at Washington, D.C.; Charlestown, Massachusetts; Philadelphia, Pennsylvania; Brooklyn, New York; and Gosport, Virginia. The site at Gosport had been an active shipyard since 1767 and was to become the Norfolk Naval Shipyard. The other sites became respectively the Washington Navy Yard, the Boston Naval Shipyard, the Philadelphia Naval Shipyard, and the New York Naval Shipyard.

2. Ibid.

3. *Current Status of Shipyards, 1974*, hearings before the Seapower Subcommittee of the Committee on Armed Forces, House of Representatives, 93d Cong., 2d sess., Part 1 of 3 parts, p. 11.

4. Ibid., p. 109. This mission statement was also true in the 1960s when eleven shipyards were operating. In reducing them, to the eight now existing, Boston, New York, and San Francisco Naval Shipyards were closed as a result of base closure programs to achieve lower Department of Defense budgets during the 1960s and 1970. These three facilities are now operated under lease to private ship repair firms.

5. While the reporting chain of command for naval shipyards is directly to the Commander, Naval Sea Systems Command, additional duty responsibilities are included in naval shipyard commanders' orders for them to report to local naval base commanders to effect local area liaison. While engineering duty officers commanded NavSea from 1974 to 1985, in June 1985 an unrestricted line officer, Vice Admiral W. H. Rowden, USN, relieved Vice Admiral E. B. Fowler, USN, as Commander, Naval Sea Systems Command.

6. Sue Leammon and E. D. Wichels, *Sidewheelers to Nuclear Power*, p. 96. Those who knew Irv Whitthorne respected his dedication, wisdom, and absolute commitment to excellence. Mare Island pipe-work in submarines was distinctive in quality under his leadership. The floor of the pipe-shop was kept showplace clean. He was of the old school for whom a master of the shop was precisely that, and other supervisors and employees reacted accordingly. He began work at Mare Island in July 1908 as a helper plumber. At the time for his mandatory retirement in 1960, he was the master pipefitter, but at the request of the Navy, he continued in his employment and became the machinery group superintendent. His spirit is typical of the majority of civil service workers in naval shipyards. They are extremely proud of their role, but recognize that improvement is always possible and work diligently to that end.

7. Captain J. J. Fee, USN, "Evolution of the Engineering Duty Officer in the United States Navy," *Naval Engineers Journal*, Vol. 97, No. 3, March 1985, pp. 58–64. Most of the information concerning the history of engineering duty officers as it pertains to naval shipyards has been developed from this timely article.

8. As a result of the Personnel Act of 1899, sponsored by then–Assistant Secretary of the Navy Theodore Roosevelt, the Engineer Corps input was dried up, and all new engineering duty only (EDO) officers were made part of the line of the Navy. In 1910, all machinery and electrical responsibilities were transferred to the Bureau of Steam Engineering, and by 1914 the Bureau of Equipment, which was previously responsible for electrical machinery, ceased to exist. The Bureau of Ships was formed in 1940 as a combination of the Bureaus of Construction and Engineering.

9. The new bureau was judged to be a success by the Naval Committee of the House of Representatives, whose 1944 report stated: "It is no exaggeration to state that the naval shipbuilding and ship repair and maintenance accomplishments of the past four years could not possibly have been achieved under the two bureau system."

10. Fee, "Evolution of the Engineering Duty Officer in the United States Navy," *Naval Engineers Journal*, p. 63.

11. This command relationship can be expected to prevail after the reorganization that eliminated the Naval Material Command, the command to which the several logistics commands reported until early 1985.

12. Clinton H. Whitehurst, Jr., "Is There a Future for Naval Shipyards?" *U.S. Naval Institute Proceedings*, April 1978, pp. 30–40.

13. *U.S. Shipping and Shipbuilding: Trends and Policy Choices* (Washington, D.C.: Congressional Budget Office, August 1984), pp. 39–40.

14. Ibid., pp. 57–58.

15. Charles F. Elliot, "The Genesis of the Modern Navy," *U.S. Naval Institute Proceedings*, March 1966, pp. 62–69.

16. Steven Eisenstat. "Demise of NAVMAT Confirmed" *Navy Times*, 15 April 1985, p. 3.

17. *Navy Times*, 15 April 1985.

18. See "USS *Saratoga*: A Taxpayer and Military Preparedness Issue," *Congressional Record—Senate*, 30 April 1979, pp. S4916–S4922 and 2 May 1979, pp. S5163–S5166 for the arguments introduced into the record by Senator John Warner (R-VA) in response to reasons supporting the assignment of *Saratoga* SLEP conversion to the Philadelphia Naval Shipyard. A final point made by this plea to assign the SLEP to the Newport News Shipbuilding and Dry Dock Company was as follows: "The uniformed Navy in the normal Navy procurement process selected Newport News both on cost and military grounds as the appropriate yard to modernize the *Saratoga*. On two occasions, however, in 1978 and 1979, the senior Navy procurement officials were overruled at the highest levels of Government." It is commonly understood that this assignment was made specifically to fulfill campaign promises made by Vice President Mondale to the Philadelphia area constituency. The ongoing assignment of continued SLEP conversions is a demonstration that naval shipyards can be counted on to perform ambitious tasks once the commitment to them is clear.

19. *Current Status of Shipyards, 1974*, p. A6.

20. Marianne Bowes, "Overhaul Costs in Public and Private Shipyards: A Case Study," CRC 4429 (Revised) (Alexandria, Va.: Center for Naval Analyses, October 1981).

Chapter 8

1. U.S., Department of Transportation, Maritime Administration, *Report on Survey of U.S. Shipbuilding and Repair Facilities 1984*, pp. 117–33. All ASIB yards are included. An additional 137 yards were listed as having major topside repair facilities for ships 400 feet or longer.

2. In his 1985 posture statement, Secretary of the Navy John Lehman noted that "The Navy shipbuilding and repair programs now account for over 80 percent of all employment in that industry in the United States."

3. U.S., Congress, House, Subcommittee on Merchant Marine, *Hearings, Maritime Redevelopment Bank Act*, pp. 1007–9 and U.S. International Trade Commission, *Analysis of the International Competitiveness of the U.S. Commercial Shipbuilding and Repair Industry*, p. 5.

4. Shipbuilders Council of America, *Statistical Summary*, January 1985, p. 3.

5. U.S., Congress, Office of Technology Assessment, *An Assessment of Maritime Trade and Technology*, p. 109.

6. Other shipyard unions, in addition to the four large unions already cited, include: International Union of Operating Engineers, International Association of Bridge, Structural and Ornamental Iron Workers, International Longshoremens' Association, International Association of Machinists and Aerospace Workers, International Brotherhood of Electrical Workers, Internatiaonal Brotherhood of Painters and Allied Trades, Pacific Coast Metal Trades Union, Teamsters, Shipwrights Union, United Brotherhood of Carpenters and Joiners, and United Industrial Workers of North America.

7. National Research Council, *Toward More Productive Naval Shipbuilding*, p. 22.

8. U.S., Congress, House, *Hearings, Maritime Redevelopment Bank Act*, p. 59.

9. Tim Neale, "Root Causes," *American Shipper*, November 1982, p. 26.

10. "Developments in Industrial Relations," *Monthly Labor Review*, December 1983, pp. 55–56.

11. "Improve Productivity, Todd Shipyards Told," *The Journal of Commerce*, New York 15 February 1985, p. 10.

12. Raymond Ramsay, "A Time for Shipbuilding Renaissance," *Naval Engineers Journal*, September 1983, p. 59.

13. "After Six Months, Management and Labor at Penn Shipbuilding Are Happy with Work Rule Changes—14% Profit Sharing," *American Shipper*, October 1982, p. 31. Labor negotiations in 1985, however, exhibited an uneven pattern. In April, Electric Boat concluded a new 42-month agreement with the AFL-CIO Metal Trades Council without acrimony. On the other hand, on 30 June 1985, the 4,500 workers at Bath Iron Works voted overwhelmingly to strike the company, primarily over a proposed two-tier wage system. The strike ended

in October 1985 when the Industrial Union of Marine Shipbuilding Workers agreed to a three-year wage freeze and a temporary two-tier wage system for new workers.

14. "Work Rules Axed," *American Shipper*, August 1982, p. 11.

15. Interview with Page Groton, director of the Shipbuilding Division, International Brotherhood of Boilermakers, Iron Shipbuilders, Blacksmiths, Forgers, and Helpers, 20 May 1985.

16. The view that shipyard skills *are not* unique is held by Raymond Ramsay, director of the Office of Maritime Affairs and Shipbuilding Technology, Naval Sea Systems Command. See note 12.

17. Most major studies on shipyards and shipbuilding/ship repair forecast lower shipyard employment levels as the naval building program tapers off in the early 1990s and there are no new government initiatives in support of shipyards. However, disagreements occur as to whether these numbers (of workers) would be sufficient to support a mobilization at some time in the future.

18. Ramsay, "A Time for Shipbuilding Renaissance," *Naval Engineers Journal*, p. 56.

19. U.S., Congress, House, *Hearings, Maritime Redevelopment Bank Act*, p. 1190 and U.S. International Trade Commission, *Analysis of the International Competitiveness of the U.S. Commercial Shipbuilding and Repair Industry*, p. 20.

20. Interview with Rudy Matzner, vice-president for finance and administration, Braswell Shipyards, Inc., Charleston, S.C., 15 March 1985. Matzner indicated that it cost the shipyard approximately $800 to have an already qualified welder certified for shipyard work by the American Bureau of Shipping.

21. Another consideration is that the multiskilled worker in a small facility, although somewhat older than the typical worker in a larger shipyard, would have greater than average experience. Here, older would definitely seem to be better. For another view of the small shipyard, see note 17, Chapter 6.

22. U.S., Congress, Office of Technology Assessment, *An Assessment of Maritime Trade and Technology*, p. 109.

23. U.S., Congress, House, *Hearings, Maritime Redevelopment Bank Act*, p. 1009.

Chapter 9

1. U.S., Congress, Congressional Budget Office, *U.S. Shipbuilding Trends and Policy Choices*, p. 41.

2. U.S., Congress, Office of Technology Assessment, *An Assessment of Maritime Trade and Technology*, p. 97.

3. A. J. Ambrose, ed., *Jane's Merchant Shipping Review*, p. 86.

4. H. K. Ullman and P. J. Pettavino, *Forecasts for U.S. Maritime Industries in 1989: Balancing National Security and Economic Considerations*, p. 8.

5. National Research Council, *Toward More Productive Naval Shipbuilding*, p. 13.

6. U.S., Congress, House, *Hearings, Maritime Redevelopment Bank Act*, p. 26 (statement of W. James Amoss).

7. U.S., Congress, House, Seapower Subcommittee, *Hearings on Current Status of Shipyards, 1974*, p. 855.

8. In manufacturing multiple units of a product (series building in shipyards), the amount of time and the quantity of resources, including labor, to build each successive unit have been observed to decrease. This reduction in inputs is known as the *learning curve effect*. An example of decreasing costs in a manufacturing process in which costs follow a 70 percent learning curve would be: 1st unit cost is $1,000, 2d unit is $1000 × .70 = $700, the 4th unit cost is $700 × .70 = $490, and the 8th unit cost is $490 × .70 = $343.

9. The carriers are the *Theodore Roosevelt*, *Abraham Lincoln*, and *George Washington*. It must be noted, however, that there are trade-offs between innovation, particularly in design on the one hand and risk of failure on the other. Thus, while a design innovation might theoretically lower costs and significantly improve performance, there is always the risk that it might not work. These trade-offs are discussed in an excellent article by Robert A. Johnson ("Innovation in Ship Design") in the *Naval Engineers Journal*, January 1985, p. 64.

10. National Research Council, *Toward More Productive Naval Shipbuilding*, p. 22.

11. Navy League of the United States, *The Almanac of Seapower 1984*, Table M-11, p. 191.

12. Ibid., p. 19.

13. If the bid-off for repair and overhaul work discussed in Chapter 6 clearly comes out in favor of the private yards, a significant increase in private yard work forces would probably come about.

14. The National Advisory Committee on Oceans and Atmosphere notes that in 1982 the United States, with around 1 percent of the world's orders for commercial shipping, had more shipyard employees than Japan with over 40 percent. A large part of the explanation was that U.S. yards are primarily engaged in building and repair of technologically complex naval combatant ships, which is more labor-intensive than building and repairing commercial vessels.

15. National Research Council, *Toward More Productive Naval Shipbuilding*, p. 42.

16. Ibid., p. 15.

17. U.S., Congress, Office of Technology Assessment, *An Assessment of Maritime Trade and Technology*, p. 88.

18. National Research Council, *Toward More Productive Naval Shipbuilding*, p. 168.

19. Ibid.

20. Ibid., pp. 168–69.

21. Ibid., p. 169.

22. U.S., Congress, Congressional Budget Office, *U.S. Shipbuilding: Trends and Policy Choices*, p. 44.

23. U.S., Congress, House, *Hearings on Maritime Redevelopment Bank Act*, p. 59. South Korean costs were also contrasted in the Shipbuilders Council study and found to be lower than those of Japan. The Shipbuilders Council study found that if one-third of shipbuilding material was purchased from foreign sources, and

more than ten vessels were built in series, the U.S. cost would be approximately $25 million, a figure that does not include a profit allowance.

24. Ibid.

25. Ibid., p. 994 (statement of L. D. Chirillo). Recent and past recommendations for series building include those made in the National Research Council study, *The Role of the U.S. Merchant Marine in National Security*, 1959, and Ambrose, ed., *Jane's Merchant Shipping Review*, 1984.

26. U.S., Congress, Office of Technology Assessment, *An Assessment of Maritime Trade and Technology*, p. 97.

27. U.S., Congress, *Hearings on Maritime Redevelopment Bank Act*, p. 64.

28. National Research Council, *Toward More Productive Naval Shipbuilding*, p. 30.

29. Oil rigs are generally cited as high-technology builds and presumably a field where the United States might be competitive. In 1984, out of 32 rigs ordered worldwide, three were built in the United States. In earlier years when orders were booming, U.S. yards had a larger percent of the market.

30. Sources suggesting this alternative include Office of Technology Assessment, the National Research Council, the authoritative maritime publication *Marine Engineering/Log*, and the naval authority Norman Polmar.

31. "U.S. Yards Could Build Diesel Subs," *Marine Engineering/Log*, September 1984, p. 11, and "Finding World Markets for Warships," *Marine Engineering/Log*, January 1985, p. 29. See also note "a" Table 4.3.

Chapter 10

1. "Far East Leading Way in Shipbuilding Projects," *Journal of Commerce*, 26 March 1985, p. 22B.

2. "World Shipbuilding," *Marine Engineering/Log*, June 1985, pp. 54–55.

3. "Canadian Group Details Plans for Shipbuilding," *Journal of Commerce*, 12 February 1985, p. 3B.

4. "New Yard Group Formed in India," *Journal of Commerce*, 15 February 1985, p. 1B.

5. "UK Shipbuilders Facing Order Loss," *Journal of Commerce*, 19 February 1985, p. 3B.

6. "Dutch Shipyards Seek Government Assistance," *Journal of Commerce*, 22 February 1985, p. 24B.

7. "Singapore Shipyards Gain but Jobs Still Being Cut," *Journal of Commerce*, 8 March 1985, p. 22B.

8. "Niarchos Shuts Down Hellenic Shipyard," *Journal of Commerce*, 3 April 1985, p. 14A.

9. "Australian Owners Cite Ship Repair 'Blackmail'," *Journal of Commerce*, 23 April 1985.

10. J. Gwarthnly, J. R. Clark, and R. Stroup, *Essentials of Economics*, 2d ed. (Orlando, Fla.: Academic Press, 1985), p. 43.

11. In 1983 the New England Collier Company took delivery of the 32,000-dwt coal-fired *Energy Independence*. The vessel was built by General Dynamics at its Quincy, Massachusetts shipyard.

12. "U.S. Shipbuilding Outlook," *Marine Engineering/Log*, June 1984, p. 14.

13. "World Shipbuilding," *Marine Engineering/Log*, June 1983, p. 61.

14. "World Shipbuilding," *Marine Engineering/Log*, June 1985, p. 55.

15. It should not be inferred that only West European nations have developed strategies to remain in the world shipbuilding market. Other nations that are aggressive competitors include Brazil, Finland, India, and Singapore.

16. The Soviet Union has a total of 51 shipyards on all its coasts and along its inland waterways. These yards employ approximately 220,000 workers. Major yards are located on the Black Sea (15), Baltic Sea (13), inland waters (13), Pacific Ocean (5), and Arctic Ocean (5). See also Chapter 12 for more details on Soviet Union shipyards.

Chapter 11

1. Federal support for shipbuilding includes (a) deferral of federal income taxes on funds deposited into a government-sponsored Capital Construction Fund (CCF) program by shipowners. Section 607 of the Merchant Marine Act of 1936 allows: (a) deferral of income tax if the funds are used to construct a firm's replacement vessel(s) in U.S. shipyards; (b) deferral of federal taxes on capital gains realized from the sale of a vessel(s) if the net proceeds are placed in a Construction Reserve Fund (CRF) and used to construct a new vessel in a U.S. shipyard within three years. Title XI of the Merchant Marine Act of 1936 provides a U.S. government credit guarantee on debt obligation of U.S. citizen shipowners when financing or refinancing the purchase of a U.S.-built (or rebuilt) vessel. The Export-Import Bank provides loans and loan guarantees to foreign buyers purchasing vessels in U.S. shipyards. The Tariff Act of 1930 imposes a 50 percent ad valorem tax on repairs and equipment purchased abroad for use in U.S.-flag vessels. Section 27 of the Merchant Marine Act of 1920, which mandates U.S.-built vessels in American domestic ocean commerce, is discussed in Chapter 5.

2. For another view on an operator splitting his construction between U.S. and foreign shipyards, see testimony of W. James Amoss, Jr., president of Lykes Lines, in U.S., Congress, House, *Hearings, Maritime Redevelopment Bank Act*, pp. 28–33.

3. U.S., International Trade Commission, *Analysis of the International Competitiveness of the U.S. Commercial Shipbuilding and Repair Industries*, p. 10.

4. U.S., Department of Transportation, Maritime Administration, *Annual Report FY 1983*, p. 53. The last vessel constructed under CDS was delivered in January 1984.

5. While the CDS program undoubtedly encouraged shipyard inefficiencies, no misuse of funds occurred during its 45-year history on scale of that made public in the spring and summer of 1985 with respect to major defense contracts. In this regard, General Electric pleaded guilty to defrauding the Air Force of $800,000 and was barred from bidding on government contracts for up to three years; the United States withheld $244 million due General Dynamics in disputed overhead payments; two naval admirals were administratively relieved of their duties for failure to comply with orders to tighten up on defense contractor purchasing procedures; and Admiral Hyman G. Rickover, USN (Ret.), was censured by the

secretary of the navy for using his position to obtain favors from defense contractors. It was, however, the trivial items that brought on the most public outrage (e.g., $748 for a pair of Air Force pliers, $436 for a naval hammer, $640 for a naval toilet seat, and $7,600 for an Air Force coffeepot).

6. "Navy Programs Will Not Support Private Yards at Efficient Level," *Shipyard Weekly*, 2 May 1985, p. 1.

7. U.S., Department of Commerce, Maritime Administration, *Annual Report FY 1980*, p. 5. In contrast, the CDS cost to construct a 27,000-dwt containership was $38.9 million.

8. For a discussion of using foreign-built components in U.S.-built ships, see U.S. International Trade Commission, *Analysis of the International Competitiveness of the U.S. Commercial Shipbuilding and Repair Industries*, pp. 29–30.

9. If a 35 percent CDS program for bulk carriers is feasible, then the CDS cost to build a foreign trade fleet of 75 tankers and 75 bulk carriers is approximately $1.5 billion or about the cost of an *Ohio*-class Trident submarine. A 150 bulk/tanker build program was proposed by Clinton H. Whitehurst, Jr. in *The U.S. Merchant Marine: In Search of an Enduring Maritime Policy*.

10. Most analysts hold the lack of new and efficient bulk and tanker vessels in the U.S. foreign trade fleet as being the weak link in the nation's maritime defense posture. In this respect, in 1982 the nonliner U.S. share of its foreign trade was 1 percent; its tanker share was 4.7 percent. By contrast, the liner share was 26.2 percent. The numbers matched the percents. There were 169 U.S.-flag freighters but only 26 tankers and dry bulk carriers.

11. Under the UN Code of Conduct for Liner Conferences, each trading partner would carry a maximum of 40 percent of its respective trades, while 20 percent would be available to third-nation carriers.

12. The bilateral with the Soviet Union expired on 31 December 1981; that with the People's Republic of China on 17 December 1983.

13. U.S., General Accounting Office, *Economic Effect of Cargo Preference Laws*, pp. iv, v.

14. Center for Naval Analyses, *Defense and Economic Aspects of HR 1242*, p. I-5.

15. Ibid., pp. 3–11.

16. Ibid., pp. 3–13.

17. *1985 Almanac and Yearbook* (Pleasantville, N.Y.: Reader's Digest Association, 1985), p. 193.

18. U.S., Congress, Office of Technology Assessment, *An Assessment of Maritime Trade and Technology*, p. 191.

19. Ibid., pp. 190–91.

20. The U.S. Department of State historically has stressed the likely displeasure of America's trading partners should it enact commercial cargo preference legislation. This, on many occasions, prompted the late Paul Hall, dean of maritime labor statesmen, to lament the fact that there was no "American desk" at the State Department.

21. U.S., Department of Transportation, Maritime Administration, *U.S. Merchant Marine Data Sheet*, February 1985, p. 3.

22. Whitehurst, *The U.S. Merchant Marine: In Search of an Enduring Maritime Policy*, p. 227.

23. Center for Naval Analyses, *Defense and Economic Aspects of HR 1242*, p. 2–13.

Chapter 12

1. Ronald Reagan, "A Program for the Development of an Effective Maritime Strategy," Reagan–Bush Committee, 22 September 1980. One of seven points in the presidential candidate's naval–maritime program proposal.

2. W. M. Fowler, Jr., "Disaster on the Hudson," *Proceedings/Supplement*, U.S. Naval Institute, March 1985, pp. 2–9.

3. Milton M. Klein, "The Contest for the Mississippi," *Proceedings/Supplement*, U.S. Naval Institute, March 1985, p. 25.

4. Timothy D. Gill, *Industrial Preparedness*, NSA monograph 84-6 (Washington, D.C.: National Defense University Press, 1984), pp. 4–6.

5. U.S., Maritime Commission, *Merchant Marine for Trade and Defense*, 1949.

6. Gill, *Industrial Preparedness*, pp. 12–16.

7. *Federal Preparedness Circular FPC-2*, Federal Emergency Management Agency, 27 October 1983.

8. U.S., Department of Defense, *Master Mobilization Plan (MMP)*, 1 June 1982.

9. U.S., Department of Defense, *Defense Guidance FY 86–90*, pp. 74–75. A "warm" production base consists of one domestic producer for each critical weapon system and related secondary items, producing at a minimum sustaining rate.

10. Interagency Maritime Study, October 1978; Shipyard Mobilization Base Study (SYMBA), February 1984; National Defense Shipyard Study (NADES), February 1985. See particularly P. E. Tobin et al., *The U.S. Shipyard Mobilization Base: Is It Ready For War?*, Industrial College of the Armed Forces Report MSP-61, April 1984.

10. Interagency Maritime Study, October 1978; Shipyard Mobilization Base Study (SYMBA), February 1984; National Defense Shipyard Study (NADES), February 1985. See particularly P. E. Tobin, et al., *The U.S. Shipyard Mobilization Base: Is It Ready For War?*, Industrial College of the Armed Forces Report MSP-61, April 1984.

11. James R. Fisher and Philip J. Coady, *U.S. Shipbuilding: The Seventies in Retrospect/The Prospects For the Eighties*, National Defense University, NSA Issue Paper 81-2, June 1981, p. 6.

12. Secret MUL issued periodically by the secretary of defense. An unclassified instruction, DODI 4410.3, describes the priority system. An item appears on the list by presidential directive for systems that support the highest national objectives, but may also appear if military essentiality is clear or if production bottlenecks are anticipated.

13. Gill, *Industrial Preparedness*, pp. 31–33. Also see Roderick L. Vawter,

Industrial Mobilization: The Relevant History (Washington, D.C.: National Defense University Press, 1983), pp. 83–88.

14. U.S., Department of Transportation, Maritime Administration, *Report on Survey of U.S. Shipbuilding and Repair Facilities, 1984*, p. 1.

15. Department of Defense, Coordinator of Shipbuilding, Conversion and Repair/Commander, Naval Sea Systems Command, 21 September 1984.

16. Naval Sea Systems Command, Office of Maritime Affairs (code 90M).

17. Secretary of the Navy Instruction 4860.42C, 3 October 1984.

18. Secret study. Limited distribution of draft report to government agencies with a need-to-know: Assistant Secretary of the Navy (Shipbuilding and Logistics) or Associate Administrator for Policy and Administration, U.S. Maritime Administration.

19. Such as the secret Department of Defense Sealift Study, March 1984, which established program requirements for prepositioning and strategic sealift for a conventional global war. Controlled by Office of Program Analysis and Evaluation.

20. Availability of workforce in order to expand at all has been the subject of persistent debate. Some yards claim that five years are required to train a skilled worker. The Shipbuilders Council doubts that sufficient skilled or semiskilled workers would respond to a mobilization call, having been assimilated into other occupations once laid off from shipbuilding. Yet, in the first quarter after December 1941, 200,000 workers joined the nation's yard workforces. The 1977–81 industry reached a post–World War II high, with 1981 employment 115 percent of 1971. In 1983, employment only fell to the mid-1970s level, and forecasts are for increases in employment through the late 1980s. During the Vietnam War, a naval combatant was reactivated at Long Beach Naval Shipyard, and 4,000 workers were recruited in three months from all over the country.

21. Robert Dillman and Samuel Major, *The United States Shipyard Mobilization Base: Manpower Requirements*, National Defense University Report MSP-69, March 1985, executive summary.

22. Hearings before the Committee on Armed Services, U.S. Senate, 6 February 1985, Posture Statement of the Secretary of the Navy. Response to a question by Senator Wilson.

23. Department of Transportation, Maritime Administration, *Regulatory Analysis of Proposed Relaxation of the Buy American Requirement for Maritime Administration Title XI Program Vessels*, June 1983.

24. *Federal Register*, 21 March 1985. Requested public comments on four alternatives.

25. Vawter, *Industrial Mobilization*, pp. 76–77.

26. Material in this section was obtained from the Naval Sea Systems Command, Office of Maritime Affairs (code 90M), and Institute for Defense Analysis Study S-538, *The Reinstitution of the Construction of U.S. Navy Combatant Ships in U.S. Government Owned Shipyards*, January 1982. However, the NavSea Deputy Commander for Acquisition and Logistics has stated that there are no plans for building any ships in the naval shipyards.

27. Department of Defense, Coordinator of Shipbuilding, Conversion and Repair, *Annual Report on the Status of the Shipbuilding and Ship Repair Industry*

of the United States, 1983. Information was derived from an Institute for Defense Analysis study, *The Shipbuilding Industries of the U.S. and U.S.S.R. as Bases for National Maritime Policies,* and from the Naval Intelligence Support Center.

28. U.S., Department of Defense, *Soviet Military Power 1985,* April 1985, p. 142.

29. Remarks made at the three-day, Third Biennial Shipbuilding Conference, Washington, D.C., November 1984, cited in *Shipyard Weekly,* 22 November 1984, pp. 1–2.

30. Ibid., p. 2.

31. A paper presented to the Shipbuilding Panel, seminar on "The American Merchant Marine: An Industry in Transition," Center for Ocean Law and Policy, University of Virginia School of Law, 30 March 1985.

Chapter 13

1. U.S., Department of Transportation, Maritime Administration, *A Report to the Congress on the Status of the Public Ports of the United States, August 1984,* p. 6.

2. Ibid., p. 7.

3. Ibid., p. 23.

4. U.S., Department of the Army, Military Traffic Management Command, *An Analysis of Ports for National Defense.* In 1985 the Military Traffic Management Command and five other federal agencies signed a memorandum of understanding to ensure full support by federal agencies at key ports during a mobilization.

5. Included are: U.S., General Accounting Office, *American Seaports— Changes Affecting Operation and Development* (1979) and *Observations Concerning Plans and Programs to Assure the Continuity of Vital Wartime Movements through United States Ports* (1983); U.S., Department of Transportation, Maritime Administration, *National Port Assessment 1980/1990* (1980) and *A Report to the Congress on the Status of the Public Ports of the United States* (1984). The American Association of Port Authorities sponsored a major conference, "U.S. Ports and National Defense Strategies," in November 1984, at Charleston, South Carolina.

6. U.S., Department of Transportation, Maritime Administration, *Report on Survey of U.S. Shipbuilding and Repair Facilities 1984,* pp. 118–27.

7. These yards were located at Bath, Maine; Portland, Maine; Middleton, Rhode Island; Newport, Rhode Island; San Juan, Puerto Rico; Port Everglades, Florida; Pascagoula, Mississippi; Brownsville, Texas; Honolulu, Hawaii; Sturgeon Bay, Wisconsin (2); and Superior, Wisconsin.

8. The American Association of Port Authorities (AAPA) estimated that U.S. ports have invested over $15 billion in new cargo facilities since the end of World War II. The Maritime Administration estimates that another $5 billion will be spent by 1990.

9. John J. Ettore, "Senate–White House Pact May Key Port Development Bill This Year," *Traffic World,* 1 July 1985, p. 69.

10. U.S., General Accounting Office, *American Seaports—Changes Affecting Operations and Development,* p. 11.

11. Some ports having significant national defense utility such as a large naval base (e.g., Norfolk, Virginia and Charleston, South Carolina) could count on continued federal support irrespective of any cost-sharing arrangement. See Clinton H. Whitehurst, Jr., "Small Ports and Shipyards: Mobilizable?" *U.S. Naval Institute Proceedings*, February 1984, p. 100.

12. U.S., Congress, House, *Hearings, Maritime Redevelopment Bank Act*, p. 294.

13. Center for Naval Analyses, *Defense and Economic Aspects of HR 1242*, p. A-7.

14. U.S., Congress, House, *Hearings, Maritime Redevelopment Bank Act*, p. 294.

15. Center for Naval Analyses, *Defense and Economic Aspects of HR 1242*, pp. A-8, 9.

16. A classic case in this respect was the legal action taken by Charleston, South Carolina against Savannah, Georgia and the consulting firm hired by the Port of Savannah, in 1984. Charleston alleged the consultant's report was factually in error and misrepresented Charleston's competitive position. Savannah withdrew the report from circulation, and the matter was settled out of court.

17. Drewry Shipping Consultants, *The Future of World Shiprepairing* (London: Drewry Shipping Consultants, Ltd., 1984).

18. "Worldwide Ship Repair," *Marine Engineering/Log*, May 1985, p. 27.

19. "Ports Woo Shipping Lines with Better Facilities and Access," *Marine Engineering/Log*, March 1985, p. 25.

20. U.S., Department of Transportation, Maritime Administration, *Merchant Fleets of the World*, p. 2.

21. "Navy Cannot Save Maritime Industry," *Shipyard Weekly*, 4 July 1985, p. 3.

22. A "load center" is a strategically located container port with respect to a heavy-volume trade route (e.g., U.S. east coast–North Europe). Small shipments are fed into the load center for transshipment in large containerships. In terms of a port's economic viability, being designated a load center by a major shipping line is a prized accomplishment.

23. Alan Schoedel, "Joint Ventures 'Key' to Port Funding," *Journal of Commerce*, 25 August 1984, p. 1.

Chapter 14

1. In the FY 1981 Department of Defense *Annual Report* to Congress, funds were requested to acquire 14 maritime prepositioned ships. These ships would be stationed in remote areas of the world where U.S. forces might be deployed. This is the so-called T-AKX program. Another program was DoD's purchase of eight Sea–Land container ships to be modified as military logistic support vessels. These ships would be maintained on a standby basis in U.S. ports. This was the T-AKRX program. Both programs were funded and are nearing completion.

2. The effective U.S. control (EUSC) concept is based on the premise that in an emergency, U.S.-owned vessels registered in certain foreign countries and crewed by foreign nationals would be returned to U.S. control. The concept has

been roundly criticized and is so logically flawed that little weight is given to EUSC shipping in defense planning.

3. *Shipyard Weekly*, Shipbuilders Council of America, 29 August 1985, p. 2.

Chapter 15

1. U.S., General Accounting Office, *Letter Report B-118779*, 30 December 1975.

2. Paper by Everett Pyatt, Assistant Secretary of the Navy for Shipbuilding and Logistics, read at a seminar, "The American Merchant Marine: An Industry in Transition," sponsored by the Center for Ocean Law and Policy, University of Virginia Law School, 30 March 1985.

3. Ralph V. Buck, Captain USN, "Comment—Tomorrow's Fleet," *U.S. Naval Institute Proceedings*, August 1984, p. 31.

4. Letter, with enclosure, to James Goodrich, Undersecretary of the Navy, from Rear Admiral N. R. D. King, Royal Navy, 26 July 1985.

5. U.S., Department of Commerce, Maritime Administration, Office of Ship Construction.

6. U.S., Congress, *Congressional Record–House*, pp. H-3436–39, 22 April 1977.

7. "People in the News," *Marine Engineering/Log*, December 1983, p. 7.

8. J. J. Henry's design achievements include designing the first liquid natural gas (LNG) tanker and the hull and engine room of the NS *Savannah*.

9. "Soviets Soon to Launch Nuclear Merchant Ship," *Daily Telegraph* (London) 28 May 1985, p. 10.

10. On 21 March 1985, the Maritime Administration proposed a relaxation of the rules requiring the use of American materials in vessels built under Title XI of the Merchant Marine Act of 1936. Title XI provides federal government guarantees for loans used to construct vessels for U.S. registry. Waivers of the requirement can be granted on the finding that materials were not available in the United States or that using American materials would cause an unreasonable delay in the vessel's construction. See also Chapter 9.

11. Clinton H. Whitehurst, Jr., *The U.S. Merchant Marine: In Search of an Enduring Maritime Policy*, p. 95.

12. Interview with Chengi Kuo, Glasgow, Scotland, Professor of Ship and Marine Technology, Strathclyde University, 23 May 1985.

13. It has been repeatedly urged that U.S. building costs can be cut, although never enough to match foreign competitors; so a U.S. merchant ship building program must be financed by some type of construction differential subsidy. Reinstituting a CDS program, however, raises the question of what is a reasonable construction differential percent. Studies cited in Chapters 9 and 11 suggest that for bulk and tank vessels on the order of 35,000 to 50,000 dwt, built in series, a federal subsidy of 35 percent is an attainable goal.

14. Jane Couch Nutter, ed., *Political Economy and Freedom*, p. 263.

15. Center for Naval Analyses, *Defense and Economic Aspect of HR 1242*, p. 1–7.

16. U.S., Congress, *Congressional Record—Senate*, 4 June 1920, p. 8469.

17. The Maritime Advisory Committee was made up of W. J. Amoss, Jr., President, Lykes Brothers Steamship Company; James R. Barker, Chairman of the Board, Moore McCormack Resources, Inc.; William B. Burhmann, President, USS Great Lakes Fleet; Jesse Calhoun, President, Marine Engineers Beneficial Association; Vincent Cannaliato, Jr., First Vice-President, Smith Barney, Harris, Upham and Co.; Thomas Crowley, Crowley Maritime Corporation; F. Eugene Dixon, Jr., Delaware River Port Authority; Arthur E. Erb, President, Eller and Company; J. T. Gilbride, Chairman, Todd Shipyards Corporation; Thomas Gleason, President, International Longshoremen's Association; Don Griffin, Vice-President, Pittsburgh Plate Glass Company; Ran Hettena, President, Maritime Overseas Corporation; Charles I. Hiltzheimer, Chairman and President, Sea–Land Industries; Rear Admiral Roy Hoffman, USN (Ret.), Milwaukee Municipal Port Board of Harbor Commissioners; Charles Hardlicks, Foster, Meadows and Ballard; Adolph B. Kurz, President, Keystone Shipping Company; Milton G. Nottingham, Jr., U.S. Merchant Marine Alumni Association; Frank T. Stegbauer, Southern Towing Company; Stephen Van Dyke, President, Sonat Marine, Inc.; Shannon J. Wall, President, National Maritime Union; and Archie L. Wilson, President, Dixie Carriers, Inc.

18. Paula J. Pettavino and Harlan K. Ullman, *Maritime Policy in Perspective: Choices, Capabilities and Costs* (draft report), p. 14.

Glossary

ACTIVE SHIPBUILDING INDUSTRIAL BASE. As defined by the Maritime Administration, shipyards seeking, as well as having, the capability of constructing naval and/or large merchant vessels.

BILATERAL SHIPPING AGREEMENT. An agreement by which trading partners set down the conditions under which cargo is moved between their two countries. As a rule, each country reserves a certain percent of such cargo to its national flag carriers.

CAPITAL CONSTRUCTION FUND (CCF). A government-administered account into which ship operator earnings can be deposited on a tax-deferred basis for the ultimate purpose of building or acquiring U.S.-flag, U.S.-built vessels.

CODE OF CONDUCT FOR LINER CONFERENCES. A UN-endorsed cargo-sharing arrangement between trading partners with respect to the movement of general cargo. Each trading partner may reserve up to 40 percent of such trade for its national flag carriers, with 20 percent left for third-country vessels.

CONSTRUCTION, ALTERATION, AND REPAIR (CAR). The types of shipyard work performed on naval vessels.

CONSTRUCTION DIFFERENTIAL SUBSIDY (CDS). A subsidy paid to U.S. shipyards by the federal government. The amount of the subsidy equals the difference in dollar cost between building a vessel in the United States and building overseas. Payments historically have had an upper limit of 50 percent; that is, the government paid 50 percent of the U.S. shipyard price.

CONTINGENCY. A military term usually denoting a quick-breaking situation in which national interests are threatened but not so threatened that a national mobilization is declared.

DEADWEIGHT TONS (DWT). A vessel's carrying capacity in tons of 2,240 pounds each.

EFFECTIVE U.S. CONTROL (SHIPPING) (EUSC). U.S.-owned ships registered under the flags of Liberia, Honduras, and Panama.

FEDERAL SHIP FINANCING GUARANTEE PROGRAM (Title XI of the Merchant Marine Act of 1936, as amended). A program by which the U.S. government insures full payment to a private lender should the mortgagee (vessel owner) be in default.

FLAG OF CONVENIENCE SHIPPING. Ships owned by nationals of one country that fly the flag of another. U.S.-owned foreign flag shipping is registered primarily, but not only, under the flags of Liberia, Honduras, and Panama.

FREE SHIP. A term used to describe a shipowner's option of purchasing his ship(s) anywhere in the world without any restraint by his government.

GROSS TONS (GT). The internal cubic capacity of a vessel's cargo space expressed in tons of 100 cubic feet each.

JONES ACT. Legislation that prohibits foreign-flag shipping from engaging in U.S. domestic ocean and Great Lakes trades. Specifically, Section 27 of the Merchant Marine Act of 1920.

LIGHTER ABOARD SHIP (LASH). A general cargo vessel that carries barges loaded with cargo. Barges are floated to and from the ship and loaded or unloaded by an elevator crane on the ship's stern.

LIQUID NATURAL GAS CARRIER (LNG). A vessel specifically designed to transport liquid natural gas.

MODULAR CONSTRUCTION. A technique of ship construction by which parts of a ship are built in separate sections and later joined.

NATIONAL DEFENSE FEATURE (NDF). An addition to a merchant vessel that enhances its usefulness as a naval or military auxiliary; for example, radio equipment capable of communicating with naval ships.

NAVAL SEA SYSTEMS COMMAND. An agency within the Department of the Navy with responsibility for coordinating naval shipbuilding, repair, and conversion.

OPERATING DIFFERENTIAL SUBSIDY (ODS). A subsidy paid by the federal government to U.S.-flag operators meeting specific criteria. The amount of the subsidy equals the difference between operating a vessel under the U.S. flag and operating it under competing foreign flags on a particular trade route. ODS is paid in a number of categories; wages account for the largest amount.

ORGANIZATION FOR ECONOMIC COOPERATION AND DEVELOPMENT. An organization of economically developed (industrialized) Western nations.

RAPID DEPLOYMENT FORCE (RDF). Ships loaded with military supplies and located at likely world trouble spots; for example, ships, including loaded tankers and general cargo ships, based at Diego Garcia in the Indian Ocean. Also, government-owned or -controlled cargo ships that are kept in a high state of readiness in the United States and that could be rapidly deployed worldwide if the need arose.

READY RESERVE FORCE (RRF). A part of the National Defense Reserve Fleet that can be broken out and on berth in five to ten days.

ROLL-ON/ROLL-OFF (RO/RO). A type of general cargo vessel that primarily carries highway trailers/trucks. Vehicles drive on and off the ship.

SEA SHED. A cargo module that fits into a container ship's cell guides. Essentially, the module converts a container ship into a break-bulk ship. The module can also be used in bulk carriers.

SERVICE LIFE EXTENSION PROGRAM (SLEP). A Navy Department program under which naval vessels approaching the end of their normal service life are completely overhauled/reconstructed and fitted with the latest state-of-the-art technology with respect to weapons, communication, and navigation systems.

SHIPBUILDERS COUNCIL OF AMERICA. An industry organization representing major American shipyards. The organization is headquartered in Washington, D.C. and represents shipyard interests before Congress and the executive branch of government.

SHIPYARD MOBILIZATION BASE. Active U.S. shipyards that would form the nucleus for expansion of the nation's shipbuilding/ship repair capability in a war or national emergency.

T-SHIP PROGRAMS. A term used to describe two ship modification programs administered by the Military Sealift Command (MSC). In the first program (T-AKRX), MSC converted eight U.S.-flag container ships to fast logistics support vessels. The container ships were converted to a roll-on/roll-off mode. In the second program (T-AKX), MSC acquired and converted a number of ships that would be combat-loaded and pre-positioned in likely world trouble spots.

UNDERWAY REPLENISHMENT (UNREP). At sea replenishment (with stores, fuel, ammunition, etc.) of combatant naval vessels by other combatants, noncombatant naval, or civilian-manned ships.

ZONE OUTFITTING. A ship construction technique by which components of a major unit are preassembled and tested before installation in the ship's hull.

Bibliography

Primary Sources

U.S. Maritime Administration

The Maritime Administration publishes a wealth of information of interest to the observer or student of maritime affairs. In addition to its annual reports, cited extensively in this book, the agency periodically publishes statistics on world merchant fleets; U.S.-owned, foreign-flag shipping, including those vessels regarded as being under effective U.S. control; an American-flag-vessel inventory report; and data on new American and worldwide construction. Of particular interest on the shipbuilding side is the annual report on U.S. shipbuilding and repair facilities. Domestic ocean trade data are extensively reported in a triennial report, while a profile of U.S. maritime activities is reported monthly in a U.S. merchant marine data sheet. These and other agency publications can be found in the Maritime Administration section of the main library of the Department of Transportation. Many Maritime Administration publications can be found in college and university libraries that serve as full or partial depositories for government documents.

U.S. General Accounting Office

A primary research source for those interested in maritime affairs, particularly contemporary issues, consists of the various reports to Congress published by the General Accounting Office. This book has relied upon a number of such reports.

Investigations by the General Accounting Office (and the subsequent reports to Congress) are requested by individual members of Congress or congressional committee chairpersons. The agency also independently initiates work in the maritime field. Over the decade 1976–85, the General Accounting Office issued reports on shipbuilding, shipping subsidies, cargo preference legislation, and several reports dealing with U.S. seaports. The researcher may request to be put on GAO's monthly publications mailing list. Reports may be requested free of charge by, among others, members of the press, college libraries, faculty members, and students.

Marine Engineering/Log

This monthly periodical is required reading for any author writing on present-day maritime issues. The content scope is worldwide. Articles on technological innovations taking place within the industry are current and authoritative, while the annual review issue (June) provides up-to-date statistics on shipping and shipbuilding. Of particular significance in this respect is that data published in the review issue are the most timely in all maritime publications, generally leading agency publications, for example, those of the Maritime Administration and the Navy, by three to six months. A number of specific *Marine Engineering/Log* references are cited in the secondary sources section of this bibliography; many more provided initial information that led to further research in particular subject areas.

Published Histories

Occasionally the maritime researcher comes to rely on a particular published work, not just for specific statistical data, but as a "must" background source. Such a volume is John G. B. Hutchins's *The American Maritime Industries and Public Policy, 1789–1914: An Economic History*. Chapters 2 through 4 of this book are indebted to Hutchins's detailed, comprehensive, and scholarly treatise.

A general economic history text that gives more than usual attention to America's historical maritime role is Harold Underwood Faulkner's *American Economic History* (8th edition). Of particular importance to the scholar is an understanding of the overall economic setting in which American maritime investment took place. The Faulkner text is superb in that respect and as such must be considered a primary research source for this volume, in particular Chapters 2, 3 and 4.

American Enterprise Institute for Public Policy Research

A number of studies, reports, and analyses published by the American Enterprise Institute served as major reference sources. Very important were transportation studies over the past 15 years dealing with the effects of economic regulation in general. Also, articles in the defense area published in the quarterly *Foreign Policy and Defense Review* proved most helpful. The major AEI reference source with respect to this book was a special analysis by Clinton H. Whitehurst, Jr., *American Domestic Shipping in American Ships: Jones Act Costs, Benefits, and Options*

(1985). Publications of the American Enterprise Institute can be found in most major university libraries or can be obtained from AEI's Washington, D.C. office.

Secondary Sources

"A Cost Watching Navy Snubs U.S. Shipyards." *Business Week*, 10 November 1980, 39–40.

"A Double Disadvantage for U.S. Builders." *Seapower* 27 (October 1984): 13.

A Study of the U.S. Deep Sea Coastal Cruise Market and U.S. Built Deep Sea Cruise Ships. Washington, D.C.: Harbridge House, Inc., March 1984.

Abrahamson, Bernhard J. *Imternational Ocean Shipping*. Boulder, Colo.: Westview Press, Inc., 1980.

Ambrose, A. J., ed. *Jane's Merchant Shipping Review*. New York: Jane's Publishing Company, Ltd., 1984.

Andrews, Phillip, and Engel, Leonard. *Navy Yearbook*. New York: Duell, Sloan and Pearce, 1944.

Baker, G. S. *The Merchant Ship: Design Past and Present*. London: Sigma Books, Ltd., 1948.

Bonsor, N. R. P. *North Atlantic Seaway*. New York: Arco Publishing Co., 1975.

Bowes, Marianne, "Overhaul Costs in Public and Private Shipyards: A Case Study," CRC 4429 (Revised). Alexandria, Va.: Center for Naval Analyses, October 1981.

Branch, Alan E. *Economics of Shipping Practice and Management*. New York: Chapman and Hall, Ltd., 1982.

Brown, Kenneth M. *The R&D Tax Credit: Issues in Tax Policy and Industrial Innovation*. Washington, D.C.: American Enterprise Institute for Public Policy Research, 1984.

Bunker, John G. *Liberty Ships: The Ugly Ducklings of World War II*. Annapolis, Md.: Naval Institute Press, 1972.

Campbell, George F. *China Tea Clippers*. New York: David McKay Company, 1974.

Center for Naval Analyses. *Defense and Economic Aspects of HR 1242 (Competitive Shipping and Shipbuilding Act of 1983)*. Alexandria, Va.: Center for Naval Analyses, 1983.

Center for Oceans Law and Policy, University of Virginia Law School. *The American Merchant Marine: An Industry in Transition*. New York: Oceana Publications, Inc., 1985.

Cole, Brady M. *Procurement of Naval Ships: It Is Time for the U.S. Navy to Acknowledge Its Shipbuilders May Be Holding a Winning Hand*. Washington, D.C.: National Defense University Research Directorate, 1979.

Committee of American Steamship Lines. *A Legislative History of Shipbuilding Subsidies under the Merchant Marine Act of 1936*. Washington, D.C.: Committee of American Steamship Lines, 1959.

Cradle of American Shipbuilding, Portsmouth Naval Shipyard, Library of Congress #LC78-600146. Portsmouth, N.H., 1978.

Cutler, Carl C. *Greyhounds of the Sea*. Annapolis, Md.: Naval Institute Press, 1960.

Department of Ship and Marine Technology, University of Strathclyde. *Marine Technology Next Century's Challenge*. Glasgow: Bell and Bain, Ltd., 1982.

Dillman, Robert, and Major, Samuel. *The U.S. Shipyard Mobilization Base: Manpower Requirements*. Washington, D.C.: National Defense University, 1985.

Dorn, David R. "Ships for Victory." *U.S. Naval Institute Proceedings* 111 (February 1985): 68.

Eames, Michael C. "Future Naval Surface Ships." *Naval Engineers Journal* 97 (February 1985): 65.

Elliott, Charles F. "The Genesis of the Modern Navy." *U.S. Naval Institute Proceedings* (March 1966): 62.

Ettorre, John. "Ports Look to Automated Cargo Systems to Improve Service." *Traffic World* (24 September 1984): 47.

"European Ports Launch a Variety of Programs to Attract Shippers." *Journal of Commerce* (25 September 1984): 13A.

Faulkner, Harold U. *American Economic History*, 8th ed. New York: Harper & Brothers, 1960.

Fee, J. J. "Evolution of the Engineering Duty Officer in the United States Navy." *Naval Engineering Journal* 97 (March 1985): 58.

Foss, Murray F. *Changing Utilization of Fixed Capital*. Washington, D.C.: American Enterprise Institute for Public Policy Research, 1984.

Frankel, E. G. *Destructive Shipping Practices: Boom or Blight for Developing Countries*. Seattle, Wash.: Institute for Marine Studies, 1985.

Frankel, Ernst. *Management and Operations of American Shipping*. Boston: Auburn House Publishing Co., 1982.

Frankel, Ernst. *Regulation and Policies of American Shipping*. Boston: Auburn House Publishing Co., 1982.

Fries, P. A., et al. *Sea Shed Test and Evaluation Program: Final Report*. Arlington, Va.: Information Spectrum, Inc., 1984.

Frump, Robert R. "The Maritime World in 1984." *U.S. Naval Institute Proceedings* 111 (May 1985): 82.

Gibson, Charles E. *The Story of the Ship*. New York: Henry Schuman, 1948.

Griffiths, Maurice. *Man the Shipbuilder*. London: Priory Press, Ltd., 1973.

Haskell, Arthur J. "Discussion—The Jones Act: Foreign Built Vessels and the Domestic Shipping Industry." *Society of Naval Architects and Marine Engineers, Transactions* 91 (1983): 184.

Hessdoerfer, R. C. *Maritime Options for the Future—The Means to Revitalize the U.S. Merchant Marine*. Monterey, Calif.: Naval Postgraduate School, 1984.

Heyerdahl, Thor. *Kon-Tiki: Across the Pacific by Raft*. New York: Rand McNally and Company, 1950.

Howe, O. T., and Matthews, F. C. *American Clipper Ships 1833–1858*. New York: Argosy, Antiquarian, 1967.

Hutchins, John G. B. *The American Maritime Industries and Public Policy, 1789–1914: An Economic History*. Cambridge, Mass.: Harvard University Press, 1941.

Iarossi, Frank J. "Future of U.S. Flag Tanker Industry." Address before American Petroleum Institute Tanker Conference, Boca Raton, Fla., 3 June 1984.

International Brotherhood of Boilermakers, Iron Shipbuilders, Blacksmiths, Forgers and Helpers. *An Analysis of Shipbuilding and Marine Industry Labor Agreements.* Prepared for 1983 Conference of Shipbuilding and Marine Industry, 16 March 1983, Washington, D.C.

Jackson, G. Gibbard. *The Book of the Ship.* London: D. Appleton-Century Company, 1938.

Jantscher, Gerald R. *Bread upon the Waters: Federal Aids to the Maritime Industries.* Washington, D.C.: The Brookings Institution, 1975.

Johnson, Robert A. "Innovation in Ship Design: Are We Willing to Risk?" *Naval Engineers Journal* 97 (January 1985): 64.

Johnson, Robert A. "Naval Ship Design: The Shipbuilders' Emerging New Role." *Naval Engineers Journal* 97 (May 1985): 37.

Kendall, Lane C. "U.S. Merchant Marine in 1984." *U.S. Naval Institute Proceedings* 111 (May 1985): 66.

Kilmarx, Robert A., ed. *America's Maritime Legacy: A History of the U.S. Merchant Marine and Shipbuilding Industry since Colonial Times.* Boulder, Colo.: Westview Press, 1979.

Kiskaddon, Charles G., Jr. and Stewart, J. Todd. "UNCTAD and the International Bulk Trades: Two Viewpoints." Addresses before Annual General Meeting of the International Association of Independent Tanker Owners, Washington, D.C., 1 April 1981.

Kurtz, Howard, and Isikoff, Michael. "SOS! Industry Overboard." *The Washington Post (National Weekly Edition),* 19 August 1985.

LaDage, John H. *Modern Ships: Elements of Their Design, Construction and Operation.* Centreville, Md.: Cornell Maritime Press, 1953.

"Last Chance for U.S. Shipbuilders." *Seapower* 27 (December 1984): 18.

Lawrence, S. A. *International Sea Transport: The Years Ahead.* Lexington, Mass.: D. C. Heath and Company, 1972.

Leammon, Sue, and Wichels, E. D. *Sidewheelers to Nuclear Power.* Annapolis, Md.: Leeward Publications, 1977.

Leback, Warren G., and McConnell, John W. "The Jones Act: Foreign Built Vessels and the Domestic Shipping Industry." *Society of Naval Architects and Marine Engineers Transactions* 91 (November 1983): 169.

MacGregor, David R. *Merchant Sailing Ships 1815–1850.* Annapolis, Md.: Naval Institute Press, 1984.

Maddocks, Melvin. *The Great Liners.* Alexandria, Va.: Time-Life Books, 1978.

Mahan, Alfred Thayer. *The Influence of Seapower Upon History 1660–1783.* New York: Sagamore Press, 1957.

Maclay, Edgar S. *A History of American Privateers.* Freeport, N.Y.: Books for Libraries Press, 1899.

Marine Engineering/Log. *Marine Directory, 1983–84.* New York: Simmons-Boardman Publishing Corp., 1984.

Marine Engineering/Log. *Annual Yearbook and Maritime Review.* New York: Simmons-Boardman Publishing Corp., 1984.

Marine Engineering/Log. *Annual Yearbook and Maritime Review*. New York: Simmons-Boardman Publishing Corp., 1985.

McDowell, Carl E., and Gibbs, Helen M. *Ocean Transportation*. New York: McGraw-Hill Book Co., 1954.

McKelvey, Michael J. "The Economic and Trade Outlook to 1995 for the U.S. Economy and the Transportation Industry." Lexington, Mass.: Data Resources, Inc., 1985.

Morison, Samuel E., and Commager, Henry S. *The Growth of the American Republic*. New York: Oxford University Press, 1950.

National Academy of Sciences. *Defense Utility of Commercial Vessels and Craft*. Washington, D.C.: National Academy of Sciences, 1980.

National Academy of Sciences, Maritime Transportation Research Board. *Innovation in the Maritime Industry*. Washington, D.C.: National Academy of Sciences, 1979.

National Academy of Sciences, Maritime Transportation Research Board. *Innovation in the Maritime Industry, Appendix*. Washington, D.C.: National Academy of Sciences, 1979.

National Academy of Sciences, Maritime Transportation Research Board. *Personnel Requirements for an Advanced Shipyard Technology*. Washington, D.C.: National Academy of Sciences, 1980.

National Academy of Sciences. *The Role of the U.S. Merchant Marine in National Security*. Washington, D.C.: National Academy of Sciences, 1959.

National Advisory Committee on Oceans and Atmosphere. *Shipping, Shipyards and Sealift: Issues of National Security and Federal Support* (discussion draft report). Washington, D.C.: National Advisory Committee on Oceans and Atmosphere, 1985.

National Research Council. *Toward More Productive Naval Shipbuilding*. Washington, D.C.: National Academy Press, 1984.

National Technical Information Service. *Shipbuilding and Shipping Industries: Government Regulations (February 1984–May 1985)*. Citations from the Ocean Abstracts Database, June 1985.

Naval Amphibious School, Little Creek, Virginia. *Senior Officers Forum Position Papers*. May 1983.

Navy League of the United States. *The Almanac of Seapower 1984*. Washington, D.C.: Navy League of the United States, 1984.

Navy League of the United States. *The Almanac of Seapower 1985*. Washington, D.C.: Navy League of the United States, 1985.

Nelson, Richard R. *High Technology Policies: A Five-Nation Comparison*. Washington, D.C.: American Enterprise Institute for Public Policy Research, 1984.

Nersesian, Roy L. *Ships and Shipping: A Comprehensive Guide*. Tulsa, Okla.: Penn Well Publishing Company, 1981.

Nutter, Jane Couch, ed. *Political Economy and Freedom*. Indianapolis: Liberty Press, 1983.

Oceanic Abstracts. *Shipbuilding and Shipping Industries: Government Regulations*. Springfield, Va.: National Technical Information Service, 1985.

Pettavino, Paula J., and Ullman, Harlan K. *Maritime Policy in Perspective: Choices, Capabilities and Costs* (draft report). Washington, D.C.: Center for Strategic and International Studies, 1985.

"Ports Woo Shipping Lines with Better Facilities and Access." *Marine Engineering/Log* (March 1985): 26.

Potter, E. B. *The Naval Academy Illustrated History of the U.S. Navy.* New York: Crowell Press. 1971.

Prothero, I. J. *Artisans and Politics in Early Nineteenth Century London.* Baton Rouge, La.: Louisiana State University Press, 1979.

Ramsay, Raymond. "A Time for Shipbuilding Renaissance." *Naval Engineers Journal* 95 (September 1983): 33.

Schmitz, Andrew. *The U.S. Sugar Program under Price Uncertainty.* Washington, D.C.: American Enterprise Institute, 1984.

Schonknecht, Rolf, Lusch, Jurgen, Schelzel, Manfred, and Obenaus, Hans. *Ships and Shipping Tomorrow.* Centreville, Md.: Cornell Maritime Press, 1983.

Shipbuilders Council of America. *Statistical Summary.* Washington, D.C.: Shipbuilders Council of America, 1985.

Smith, J. Russell. *Influence of the Great War upon Shipping.* New York: Oxford University Press, 1919.

Stern, Philip. *The Confederate Navy: A Pictorial History.* New York: Bonanza Books, 1962.

Thomas, Vincent C., Jr. "Shipbuilding: The Challenge of the 80s." *Seapower* 26 (April 1983): 83.

Tobin, P. E., et al. *The U.S. Shipyard Mobilization Base: Is It Ready for War?* Washington, D.C.: Industrial College of the Armed Forces, 1984.

Tunis, Edwin. *Oars, Sails and Steam.* New York: The World Publishing Company, 1952.

Ullman, Harlan K. *Crisis or Opportunity? U.S. Maritime Industries and National Security.* Washington, D.C.: Center for Strategic and International Studies, 1984.

Ullman, Harlan K., and Etzold, Thomas H. *Future Imperative: National Security and the U.S. Navy in the Late 1980s.* Washington, D.C.: Center for Strategic and International Studies, 1985.

Ullman, Harlan K., and Pettavino, Paula J. *Forecasts for U.S. Maritime Industries in 1989: Balancing National Security and Economic Considerations.* Washington, D.C.: Center for Strategic and International Studies, 1984.

Ullman, Harlan K., and Pettavino, Paula J. *Maritime Policy in Perspective: Choices, Capabilities and Costs* (draft report). Washington, D.C.: Center for Strategic and International Studies, 1985.

Ullman, Harlan K., and Pettavino, Paula J. "The Dreary Future of U.S. Maritime Industries." *U.S. Naval Institute Proceedings* 111 (May 1985): 137.

United States, Congress. *Congressional Record, May 25, 1920 to June 5, 1920.*

United States, Congress. Merchant Marine Act of 1920, Section 27 (41 Stat. 988, Chapter 250).

United States, Congress, Committee on Merchant Marine and Fisheries. *The

Merchant Marine Act of 1936, the Shipping Act of 1916 and Related Acts. 96th Cong., 1979.

United States, Congress, Congressional Budget Office. *U.S. Shipping and Shipbuilding: Trends and Policy Choices*. 1984.

United States, Congress, House, Subcommittee on Merchant Marine. *Hearings, Maritime Redevelopment Bank Act*. 98th Cong., 1984.

U.S. Congress, House, Seapower Subcommittee of Committee on Armed Services. *Hearings on Current Status of Shipyards, 1974*, Part 2. 93d Cong., 2d Sess., 1974.

United States, Congress, Office of Technology Assessment. *Alternative Approaches to Cargo Policy*. August 1985.

United States, Congress, Office of Technology Assessment. *An Assessment of Maritime Trade and Technology*. 1983.

United States, Congressional Budget Office. *U.S. Shipping and Shipbuilding: Trends and Policy Choices*. August 1984.

United States, Department of the Army, Corps of Engineers. *Transportation Lines of the United States, 1983–84*. Springfield, Va.: National Technical Information Service, July 1985.

United States, Department of the Army, Military Traffic Management Command. *An Analysis of Ports for National Defense*. Newport News, Va.: Military Traffic Management Command, 1978.

United States, Department of Defense. *Annual Report, Fiscal Year 1986*. February, 1985.

United States, Department of the Navy. *Annual Report on the Status of the Shipbuilding and Repair Industry of the United States*. 1982.

United States, Department of the Navy. *National Defense Shipyard Study (NADES)* (draft report). Washington, D.C.: Department of the Navy, 1985.

United States, Department of the Navy, Military Sealift Command. *Ship Register*. Washington, D.C.: Military Sealift Command, January 1985.

United States, Department of the Navy and Department of Transportation, Maritime Administration. *Shipyard Mobilization Base (SYMBA) Study* (Executive Summary). Washington, D.C.: Department of the Navy, 1984.

United States, Department of Transportation. *National Transportation Statistics*. August 1984.

United States, Department of Transportation, Maritime Administration. *A Report to the Congress on the Status of the Public Ports of the United States, August 1984*. 1984.

United States, Department of Transportation, Maritime Administration. *Bulk Carriers in the World Fleet as of January 1, 1981*. December 1981.

United States, Department of Transportation, Maritime Administration. *Domestic Waterborne Trade of the United States 1978–82*. November 1984.

United States, Department of Transportation, Maritime Administration. *Effective U.S. Control (EUSC)*. July 1984.

United States, Department of Transportation, Maritime Administration. *Foreign Flag Merchant Ships Owned by U.S. Parent Companies, July 1, 1984*. July 1984.

United States, Department of Transportation, Maritime Administration. *Maritime Subsidies*. February 1983.

United States, Department of Transportation, Maritime Administration. *Merchant Fleets of the World as of January 1, 1984*. March 1985.

United States, Department of Transportation, Maritime Administration. *New Ship Construction 1983*. January 1985.

United States, Department of Transportation, Maritime Administration, *Relative Cost of Shipbuilding*. October 1984.

United States, Department of Transportation, Maritime Administration. *Report on Survey of U.S. Shipbuilding and Repair Facilities 1984*. December 1984.

United States, Department of Transportation, Maritime Administration. *Vessel Inventory Report*. July 1984.

United States, Department of Transportation. *National Transportation: Trends and Choices to the Year 2000*, January 1978.

United States, General Accounting Office. *American Seaports—Changes Affecting Operations and Development*. 1979.

United States, General Accounting Office. *Cargo Preference Programs for Government Financed Ocean Shipments Could Be Improved*. 1978.

United States, General Accounting Offic. *Economic Effects of Cargo Preference Laws*. 1984.

United States, International Trade Commission. *Analysis of the International Competitiveness of the U.S. Commercial Shipbuilding and Repair Industries*. 1985.

United States, Maritime Commission. *Economic Survey of the American Merchant Marine*. November 1937.

United States, Office of Managment and Budget. *Standard Industrial Classification Manual*. Washington, D.C.: Government Printing Office, 1972.

"U.S. Merchant Shipbuilding: 1607–1976." *Marine Engineering/Log* 81 (August 1976): 65.

"U.S. Naval Shipbuilding Program 1982." *U.S. Naval Institute Proceedings* 109 (January 1983): 120.

Vawter, Roderick L. *Industrial Mobilization: The Relevant History*. Washington, D.C.: National Defense University, 1983.

Vego, Milan. "Shipbuilding, Soviet Style." *Seapower* 28 (July 1985): 46.

Whitehurst, Clinton H., Jr. "Is There a Future for Naval Shipyards?" *U.S. Naval Institute Proceedings* 104 (April 1978): 30.

Whitehurst, Clinton H., Jr. "Small Ports and Shipyards: Mobilizable?" *U.S. Naval Institute Proceedings* 110 (February 1984): 100.

Whitehurst, Clinton H., Jr. "The Aging Mariners." *U.S. Naval Institute Proceedings* 106 (April 1980): 124.

Whitehurst, Clinton H., Jr. *The U.S. Merchant Marine: In Search of an Enduring Maritime Policy*. Annapolis, Md.: Naval Institute Press, 1983.

Whitehurst, Clinton H., Jr. "U.S. Flag Passenger Ships and National Security." *Marine Policy Reports* 7 (September 1984): 1.

Index